AF540515

AGRO-AFFORESTATION MANAGEMENT ON WASTELANDS

About the Author

H.R. Yadav obtained degrees of M. Phil. and Ph. D. from Jawaharlal Nehru University, New Delhi, worked with CSIR for Eight years having authored six books and published 53 research papers. He has been the member of various Wastelands Development Boards besides being founder Member Secretary and Director, Institute of Wasteland Reclamation and Rural Development (1990) Institute of Science and Technology for Rural Development (1994) and RIWARD, Post Graduate College, Hanumanganj, Sultanpur. Presently he is engaged in the implementation of women empowerment & National Rural Health Mission & Village Information System Programmes in Amethi Block, Sultanpur District.

AGRO-AFFORESTATION MANAGEMENT ON WASTELANDS
(Village Level Study)

Hridai R. Yadav

CONCEPT PUBLISHING COMPANY PVT. LTD.

NEW DELHI-110059

ISBN-13: 978-81-8069-735-7

First Published 2011

Published and Printed by

Concept Publishing Company Pvt. Ltd.
Regd. Office:
A/15-16, Commercial Block, Mohan Garden
New Delhi-110059 (India)
Phones : 25351460, 25351794, *Fax* : 091-11-25357109
Email : publishing@conceptpub.com
Website: www.conceptpub.com

Editorial Office:
H-13, Bali Nagar, New Delhi-110 015, India.

Cataloging in Publication Data--*Courtesy*: D.K. Agencies (P) Ltd. <docinfo@dkagencies.com>

Yadav, Hridai Ram, 1957-
Agro-afforestation management on wastelands : village level study / Hridai R. Yadav.
p. cm.
Includes bibliographical references (p.) and index.
ISBN 9788180697357

1. Waste lands--India--Amethi Development Block--Management. 2. Afforestation--India--Amethi Development Block--Management. 3. Reclamation of land--India--Amethi Development Block--Management. 4. Forestry projects--India--Amethi Development Block. I. Title.

DDC 333.7313709542 22

Dedicated
to

My Mentor and Our Beloved Leader

Late Shri Rajiv Gandhi

Former Prime Minister of India

as a token of his inspiration and guidance for my Publications and Research on Wastelands, his matchless Vision, Mission, Zeal and Ecouragement

Preface

India being a vast country, having diverse agro-ecological regions, planning process for better management and optimal utilization of available natural resources always has been challenged. There is consistent demand of Fuelwood, Fodder, Fibre, Foodgrain, Fruits, Fisheries (F^6), leading to ecological imbalances of the area and over exploitation of natural resources causing environmental degradation leading to an increase in the wastelands area. There has been ecological and socio-economic crisis due to examine loss of forest cover.

The Hon'ble Supreme Court of India has also been concerned and instructed the concerned implementing agencies of the Govt. of India to develop Compensatory Fund for Afforestation Programme (COMPA) to control the diversion of forest land to non-forest use but the same is not being apropriately implemented at Grass Root Level.

Hence, the reclamation of wasteland has to be progressively taken up so as to bring our country into an ecological balance. Problems and prospects of wastelands at village, block, district level are to be sorted out. Analysis of policies and planning for Agro-Afforestation Management on wastelands and strategies for reclamation of wastelands to restore the ecological imbalance and improve socio-economic crises of the area. Thus, there is an urgent need to evolve a planning strategy applicable at different levels including village as lowest unit of planning.

It gives immense pleasure to me to note that wide range of issues which are very important for the restoration of degradation land/wastelands has been analysed in this study. An attempt has been made in this study to analyse the distribution of Usar, Banjar, Waterlogged, Old Fallow, Fallow Land at village level in Amethi Block and Block Level in Sultanpur Distt. including factors, responsible for the uneven distribution of wastelands, and the process of reclamation for wastelands in the farmers field have been practically demonstrated and the cost-benefit analysis has been explained, strategies and policies, planning for the reclamation various wastelands types has been described elaborately in this book. This study has been relied upon Remote Sensing and Geographical Information System Techniques, to add in the planning process of reclamation and distribution of wastelands at village level in Amethi Block, Sultanpur.

I hope this study on Agro-Afforestation Management on Wastelands at Village Level : A Case Study of Amethi, Sultanpur would be of immense use for planners while implementing the wastelands reclamation programmes with peoples participation. It will also be useful for academic researchers, policy-makers, equally to understand the micro-level planning for wastelands, development planning process in India.

Prof. (Dr.) H.R. Yadav

Acknowledgements

Agro-Afforestation in Management in Wastelands at village level in Amethi Block, District Sultanpur as is a field, plot level study which cannot be completed without the continued support of District authorities especially District Magistrate and Sub-Divisional Magistrate Amethi and the concerned departments who deserves greetings Village Lekhpal and Pradhan and the Village beneficiaries of Amethi and D.K. Tewari deserves heartiest thanks. Author is also grateful to Mr. Ratnesh Kumar Singh, Mr. Shobhit Pipil, Mr. Pal for their co-operation, assistance in the digitalization of maps.

I thank to those who directly or indirectly supported for the completion of this study. I am grateful to Sri Ashok Kumar Mittal, Managing Director, Concept Publishing Co. Pvt.. Ltd. for publication of this book.

Last but not the least, I am indebted to my wife Reeta and beloved son Sahit Hridai without whose support writing and completion of the book would not have been possible.

Prof. H.R. Yadav

Contents

List of Maps

List of Tables

List of Figures

1

Introduction

Statements of the Problem

Tremendous growth of population in India and the growing demand of fuelwood, fodder, fibre, fruits, fisheries, foodgrain (F^6) and goods and services have imposed severe constraints on the natural resources especially on the forest and green cover. The over exploitation of natural resources continues to affect the quality of life of deprived rural people who constitutes 75 per cent of our population. State of Uttar Pradesh is one of the major State in which District Sultanpur ranks 22nd in population and 36th in area amongst all the District of Uttar Pradesh. Excessive exploitation of natural resources for meeting the growing demand of ever increasing population has led to environmental degradation and rapid growth in the wastelands area. Thus massive deforestation has taken place in the report has been fairly well documented, which really shook the nation to know that we have lost 50 per cent of our forest cover and it was partly in response to this tremendous forest degradation and the associated ecological crisis and associated socio-economic crisis related to it that the then Prime Minister Late Sri Rajiv Gandhi in his address on January 5, 1986 mentioned the establishment of

National Wastelands Development Board. Then the Prime Minister talked about ecological and economic crisis but what needs to be underlined is that the crisis affects the poor much more significantly. The major impact of deforestation and ecological degradation that has taken place has been largely on the rural poor because half of our nation depends for its fuelwood and fodder on the common lands and it is the degradation of these common lands which has made not only their poverty much more acute but the quality of life of the poor.

It has been mentioned that we have lost about 50 per cent of our forest cover out of 75 million hectares which are considered to be forest cover area. About 40 million hectares are considered without sufficient forest tree cover. But it is not only the forest area but we have lost 26 to 52 per cent of our grazing lands, so here again the impact has been largely on the poor. On the one side the productive forest resources and the grazing lands have reduced by half and on the other the population has increased very significantly and also our cattle population. Thus, it is evident that the reduction in the land resources, its productivity and its degradation and land is not producing the fuelwood and fodder which people require and tremendous growth in cattle and human population has made the crisis very significant. Therefore, the reclamation and restoration of wastelands have alluded and we have to bring our country into an ecological balance. To achieve the ecological balance we need at least 33 per cent of our land resources under forest cover, at the moment we have less than 11 per cent. Our country is having very serious ecological crisis and if we want to have ecological balance then it is absolutely necessary and imperative that we do afforestation by 50 million hectares every year. It was not in terms of the feasibility of increasing from four million hectares which was done in the Sixth Plan to 25 million hectare in the Seventh Plan. The then, Prime Minister Late Shri Rajiv Gandhi emphasized massive afforestation and the target for afforestation on wastelands, many people said, was very unrealistic. On the other hand in one of the meeting the then Prime Minister said "can we afford to do it, do we have the resources to do it," "can we afford not to do it?" Really, that was the key question and that was in the mind of Late Shri Rajiv Gandhi. Massive increase in afforestation would have been achieved through people's participation and people's movement. The specialized agencies like forest and soil conservation, wastelands or other agencies would not achieve the ear marked target because it was not people's movement. The Agri-Horti- Afforestation programme was not implemented as per the requirement, involvement, participation and people's movement, due to which the deforestation crisis is so disperate, that the crisis is so real, that we must involve everyone in this movement. In general, it is no longer only the Forest Department's concern to see that the afforestation takes place, although that is a very important concern of the Forest Department but it is everyone's concern and every villagers concern. Thus it is each villages concern that we bring to take this whole question of afforestation on wastelands on priority basis.

The increased exploitation of natural resources for meeting the growing demand of the ever increasing population and industry for food, fibre, fruits, fisheries, fodder and fuelwood (F^6) and other materials has led to environmental degradation and rapid expansion of wastelands. There are more than 175 million hectare degraded land out of the total area of only 328 million hectares. It has been indicated that our country is losing 1.3 million hectare forest per year. The continued deforestation has brought us face to face with a major ecological and socio-economic crisis. This trend must be halted.

India's present firewood requirement is more than 130 million tonnes per year, of which only 39 million tonnes are fetched from the forest. The life of tribals and scheduled caste is interwoven with the forest and unless there is replishment through positive afforestation, there will be complete break down of socio-economic system.

Excess use of chemicals and persticides and industrial growth have had serious negative impacts on the life of the common people of our country. In the historic words of Late Smt. Indira Gandhi "In his arrogance with his increasing knowledge and ability, man has ignored his dependence on the earth and has lost communion with it. He no longer puts his ear to the ground so that the earth can whisper its secret to him. The national song which inspired our freedom movement describes our land as one endowed with water, fruits, rich with greenness of growing plants, we must make this true not only of India but of all lands."

The poverty alleviation programme for the deprived rural multitudes of India and weaker sections of our society, a positive programme implementation towards providing fuelwood, fodder, fruits, foodgrain, etc. as well as for growing raw materials so as to cater the increasing needs of industries and to open up new employment avenues should be taken up. Therefore, it is the need of the hour to develop wastelands is thus paramount. The massive action envisaged will mean having a fresh look at policies and priorities, formulation of new and innovatice strategies new and more appropriate structures, fresh initiatives that will make afforestation a movement of everyone's concern and ultimately ushering in a revolution to green the wastelands.

Magnitude of the problem of wastelands and gravity of the situation are evident from the following facts:

(a) In agricultural sector out of 143 million hectare area 40-60 million hectare land is considered to be degraded land.

(b) In the forestry sector out of 75 million hectare area 40 million hectare land is degraded, 30 million hectare is without forest tree cover and 5 million hectare is with only shrubs.

(c) The pasture and grazing lands and other public lands are the most degraded ones because they have also been the most neglected areas. We are loosing about 6000 million tonnes of soil equivalent to 5.37 to 8.4 million tonnes nutrients per annum which represents a production loss of 30 to 40 million tonnes of foodgrains per year.

(d) Approximately 40 million hectare area is flood prone and 260 million hectare area is drought prone, besides soil erosion by water and wind. There are several other causes of soil degradation.

Presently, more than 1000 million population of our country requires 225 million tonnes of foodgrains, 30 million tonnes of sugar, 695 million kg/tea, 159 million kg. coffee, 10.2 million tonnes vegetables oils, 17 million bales cotton and 70 million cubic meter wood. To achieve this target, 40 million hectare area should have to be brought under foodgrain production, for fuel and other needs and 10 million hectares each for the production of crops and fodder along with 6 million hectares land for increased urbanisation. Estimated fuel requirement of our country is 230 million cubic meter.

It is evident from the above observations that points to the urgency of the following :

- Strengthening and launching of educational programmes on wastelands development and agro-afforestation by end for the farmers and government officials as well as the general public. So that the minimum requirements of deprived rural poor people, scheduled castes and scheduled tribes are met;
- A massive campaign for increasing the area under Agri-Horti-Afforestation productive use i.e., production of fuelwood, fodder, foodgrain,

vegetables, etc. and other materials for rural and cottage industries;

- Development of appropriate suitable technologies for different climatic, soil, topographic conditions for utilization of wastelands; and
- Identification of optimum patches of land in different locations with respect to water and soil resources for maximization and benefits to rural poors.

Developments of human civilization and common minimum need of the human population is being fulfilled through optimum exploitation of natural resources. In the early period need of the people was very limited which was fulfilled through maintaining ecological balance. Later on excess growth of population and increasing demand of the growing population has compelled for maximum exploitation of available natural resources. Thus the human population obtained power and facilities through optimum utilization of natural resources on the earth.

Economic progress should not be achieved on account of exploiting developmental resources of tommorrow. If the progress till now is evaluated, then it can be easily concluded that the overall progress have been obtained through exploiting environment natural resources. Thus, the sustainable development have been defined as when all strategies for development have basic theme of environmental stability; ecological balance, food, fodder, fuelwood security employment generations, raising income level and removing regional disparities, is known as sustainable development.

We are authorised to utilise the left out natural resources from our ancesstors but not snatching the happiness sources of our future generation. Sustainable development should be viewed on the basis of inter generational system. Sustainable development is called to fulfil the human needs, without disturbing natural resources for future generation and maintaining the ecological balance of the area.

Hart and Sand[1] said that "The essence of sustainability is the maintenance of natural resource productivity."

In the words of world famous agricultural scientist Swaminathan (1990)[2], "sustainability should be regarded as a dynamic concept. It has several dimensions — Ecological, Economic, Social and Cultural. Indicators of sustainable development should take into account this dynamic aspect. Unacceptable risks in areas such as soil productivity water quality and availability, biological diversity pollution and energy sources should be defined for each Agro-Ecological Zone. Indicators of sustainability should be developed."

Thus, justified development should be done, through maintaining ecological balances of the area, to meet the common minimum needs of the people - foodgrain, fuelwood, fibre, fruits, fodder, fisheries, wood, etc. These are base of sustainable development. The natural resources are limited and it should be exploited in an appropriate system. In the words of Tiwari (1990)[3], "There are three components of sustainable development - the preservation of environment, equitable development and family planning, Technological change is a dire necessity for achieving self-sufficiency in foodgrains, fodder, fuelwood, and other produce. An unbroken link with nature and life has to be reestablished. Development must aim at improving the environment for living, providing water, sanitation and shelter turning deserts green and country area habitable. Higher standard of living and increased productivity must be achieved without despoiling nature of its beauty, freshness and purity, so essential for survival."

Agro-afforestation are one of the most important eco-system of the earth. It has profound influence on human population because it fulfils the increasing demand of growing human and cattle population in the form of fuelwood, fodder, fibre, fruits, fisheries, foodgrain (F^6) etc. Agro-Afforestation provides innumerable goods and services to the human and cattle population. Agro-afforestation provides means for people's livelihood as well as succor to million people who lives in rural villages because they are dependent on agro-forestry produce. Benefits accrued from agro-forestry can continue to flow for the common needy people for the present and future on a sustained basis. But this will be possible if the agro-forestry resources are managed and maintained on the basis of principles of sustainability for future generation. Management of agro-afforestation sustainability necessiates an elaborate management system. With the objectives of minimizing the achievement of aforesaid goals for the benefits of deprived rural poor of the society at larger extent.

Environmental, ecological and socio-economic crisis emerged on account of excessive exploitation of natural land resources leading towards growth of wastelands area. Without restoring our land resources it will be very difficult to eliminate poverty from our country, because half of our population depends for its survival needs for its sustainence needs of the common lands and if a certain degree of productivity is not maintained it would be very difficult to deal with the poverty which we face from long time. Thus, the basic goal of the common people about reclamation and agro-afforestation is a very central instrument in dealing with problems of anti-poverty in India. Floods and droughts, are related to the kind of degradation hunger and famine have come and we spend crores of rupees every year in dealing with symptoms and in dealing with the crisis that overtakes common people. During the past few years, it is observed in terms of making a shift, in terms of policies, strategies, from moving away, from an entirely Government Programme to a people's programme. Policy should be made for massive involvement of schools, involvement of school children and setting up of nurseries and decentralization of nurseries instead of large government nurseries, which cannot therefore respond to local needs and what people want. Plant nurseries should be established in a cluster of two or three villages, so that these nurseries are in response to what people want for fuelwood, fodder, fibre, fruits and foodgrains, etc. If local villages want fodder, fuelwood, woodfruit plants that should be created to. This is what the nursery should be and besides this, there is much less damage in transportation and most important factor is that one can identify a small marginal farmer or a land less person, a poor man, who can raise these nurseries and generate employment through decentralized nurseries. Through decentralized nurseries alone, it can generate half a million employment in the rural areas. The reclamation of wastelands should be adopted as people's movement and co-operatives movement of common people and the voluntary sector.

Keeping the above facts into consideration it is planned to analyse the distribution of various wastelands at village level in Amethi Block, District Sultanpur. To analyse the factors responsible for the increase in the wastelands area in the various villages of Amethi Block of District Sultanpur. An attempt will be made to analyse the policies and planning for agro-afforestation management on wastelands. It is planned to analyse the reclamation process of wastelands and agro-afforestation management on reclaimed wastelands in the selected 5 villages (Benipur, Parsanwa, Mahmoodpur, Loniapur and Bhaganpur) of Amethi Block of Sultanpur District. An attempt will be made to analyse the cost-benefit analysis of reclamation of wastelands and agro-afforestation management in wastelands to meet the increasing demand of growing cattle and human population and to maintain and restore the environmental and ecological balance of the area and to improve the socio-economic crisis and eradicate the poverty among the people living below poverty line in the selected villages of Amethi Block, District Sultanpur, in the State of Uttar Pradesh.

Literature Survey

It has been observed from the detailed literature survey that very limited information or documented records on wastelands reclamation and agro-afforestation management is available on the above themes directly related to the conservation of wastelands to meet the increasing demand of growing cattle and human population and maintaining the ecological imbalances of the area and restoring the socio-economic crisis. Related to this aspect there are few relevant studies are described below —

The distribution of saline lands and its reclamation with particular reference to reclamation measures and economics of reclamation has been discussed by Godrej.[4] An effort has been made by Sharma[5] to analyse ravine lands, its distribution with special reference to Chambal valley and suggested several measures for the reclamation of ravine lands. Agricultural land reclamation with particular reference to the selected villages of Koil Tehsil of Aligarh District in Uttar Pradesh has been discussed by Singh.[6] It constitutes a new approach to wasteland studies. An exhaustive survey of land classified an other uncultivated land excluding follow's and follow's other than current fallows to locate the areas where large blocks of land are available for reclamation and resettlement have been analysed in this study.

H.R. Yadav[7] has classified the wastelands of Sultanpur District into various types viz. waterlogged, usar, banjar, old fallow, fallow and kankarili, ravine lands, etc. He has explained the distribution of wastelands in the District Sultanpur at village level, Block and Tehsil level for the year 1977-78 and 1981-82. The increase in the area of wastelands during these years has also been studied. Various environmental, human factors responsible for the formation of such wastelands were explained with the help of correlation matrix and stepwise regression analysis. The reclamation strategies for wastelands development and economics of reclamation of wastelands has been discussed in this study. It has been suggested that reclamation of wasteland should be started as a strategy to increase the net sown area under agricultural production as a means of improving the socio-economic conditions of the deprived rural population.

Identification and definition of wastelands on the basis of revenue records has been discussed in study carried out by Dhir.[8] A survey of wastelands have been attempted and its classification on land use basis too. Sarkar[9] studied the vegetation of semi-arid wastelands and various dependable indicators for accessing the extent of degradation of such wastelands. Sen[10] attempted to analyse the types and extent of wastelands in Western Rajasthan. He studied the typology of wastelands on the basis of land utilization, survey has been conducted using remote sensing techniques, topographical and aerial photography techniques. Wastelands has been classified as sandy waste, saline waste, storm waste, gravelly waste, rocky waste, rocks, with open shrubs. He also attempted to map various wasteland types in Western Rajasthan. Multi-purpose plants survival on wastelands have been studied by Saxena.[11] He has discussed the soil conservation characteristics and animal husbandary practices and economic contributions of multi-purpose trees and shrubs for wastelands development. Chopra[12] has discussed the economic importance of various horticultural plants which are suitable for planting under arid conditions and it can be easily adopted by the farmers enabling them to make good profits out of it. Shankarnaryan[13] has dealt with rehabilitation of wastelands, according to him such lands can be easily identified and used for agro-forestry purposes. It has been concluded that agro-forestry developed on the wastelands are the key to the rehabilitation of wastelands. Mittal[14] has explained the role of livestock farming on wastelands development. He has explained various livestock farming methods on wastelands where crop production is impracticable. Dhir[15] has analysed the recent awareness programmes related to ecological crisis and fuelwood and fodder shortage. Environmental degradation has caused serious problem for the rural poor masses in respect of fuelwood and fodder. He has also reviewed the work of various organisations at national and state levels involved in developmental activities in this area.

Verma[15] has analysed the principles and practices behind the gully erosion and the different approaches to gully reclamation. Chinnamani[17] has discussed the role of forestry and agro-forestry in ravine reclamation. He has described the concept of ravine land and its distribution in India. According to him, through ravine reclamation, the minimum fuel requirements of the rural poor can easily met. Singh[18] studied the distribution of wastelands in India on the basis of rainfall. He has discussed various inputs needed for the development of dry land farming.

He has also dealt with reclamation of wastelands for farming, water storage in the form of ponds and tanks, improved agriculture, social-forestry and agro-forestry including horticultural activities. According to him wastelands development work should be linked with dry land farming activities. Bhumbla[19] has discussed the reclamation of alkali soils in Uttar Pradesh. He has highlighted the essential components of wastelands development technologies which are important for the reclamation of alkali soils. Pant[20] has discussed the problem of reclamation of usar land and analysed the importance of proper planning for the reclamation of usar land. He has emphasized the role of NABARD towards reclamation of usar land. Aggarwal[21] has made an exhaustive study of usar lands in Uttar Pradesh and its reclamation for agricultural and forestry purposes.

Khanduri[22] has discussed the role of climate and topography in the formation of usar land and has emphasized the need to reclaim usar land on a large scale for agricultural and agro-forestry programmes. Srivastava[23] has explained the role of Prosopis in wastelands development. According to him Prosopis can be easily grown in soil having P^H above 9. According to him keeping in view the extent of usar and other types of wastelands there are considerable scope for planning such species in these areas, besides being a good source of fuel wood, Prosopis gives high quality charcoal. Hegde[24] has discussed wastelands development through plantation of Prosopis. According to him plantation of Prosopis on wastelands will not only enable us conservation and reclamation of the wasteland, but it will also provide large quantities. Biomass making it an economically viable programme. Sharma[25] has suggested integration of agro-forestry with goat husbandary on wastelands. He has proposed a three tier agro-forestry scheme for reclaiming wastelands with people's participation particularly of women, tribals and children. He claims that his scheme can help to bring rapid improvement in the soil status and fertility. Thereby enabiling regeneration of productive phytomass on fragile eco-zones. It has the potential to benefit the below poverty line population through production of fuelwood, fodder, fruits and food- grain.

Mustafa[26] has attributed farm land degradation to over cultivation, unskilled irrigation and overgrazing. He has also suggested various measures to check such land degradation, whereby livestock productivity can be increased without damaging the environment. He has also discussed the role of industrial pollution in the creation of wastelands. Bhumla and Khare[27] have discussed the ways in which wastelands are formed through water erosion, soil erosion, floods, waterlogging, soil salinity, alkalinisation, etc. They have also suggested the measures for reclaiming various types of wastelands. Sen[28] used photo-interpretation techniques to map and estimate the wastelands on the arid zone of Rajasthan. Shankarnarayan *et al.*[29] tried using the remote sensing techniques. They have also suggested several land utilization steps for arid land. Banerjee[30] has dealt with the reclamation of wastelands in laterite tracts of Eastern India.

Abrol and Joshi[31] have discussed the economic viability of reclamation of alkali land, with special reference to agriculture and forestry. He has also discussed the various technologies developed for afforestation along with their cost-benefit analysis. The economies of agro-forestry for wasteland reclamation has been discussed by Mathur.[32] An attempt has been made by Shah[33] to analyse the economics of wasteland development under the projects undertaken by Gujarat State Rural Development Corporation. He has also discussed various techniques being used to reclaim wastelands and cost-benefit analysis. Venkatraman[34] has discussed designing, planning and financing of tree plantation projects for wastelands. Chaudhary[35] has analysed various strategies for forestry development on wastelands with particular reference to the policy aspects and the achievements made in the wastelands development.

Srivastava[36] has tried to analyse agro-forestry for sustainable development, wastelands development, social-forestry, agro-forestry, agro-industrial forestry, tree plantation and care, and description of trees. He has also analysed forestry and horticultural wealth and watershed management in Madhya Pradesh. Bebarta[37] has attempted to analyse planning for forest resources and bio-diversity management especially the principles, organization and methodology of forest resource management. He has explained the forest resources and their silvi-cultural management and forest planning, principles, rationale and practices. He attempted to analyse the various field works and data management, report organizations and technical writing and new tools of planning for forest resources and bio-diversity management. Community participation and sustainable forest development in a global perspective has been explained by Bhattacharya.[38] He has explained sustainable forest management and sustainable development, forest policies and community participation for sustainable forest managment.

Singh[39] *et al.* has attempted to explain forest resources, economic assessment of forest and deforestation: a treatment to environment and managing forest resources. Tejwani[40] has explained agro-silviculture practices, plantation crops under shade of trees, agricultural Grops with commercial trees, forest based silvo-agriculture practices, pastoral silvi-culture practices, silvo-pastoral practices and agro-silvo-pastoral practices. He has discussed agro-forestry system in India. Yadav[41] has attempted to explain the distribution of wastelands, determinants viability of wastelands reclamation and strategies for reclamation of wastelands in the various villages of Amethi Block, District Sultanpur, Uttar Pradesh.

In view of the above literature survey it is observed that most of the studies have concentrated mainly in the problems related to reclamation of alkaline and saline soils. Very few studies have been conducted on spatial distribution of wastelands. Attempts have been made to study the possible reclamation measures along with the eonomies of reclamation of wastelands. In general, the main thrust has been on the pedogenic factors while proving into the causes of wastelands formation. The earlier studies have failed to provide satisfactory explanations for the growth of wastelands, the thrust has been limited only for a few determinants. Wastelands problems has not been examined in totality in the sense that the studies were restricted to the extent of the choosen problems. Though a variety of problems of wastelands and measures for the reclamation of wastelands have been suggested adequate attention has not been paid for its adoptability to particular land types.

Keeping the above facts into consideration, an entirely different approach to the problem has been attempted in the present study. The focus of this study is entirely on the following aspects :

- Identification of the problems of wastelands at village level in the respective contexts. No doubt analysis at grass-root level would help in explaining the relative merits and demerits of different wasteland reclamation procedures.

- Analysis of the prominent features of different types of wastelands.
- Describing the factors responsible for development of watelands at grass-root level.
- Analysis of Policies/Planning for Agro-afforestation management on wastelands.
- Reclamation of wastelands.
- Agro-afforestation management on wastelands.
- Economic/cost benefit analysis of agro-afforestation management on wastelands.
- Suggesting suitable strategies for the reclamation of wastelands for agro-afforestation.

Objectives of the Study

The main objectives of the present study are as follows :

1. To describe he problems and decadal growth of wastelands at grassroot level in Amethi, Sultanpur District.
2. Agro-Afforestation area.
3. To analyse the factors in wastelands development.
4. Reclamation of wastelands.
5. Policy, Planning for Agro-Afforestation Management on wastelands.
6. Agro-Afforestation management on wastelands.
7. Economics of Agro-Afforestation management on wastelands.
8. To explain the strategies for the reclamation of wastelands and agro-afforestation management.

Indicators of Wastelands Development

Indicators responsible for the development of wastelands in this study has been categorised into dependent and independant variables which are as follows :

A. Dependant variables (wastelands)

(a) Waterlogged land
(b) Usar land
(c) Banjar land
(d) Old fallow land
(e) Fallow land, and
(f) Other types of wasteland

B. Independent variables (Environmental and Human):

I. *Natural factors* :
(a) Slope
(b) Ruggedness number
(c) Drainage density
(d) Quality of water (pH)
(e) Water Table
(f) NPK of the soil
(g) pH value of the soil

II. *Human Factors.*

(a) Land concentration (size of land holdings)
(b) Population growth.
(c) Growth of fertilizers application.
(d) Growth in gross irrigated area.
(e) Agricultural workers.

Hypotheis

There are various wastelands (dependent indicators) and natural human (independent indicators) factors, responsible for the growth of wastelands in Amethi Block, District Sultanpur. The natural and human factors show a varying trends of inter relationship with the different types of wastelands.

It has been assumed that the waterlogged land may have a positive correlation with slope, ruggedness number and drainage density and it may have negative correlation with quality of water (pH), behaviour of water table and pH value of the soil.

The usar land may have a positive correlation with quality of water (pH) and pH value of the soil, NPK status of the soil and negative correlation with slope, ruggedness number, drainage density and behaviour of water table.

It is assumed that banjar land may have positive correlation with slope, ruggedness number, drainage density, quality of water (pH), behaviour of water table, NPK status of the soil and pH value of the soil.

The old fallow land may have positive correlation with slope, ruggedness number, drainage density, quality of water (pH), behaviour of water table, pH value of the soil, NPK status of the soil and land concentration.

It is assumed that fallow land may have a positive relationship with slope, ruggedness number drainage, quality of water (pH), behaviour of the water table, NPK status of the soil, pH value of the soil and land concentration, while other types of wastelands may have a positive correlation with slope, ruggedness number, drainage density, behaviour of water table, pH value of the soil, land concentration and negative correlation with the quality of water (pH) and NPK status of the soil.

In view of the above it is assumed that the wastelands are the result of complex interaction of processes which can be designated as compound process.

It is also felt that population and cattle growth, development of infrastructure institutions and habitats may have positive correlation with the wastelands. Excess use or over cultivation of agricultural land, over irrigation, high doses of fertilizers application, etc. are also responsible for the increase in the wastelands area. If the wastelands development is intense, the cost of its reclamation will be expensive and production from the reclaimed land will be very nominal in the initial stage.

Source of Data

The study is based on micro-level information i.e., grassroot level or village level information on the wastelands due attention has been paid for the collection of dependable data which can be used for propounding a theory. The data base vary from one theme to another according to the nature of the problem. The source of information/data base for the present study is as follows :

1. *Records*, Land revenue records from Amethi Tehsils. Village Khasara maps for the selected villages, revenue, Khasara register, Economic register from the Block Development Officers, Amethi Block, District-Sultanpur.
2. *District Statistical Hand Book* of District Sultanpur.
3. *Field work* : Most of the data have been collected through field work questionnaires involving revenue officials, village development officials, villagers. Village-Pradhan and members of Village Land Management Committees of the respective selected villages and field observations of the selected villages including action field work for reclamation of wasteland for agro-afforestation programmes to meet the increasing demand of growing cattle and human population.
4. *National Atlas for Thematic Maps Organisation* (NATMO) maps of Sultanpur District.
5. *Survey of India Topo-sheets* : 63f/10, 11, 12, 14, 15, 16. 63J/3, 4, 7, 8, 11, 12 and 63K/5, 9.
6. Annual Report of the Department of Forest, Uttar Pradesh.
7. *Primary Census Hand Book* of District-Sultanpur, 2001.

8. Action field work for the reclamation of wastelands and agro-afforestation management with the selected beneficiaries.

Methodology

Adopted methodology of the study are as follows :

Wastelands

There are 6 types of wastelands in Amethi Block which are - waterlogged, usar, banjar, old fallow, fallow and other types of wastelands while kankrili and ravine wastelands are found in other Blocks of District Sultanpur. The usar, banjar, old fallow, fallow wastelands information are available from the revenue records, while waterlogged and other types of wasteland types data are not available, therefore, for such categories data has been collected personally and by interviewing revenue officials, villagers, Village Pradhan, field observations, field work at grassroot level in the villages of Amethi Block, District Sultanpur. The extent of various types of wastelands are percentage to the total geographical area of the village has been computed.

Slope

Topo sheets of the Survey of India, has been consulted to find out the heights of various villages. The available spot heights as well as contour value has been considered and plotted on the village map. As per the local elevation, some additional spots has been plotted on the same map and then the contour lines has been drawn, the minimum and maximum contour lines has been identified. The average number of contour crossing per mile has been computed. The average slope has been calculated using Wentworth formula :

$$\text{Average slope} = \frac{\text{Average number of contour crossing/ mile} \times \text{contour interval}}{\text{3361 constant}}$$

The computed values of slope has been cross checked with the values available, with the office of the Executive Engineer, Irrigation, Khand of the Sharada Sahayak Command Pariyojana, Sultanpur.

Ruggedness Number

Drainage lines has been drawn on the actual map of the villages, as per the field observation and the total length was divided the area to compute the drainage density of the village. The value of relative relief has been computed by subtracting the minimum height from the maximum height of the village. The ruggedness number has been computed as follows :

$$\text{Ruggedness Number} = \frac{\text{Drainage Density} \times \text{Relative Relief}}{5280}$$

Drainage Density

The natural and artificial lines has been drawn for the selected villages and the length of drainage lines per unit area has been measured. The drainage density has been computed adopting the following formula :

$$\text{Drainage Density} = \frac{\text{Total drainage length}}{\text{Total area}}$$

Quality of water (pH)

The information on quality of water (pH) has been

obtained from the office of the Executive Engineer, Uttar Pradesh Jal Nigam and Tube-well Irrigation Department of Sultanpur District.

Behaviour of Water Table

Behaviour of water table data has been collected from the Office of the Executive Engineer Tube-well, Uttar Pradesh Jal Nigam and Groundwater Survey Division of the District Sultanpur. The data has been also obtained through field observation during the field work. The depth has been tape measured which has been generalised at village level.

NPK and pH Value of the Soil

Information on Nitrogen Phosphate and Potash concentrations in the soil and pH value of the soil has been obtained from the District Soil Laboratory, Sultanpur. Some of the soil samples has been also collected and got tested in the soil laboratory.

Land Concentration

Land concentration has been computed using Gini's Co-efficient ratio which enables the value of inequality of the land area.

Human Factors

Various human factors data has been collected from secondary sources at Block level while village level informations has been obtained through field observations and grassroot level field survey of the villages of Amethi Block.

Choice of the Samples

Various natural and human factors responsible for the wastelands development has been analysed covering all the Village Panchayat of Amethi Block of District Sultanpur. The main aim of the study is to workout practical reclamation strategies of wastelands as well as economics of wastelands reclamation for Agro-Forestry.

Five villages i.e., Parsanwa, Mahmoodpur, Benipur, Loniapur and Bhaganpur have been selected for grassroot level study on the basis of stratified sampling. A village having very high, high, medium, low and very low percentage of wastelands on the one hand while very high, high, medium, low and very low agro-afforested area village. In the selected five village reclamation of wastelands for fuel wood, fodder, fruits, fibre, fisheries, foodgrain, etc. has been practically demonstrated with the view to meet the increasing demand of growing human and cattle population and to utilize the available natural and human resources and to maintain the ecological imbalances of the villages.

Explanatory System

Study of casual relationships among dependent variables– waterlogged, usar, banjar, old fallow, fallow and other types of wastelands and independent variables – land concentration and various human and anthropogenic infrastructural/institutional factors are an essential concern of any scientific investigation. Precise quantitative measurements of the degree and direction of correlation were made as per Karl Pearson's coefficient of correlation. The correlation matrix has been prepared to work out the correlation of independent variables for various types of wastelands. Stepwise regression analysis has been done as the final step to study inter-relationship between wastelands and natural and human factors.

Cartographic Techniques

Various cartographic techniques has been adopted to represent and depict the data in a graphic form. Choroplathing has been used to show the distribution of wastelands. Geographic Information System (GIS) techniques has been also applied for appropriate analysis of information at village level in Amethi Block and Block level in the District Sultanpur of Uttar Pradesh.

Choice of the Study Area

The selection of an area for analysing this type of study involving grassroot level or micro-level situation is very important. In this study Block level analysis for Sultanpur District and village level for Amethi Block and field level wasteland reclamation for agro-afforestation has been practically demonstrated in the farmers field in the selected five villages viz. Parsanwa, Benipur, Mahmoodpur, Loniapur and Bhaganpur villages of Amethi Block based on extent of the problem of wastelands and acute problems of deforestation land degradation and environmental and socio-economic crisis of the village. The selection of specific five villages for field level wastelands reclamation for agro-afforestation and Block level for factors in wastelands and land degradation and village Panchayat level in Amethi Block of District Sultanpur has been ensured due to the wide variation in wastelands from the village to another. There are wide variation in wastelands at Village and Block level in District Sultanpur. The growth of wastelands and deforestation at Village and Block level has been observed to be significant. Fortunately, the area has potential agricultural, horticultural, social-forestry through reclamation of wastelands for the socio economic development of the deprived multitudes surviving in the various villages of Amethi Block of District-Sultanpur.

Choice of the Time Period

The choice of time period is very much a matter of convenince, as the analysis is based on field observations, field work and field survey. Time period for the study has been 2001 as the base year, for observation of temporal variation decadal gap has been decided. Thus, the changes in wasteland has been noted over the periods 1991 to 2001. The field work, field observations and field survey work has been essured for the recent years.

Geographic Background of the Area

The location of Sultanpur is depicted in the Map-1. The District of Sultanpur has been named after its headquarters town. Sultanpur District lies on both sides of river Gomati between 25° 58′ North and 26° 40′ North latitudes and 81° 32′ East and 82° 41′ East longitudes which is shown in the Map-2. Sultanpur District is bounded by Faizabad and Ambedkar Nagar Districts on the north, the Districts of Jaunpur and Azamgarh on the east, the District of Pratapgarh on the south and District of Raibarelli and Barabanki are on the west and north-west respectively. The administrative set up of Sultanpur is shown in the Map-3. District Sultanpur has a geographical area of 4,436 sq. km. which a total population of 31,90,926 persons comprising of 16,11,936 males and 15,78,990 females (2001) of which is 4.77 per cent are urban population. Administrately Sultanpur District has been divided into seven Tehsils *viz.* Sultanpur Sadar, Kadipur, Musafirkhana, Amethi, Gauriganj, Lambhua and Jaisinghpur and 23 Development Blocks. The geographical total area of Amethi Block is 4052 acres and 44 village Panchayats in

Amethi Block, the village administrative set up and village boundaries of the Amethi block is depicted in the Map-4.

Map. 1 : District Index : Uttar Pradesh

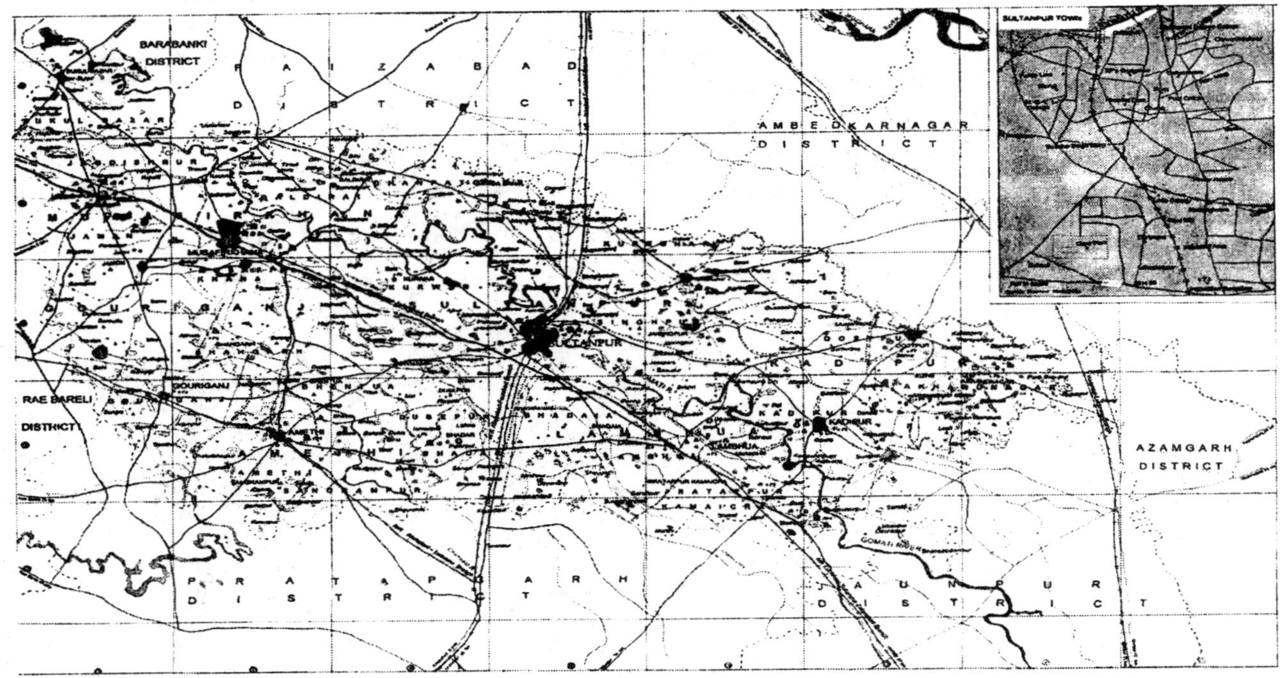

Map-2 : General Map of District Sultanpur

Source : NATMO

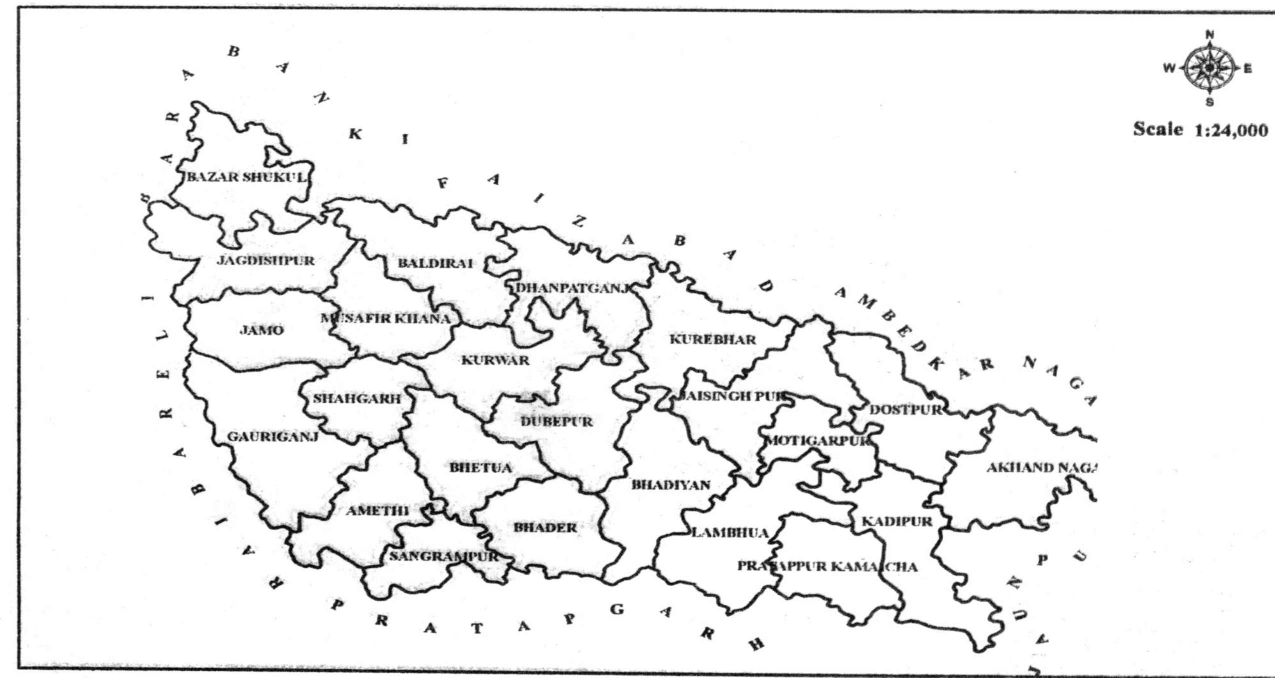

Map-3 : Blocwise Map of District-Sultanpur

Source : NATMO

Map-4 : Village Map of Amethi Block, District Sultanpur

Source : NATMO

Historical Background of the Area

Historically, the past of the District Sultanpur had been extremely famous honoured and appreciated Archaeologically, Historically, Culturally, Geographically and Industrially District Sultanpur has very important place. Inspite of several continued changes the identity of the Sultanpur has been permanent.

A. History of Sultanpur

The District Sultanpur had been the worship place of Saints like Valmiki, Durwasa, Vashishtha, etc. Saint Kanva mentioned in the *Vishnu Purana* belonged to this place. In the centre of Ayodhya and Prayag, left and right side of the Gomati river in between Sai and Tamasa rivers, the land was highly unapproachable. The rope developed by Kush and Kash and it's famous marketing place is also located here.

Traditionally in the ancient period it is known fact that a town on the left bank of river Gomati was named as Kush Bhawanpur, on the name of Kush, son of Lord Rama. Before the invasion of Mohammad Gori, the area had been ruled by Raj Bharsa having three states viz. Isauli, Koolpur, and Dadar and the parts of their ancient Forts are still available, which proves prosperity and self-sufficiency of that ancient period. According to Janashruti, Garha village is located in the west of Kurwar state, which had been one of the ten Buddhistha religious place where the king of Estate was Kalambanshi Kshtriya. His ancient name was Keshiputra whose exhistance was upto Thirteen Century. The town was held by Bhars till the end of 13th century. Historical background of the area reveals that Kush Bhawanpur was conquered by Saiyid Muhammad and Saiyid Ala-Ud-din Khilji. He attacked the Bhars and over impowered them.

After about one year's unsuccessful seize the old town of Kush Bhawanpur was reduced to ashes and a new town called Sultanpur came up in existance which was named from the rank of victor.

The district formed the part of Jaunpur Kingdom during the 15th century and after the downfall of Lodhi Dynasty, it was incorporated in Delhi empire. After the establishment made by the Akbar, the present area fell in the Subah of Oudh and partly in that of Allahabad but after 250 years, the whole District came under the Nawab of Oudh. During 1856, when Oudh was annexed a district was formed including presently Barabanki and Raibarelli District and additions were made to it from Faizabad. The district was named Sultanpur and assumed its present shape in 1869.[42]

Many ancient mounds found in the District are connected by the local tradition with the Bhars. Some of them have yielded Buddhisth relics, but no regular excavations have been done the main sacred places connected with the *Ramayana* epic are Sitakund, a bathing Ghat on the Gomati river. The other places are the ruins of a fort built by Sher Shah, which is known as Shahgarh.

B. The History of Amethi

Manohar Singh, was the only son of the first of Bandhalgotis. The six sons of Manohar Singh divided the estate between them. Raj Singh, the youngest of the six brothers succeeded in adding to his share those of his brothers, Ram Singh and Kunwar Singh who died childless. The fourth descendant Ramraj Singh, Shriram Dev had two brothers Shyam Lal and Dharamvir who owned Barna Tikar estate on the extreme west and the Tikri estate on the extreme east. Ram Sahay, the grandson of Shriram Dev was given as his share of the estate Kasranwa on the northern boundary of Amethi, while his great grandson Sultanshah obtained Shahgarh intermediate between Kasranwa and the older estates. Thus, the hold of Bandhalgotis seemed to have separate over the entire Amethi Pargana.

The next of Bandhalgotis, was Gurdatt Singh, who in 1743 defied the local authorities and ultimately flee to the neighbouring jungle of Ramnagar. His fort of Raipur was destroyed in the seige of 18 days and his state was taken over. Drigpal Singh, the son of Gurdatt Singh, recovered the estate and from his time dates the present taluqa of Amethi. The property used to be called Udaiwan. Gurdatt Singh was sometimes stylied Raja and sometimes Babu. The title of *raja* was hereditary but it is not known how long it been adopted by the head of the family. Gurdatt Singh had two sons, Harchand Singh, who obtained the bulk of his father's possessions, and Jaichand Singh who become a separate proprietor of the Kannu Kasranwa. Harchand Singh owned the whole of Amethi Pargana, except Raghipur. In 1810 he was defeated by Saadat Ali Khan and the Raja was left with only 48 villages. However, Dalpat Shah, his son whose favour he abdicated recovered in 1813 all his father's original estates. Dalpat Shah died in 1815 and was succeded by his son, Bisheshar Singh, who died childless in 1842. He was succeded by Madho Singh, nephew of Dalpat Shah. Madho Singh tried to expand his estate and had to face hostilities from the nazim of Sultanpur, Maharaja Man Singh in 1845. As the result of the hostilities was inclusive, negotiations followed and Madho Singh was given the lease of the whole pargana with the exception of a few villages. Madho Singh died in August 1891, shortly after the death of his only son, was succeded by an adopted, Raja Bhagwan Baksh Singh, son of Babu Sheodarshan Singh, a relative of the late Raja. The estate consisted of 314 villages and four *pattis*, all in Amethi Pargana.

The house of Shahgarh was founded by Sultan Shah, the brother of Bikram Shah of Amethi. It derived its name from a fort he built and called after himself. The estate consisted of 121 villages. From 1803 to 1810 Shahgarh was with the rest of the pargana, leased to Harchand Singh, but was taken away in the latter year. It then comprised 40 villages but had increased to 60 in 1846 when it was again given to Amethi.

The Kanhapurias of Sultanpur are descendants of Rahas, the second son of Kanh, the founder of the Clan. Seventh in descent from Rahas came Prashad Singh who had three sons. Janga Singh who received Ateha and Madan Singh of Simrauta. Fourth descendants of Janga Singh were Udebhan of Tiloi and Gulal Shah of Shahmau. The Raja Tiloi in the beginning of the twentieth century was the descendant of Udebhan. His property in the district consisted of Suratgarh and Naudand in pargana Gaura Jamo.

The other Sultanpur Kanhapurias are the descendants of Indrajit Singh, great grandson of Janga Singh. Balbhaddar Singh son of Indrajit Singh had four sons. Pratap Bahadur Singh, Raja of Katari who owned 13 villages in pargana Gaura Jamo was the grandson of Balbhaddar Singh. Raj Shah who founded the house of Jamo was the second son of Balbhaddar. Mahabir Bakhsha Singh of Jamo owned 17 villages of that pargana was a descendant of Raj Shah in the tenth generation. Babu Raghuraj Singh of Baraulia who owned 12 villages and the *patti* in the north of pargana Amethi was the son of Tribhubhan Shah, the third son of Balbhaddar. The whole of Kanhpuria possessions were included in the old pargana of Jais, but was broken up into four parganas of Jais, Mohanganj, Sumrauta, and Gaura Jamo by 1775

Geology

There are no noteworthy feature in the physiognomy of the District Sultanpur – Thus geologically the Sultanpur District is not important. The plain is characterised by an unrelieved monotony of alluvial deposits which completely shroud the old land surface to a depth of several thousand meters. The solid geology of the plain is totally obscured underneath the mantle.[43] Rocks and minerals of the District are depicted in the Map-5.

The *Kankar* land is found in the northern part, where some rural lands are also observed. The soils are mainly sandy-loamy and clayey and sub-divided, into *Khadar* or newer alluvium. The whole plain of the area is formed of rich alluvial soil which is of great agricultural importance but Kankar or calcarious limestones are common. Various hypothesis has been put forward to explain the geological evolution of this plain.

Geologically, the district Sultanpur does not reveal anything stricking except the ordinary Gangetic alluvium. The Kankar is only the mineral found along the bed of the Gomati. It lies at depth upto about one metre from the surface. Reh and Multani Mitti known as clay is also found in some parts of the District which are used for washing and pottery respectively. Older alluvial and saline and saline alkali are the soils found in the district Sultanpur.

Physiography

Physiographically, the district may be divided into two main physical divisions such as — Northern Tract which lied to the north of the river Gomati running from the west to east and comprised the development Block of Baldirai Dhanpatganj, Kurebhar, Jaisinghpur, Dostpur, Akhandnagar, Motigarpur, and Kadipur and Southern tract, lying to the south of river Gomati comprising-Shukulbazar, Musefirkhana, Jagdishpur, Gauriganj, Jamo, Shahgarh, Amethi, Bhnetua, Bhadar, Sangrampur, Bhadainya, Lambhua, Dubepur, Pratappur Kamicha Development Blocks. It may further be divided into three parts:

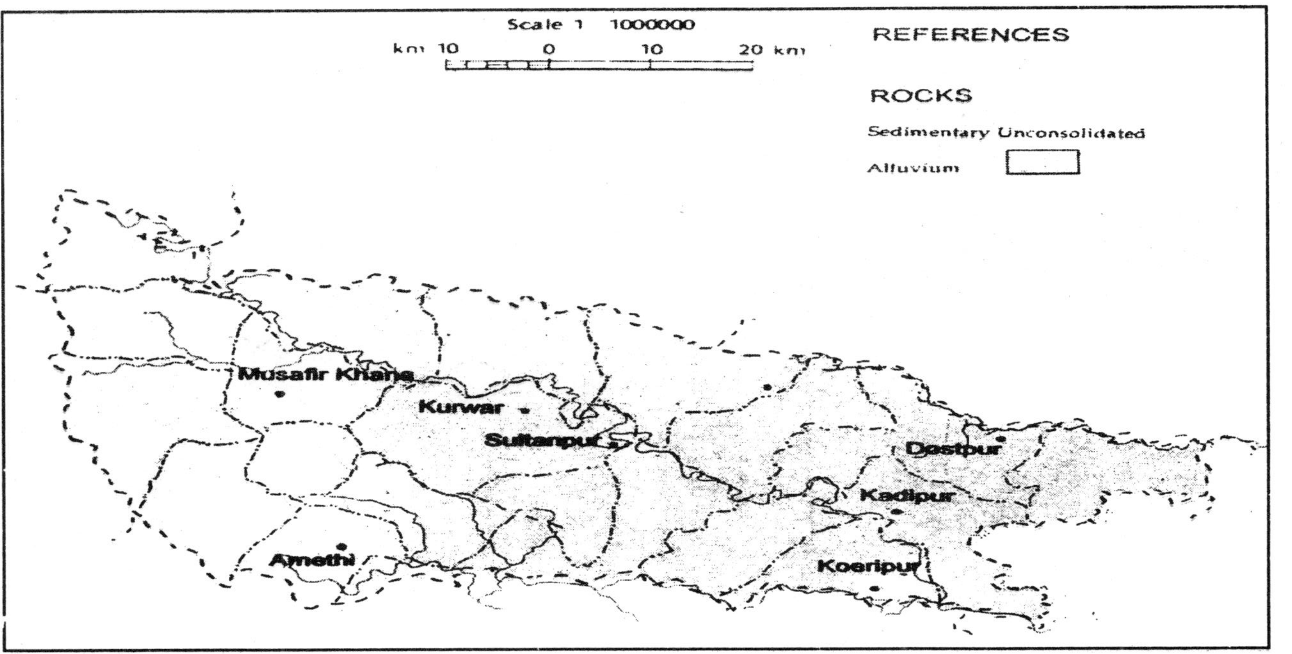

Map-5 : Rocks and Minerals

Source : National Atlas and Thematic Mapping Organisation

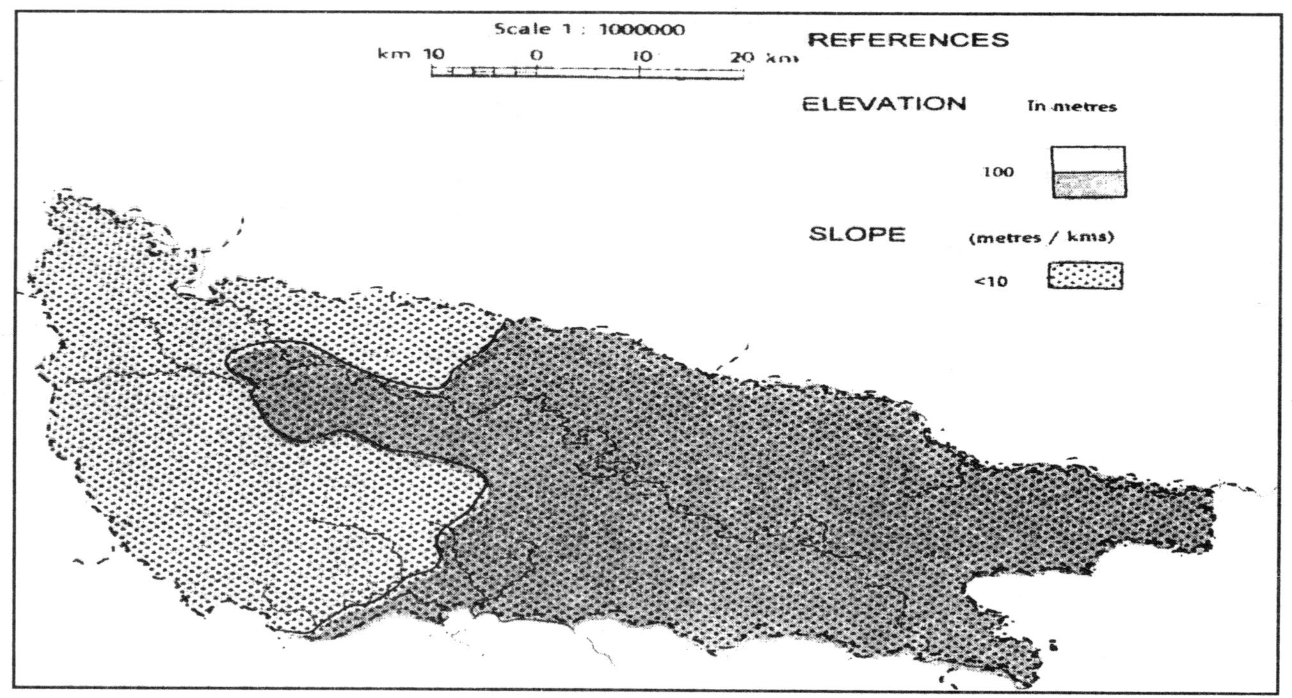

Map-6 : Relief and Slope

Source : NATMO

(a) Ravine tract of the Gomati,
(b) Central tract, and,
(c) Lake tract

The relief and slope of the Sultanpur District is depicted in the Map-6. The slope of the District runs from the north-west to south-east. The rivers which flow in the District are Gomati, Majhuai, Mangar, Chamraura, Pili and Kunwars.

The physiography of the area is gradual with a scarcely perceptible slope from north-west to south-east. The surface of the area is generally level. The average height of the area is 110 meters. Hetrogeniety of the physical landscape is caused actually by local eminences. These are the perceptible notches of banjar tracts. In real sense, the scenery is of varied character.

The Sultanpur District lies in the Ganga-Yamuna Doab which is part of the Indo-Gangetic Plain. The plain is a depression between the Himalayas in the north and the Deccan plateau in the South. This plain has been filled by the alluvium brought down by the Himalayan Rivers. The composition of this alluvium commenced after the upheaval of the mountain and has continued all through the pliestocene upto the present.[44]

Accurately, the depth of the plain is not known. Boring down mainly for artesian wells has penetrated only upto 1.606 meters is the recent alluvium strata.[45] Geologists differ in their estimates of the thickness of the alluvial deposits on the basis of observations. Glennie[46] estimated about 1.950 meters thickeness of alluvial deposits.

Drainage System of the Area

The rivers which flow in the District are Gomati, Majhuai, Mangar, Chamraura, Pili and Kunwas. The Amethi Block is a part of the integreted drainage system of the river Chamraura, although different Nalas join the stream. In general the drainage pattern of the area is dendritic and the general characteristics features throughout the plains are that the rivers meet at acute angles and several nalas from parallel or sub-parallel lines to the main stream. There are several small streams, river Chamraura flows from north-west to south-east. There are tanks, jhils and lakes. There are number of Shallow Jhils, or swamps, but none of them is of any considerable size or importance. Irrigation and hydrology of Sultanpur District is depicted in the Map-7.

Climate of the Area

Amethi Block of the District Sultanpur experiences a rhythm of seasons with reversal of prevailing winds. The reversal is regularly felt twice during the year. From November to May winds blow from the West and are of the continental character, whereas from June to October, they are of oceanic origin and come from the east. The complete reversal of direction of winds on a gigantic scale between summer and winter is responsible for the monsoon. The climatic conditions of the Sultanpur District are described in the Map-8.

The Sultanpur District experiences typical tropical climate with distinctive summer, rainy and winter seasons. The mean daily maximum temperature rises to 40.6° C. and mean daily minimum temperature dropped to 8.6° C. on an average. The average annual rainfall is 1005 mm. occurring of dust-storm and thunder-storms in the hot season is the special phenomena of the local climate in the District. The relative humidities rises to 85 per cent during south-west monsoon and decreases to 30 per cent in the summer season. The climate of the area is normal and suitable for agricultural activities.

(i) Temperature

The changes in the temperature are to out come of the monsoon currents. It tends to set up surface pressure

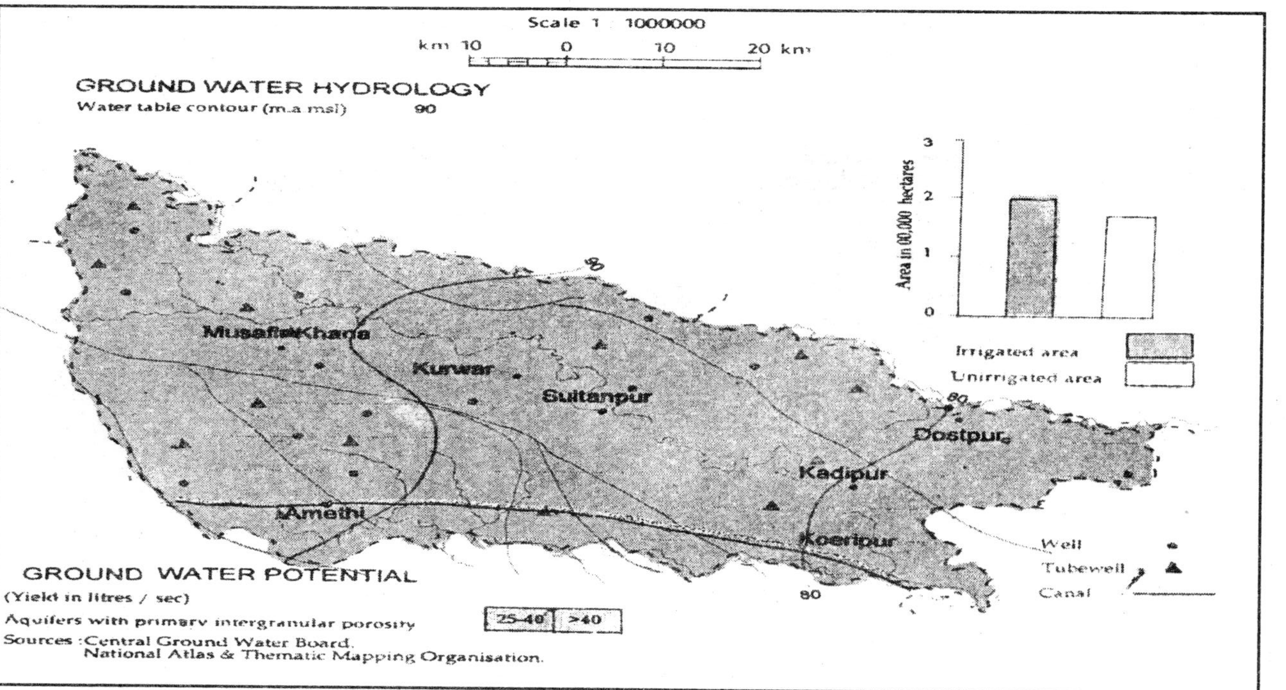

Map-7 : Irrigation and Hydrogeology

Source : NATMO

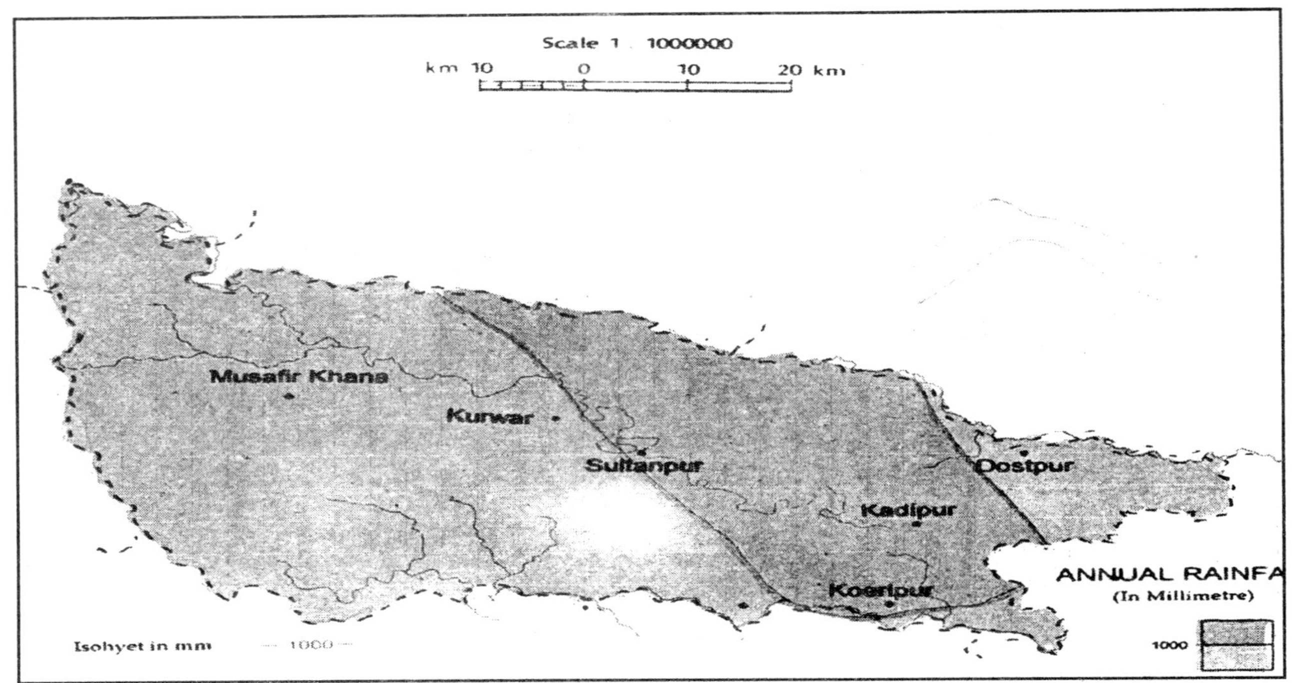

Map-8 : Climatic Conditions

Source : National Atlas and Thematic Mapping Organisation; India Meteorological Department.

differences, resulting in a low pressure over the land high pressure over the adjoining areas. May and June are the hottest months of the year. The mean temperature during these months are 32.3° C and 31.7° C respectively. The extreme maximum temperature in the month of June is 45° C. It is due to the sun's rays falling almost vertically. Conversely, the extreme minimum occurring in the month of December is 4.4° C, since the sun is low during this month owing to the earth's position during winter solstice.

(ii) Pressure and Winds

The pressure is 985 millibars during the month of June, July and August. It rises 1, 004 millibars during the month of December. A shallow cell of high pressure with sea-ward gradient develops over the land in December and January. In summer the pressure gradient is towards the land. The shallow depression visits the district in a cyclonic form ascend from the Bay of Bengal, but the high pressure wind cells in December and January reach here from west causing rough weather and little rain.

(iii) Moisture and Humidity

The principal factor which determines the potentiality of rainfall is the humidity level in the atmosphere. Humidity is high in the months of June, July, August and September. The winds are dry during the months of March, April and May. The temperature during these months is also high and the pressure is subsequently low and the relative humidity is comparatively low.

(iv) Rainfall

The annual rainfall in Sultanpur District is received within a short period of four months i.e., mid-June to October. Rainfall during the other months is scanty and sporadic. The annual rainfall for the area is 1005 mm, but it is unevenly distributed over the year.

(a) *Annual variability of rainfall* : The prosperity of the farmers depends largely on the uniform distribution of annual rainfall. An annual variability of 12 per cent or more makes an area susceptible to famine.[47] In this regard Amethi stands very often in the danger of super-abundance or deficiency of rainfall. Some areas of the district experiences drought conditions, while other areas are liable to face serious flood and waterlogging due to heavy rain.

(b) *Seasonal and monthly variability of rainfall* : Seasonal and monthly variability of rainfall is rather more significant than the annual variability from the point of view of agricultural activities. If the rainfall in the month of June is insignificent or excessive, it can delay the sowing of the easily Kharif crops and thus reduces the productions. If the rainfall is heavy and alternates with long intervals, floods and droughts are experienced simultaneously. The state of abnormality frequently causes havoc and the whole cropping pattern is affected seriously. Early or late retreat of the summer in September and October affects maturing of the Kharif crops. On the other hand heavy rainfall may cause postponment of restrictions of sowing of Rabi crops.[48]

Thus the weather elements together and considering the variations in their incidence, the year is divided into three distinct seasons :

I. The season of rain—mid-June to October.
II. The cold weather-season — November to February.
III. The hot weather season–March to mid-June.

Thus, the climate of the area is mild and healthy. Westerly winds prevail from October to June gradually increasing in strength as the hot season approaches. The northern part of the district receives more rainfall than the southern part.

Soils

Older alluvial and Saline and Saline-alkaline are the soils found in the District. Soils of the area are transported from sedimentary rocks of the Himalaya's and the product of decomposition of these rocks have been deposited over the tract through water action. Therefore, the soils of the District fall under the alluvial group of the Indo-Gangetic plain. Scientific data regarding the soils of the District are not available. The soils of Sultanpur District is shown in the Map-9.

A brief account of the soils and land classification based on the texture of the soil is, however, prepared by the revenue authorities to assess the land revenue. The main factors governing the system of classification are texture, colour, availability of water and the level of the land.[49] On the basis of texture, the soils of the district have been sub-divided into the following groups :

(i) *Bangar soil :* Bangar (upland plain) soils vary from sandy loam to stiff clay, depending upon topography and drainage. Bangar land arise on the basis of the principle that when a river grows older, it's deposits subsequently occupy a lower position along it's basin and the terraces and the flood plain are gradually left free by the spreading action of water during the old age of river. These raised uplands, which are called bangar, are again eroded by the newer channels, but they always remain above the flood plain and are never affected.

(ii) *Loamy soil :* Loamy soil is locally called "Domat Soil."

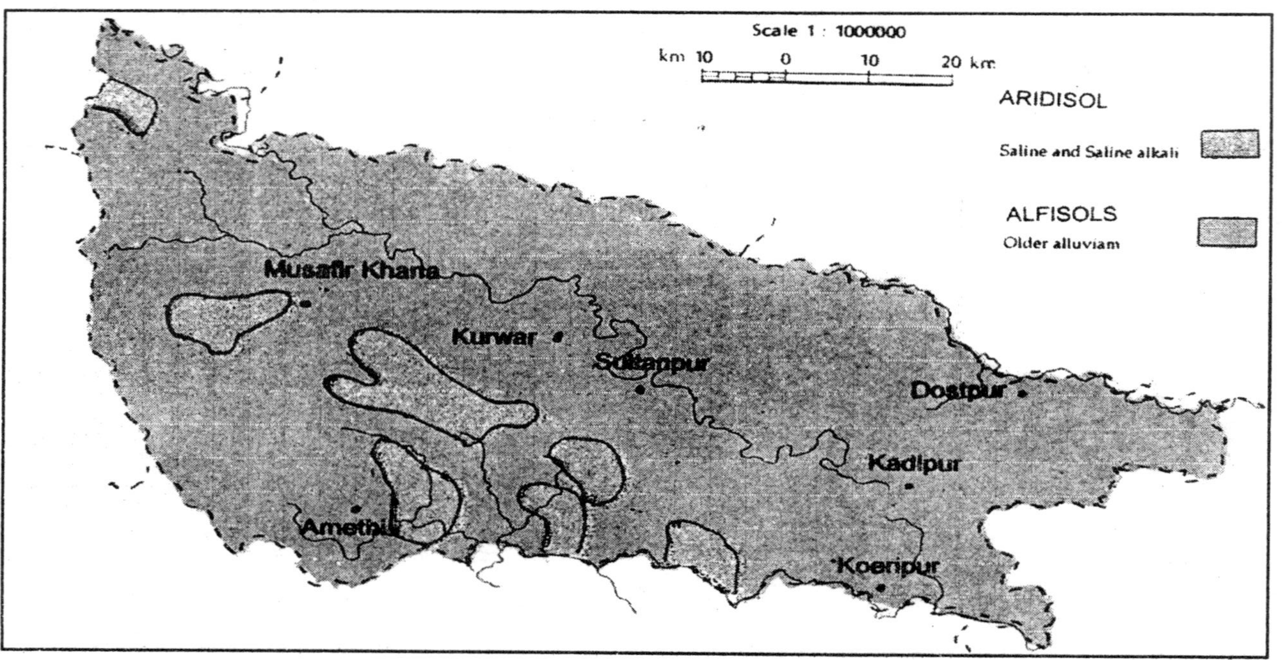

Map-9 : Soils

Source : National Atlas and Thematic Mapping Organisation.

It is extensively distributed over the bangar or upland plain. Patches of loamy soils are found in the District Sultanpur. The patches of Domat soil are very well drained. Sand and clay are present in this soil is almost equal proportions, therefore, it can be easily recognised. Depending on the fertility, Domat soil has been further divided into :–

- Domat Avval,
- Domat Doam, and
- Domat Soam

Depending upon the percentage of sand the colour varies from yellow to brown. The sub-soil is brownish and yellow, sometimes mixed together and some times with alternating layers. The water holding capacity also varies according to the texture. Loamy soil is preferred by the cultivators, since it can be used for double and multiple cropping.

(iii) *Clayey Loam* : Clayey loam soil is locally known as Matiyar Soil and it has gray or yellowish grey colour at the surface. The sub-soil is the lower horizons is dark grey in colour. In comparison to the Domat Soil, the percentage of clay in it is high, its water retention capacity is also very high. It has been observed that almost in every village Matiyar Soil is seen to occupy low level areas. Which results in accumulation of rainwater. Consequently, the soil responds well to paddy crop. Sometimes clayey loam soil is characterised by the pressure of calcareous. Concretions which are leached from the surface and get a accumulated at various depths in the form of Kankar.

(iv) *Clayey Soil* : The Clayey Soil is locally known as "Dhankhar Soil" and it is grey to dark grey colour. Dhankar Soil as its name indicates, is largely used

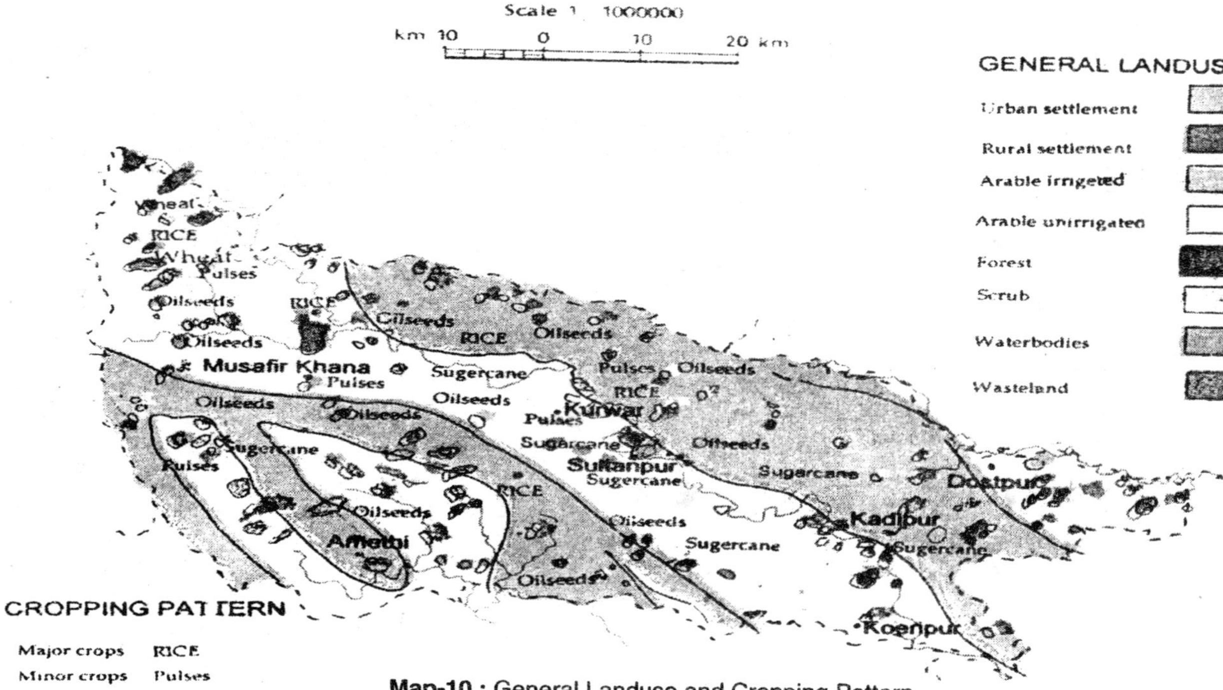

Map-10 : General Landuse and Cropping Pattern

Source : National Atlas and Thematic Mapping Organisation. Directorate of Agriculture.

for growing Dhan i.e., paddy. It has compact and cloudy structure and becomes sticky when wet and very hard when dry. It is mostly used for raising single crop of late paddy while during other parts of the year it is almost left idle. The villagers called such fields with the clayey soil as "Jadhan Khet" (type of Paddy land). Infact, ploughing and sowing are almost impossible when this land is dry. Clayey soil is found only in small patches. It mostly lies in the vicinities of Tals and Jhils and occassionaly near low lying areas.

(v) *Khadar Soil :* Khadar Soil is mainly confined to the flood plains of rivers and jhils. Khadar soil is generally light, but it is rich in calcareous matter. Beds of sand and clay are deposited as alternate layers. The soil in the vicinity of rivers has more sand in comparision to soil lying away from river beds. In various areas of the district soil is loamy and makes cultivation non-profitable. Khadar soils are found in relatively low-lying areas which are subject to occassional flooding, and therefore get freshly deposited silt, which enhances their fertility and allows growing of excellent Rabi crops in Amethi, Sultanpur District.

(vi) *Saline and Alkali Soils :* Soils which has excessive proportions of soluble salts and/or exchangeable sodium, due to which crop production is seriously hampered are locally known as "Reh/Usas." They have a high soil pH value. There is a deficiency of calcium nitrogen and micro-nutrients like zinc, extremely low water intake rate and hydraulic conductivity, resulting in poor moisture transmission characteristics. The presence of calcium carbonate nodules, called Kankar, often occurring at almost one meter depth and poor physical condition lead to hinderance in root penetration. Soils of this type are observed in almost all villages of the Amethi Block of Sultanpur District.

Natural Vegetation

The area has an almost inhabited human occupance for over three millenia and centuries of plough and pastoral culture has reduced the natural vegetation, except in pockets of Tarai and some river banks, with a moderate and healthy climate and fertile soil, the district flora presents no peculiarities. Patches of Dhok (Butea frondosa) are found here and there. The district in general, well wooded and contains magnificent groves of Mango, Jamun (*Eugenia Jambolana*) and Mahua (*Bassia Latifolia*) trees.

Religious Importance

Religious, historical and archaelogical importance can be obtained from the museum established in the super market in the city Sultanpur, in which various important photos and other materials can be seen. Religiously, District Sultanpur has been very important and the various religious places makes it clear that District Sultanpur had very important role in the ancient historical periods. Important religious places of District Sultanpur are as follows :

1. *Bijethua Mahaviran* :– It is one of the famous religious picnic spot known as 'Bijethua Mahaviran' located in Kadipur Tehsil of the District Sultanpur. There is beautiful temple of Hanumanji. Local fair/*Mela* is being organised in the Shravan Month and every Tuesday. Makari Kund is also located at Bijethua Mahaviran.
2. *Pancho-Piran* :– Very famous Pancho-Piran Mazar of Muslim saints/*Fakirs* are located at the North and South of the Gomati river. Religiously Pancho Piran Mazar is famous for the sacrifice and peace of the five Fakir brothers whose Mazars known as Sultan Shah Mazar, Sarmad Shah Mazar, Pancho-Piran

Mazar and Danka Shahid Baba Mazar, Gaus Baba Mazar, etc. Every Thursday the interested people visits these Mazars to pray the saints and local fair on the *Urs* day is also organised.

3. *Dhopap* :– Dhopap is religiously famous place located in Lambhua Block of the District Sultanpur. Many religious people used to take bath on *Jyeshtha Shukla Dashmi* and *Ram Navami*. It is the feeling of the local people that the soul of the people gets peace in heaven while taking bath at Dhopap.
4. *Sitakund* :– Sitakund is located at the bank of the river Gomati in the Sultanpur city. Chait Ram Navami Magh Amavasya, Kartik Purnima are the important occassions when the maximum people takes bath in the Gomati River. According to the common peoples version, lastly Sita Ma took place in the earth, due to which it is famous and known as Sita Kund.
5. *Kalikan* :– Kalikan Bhawani Temple is located is Sangrampur Block of District Sultanpur, which is linked with Maharshi Chayavan. Chayavan Pras Medicine has been developed here it is the belief of the local people. Local fair is being organised on every Monday at Kalikan.
6. *Nand Mahar* :– Nand Mahar is famous religious place of Yadav's located at Musafir Khana Tehsil of District Sultanpur. According to the local people Lord Krishna's religious Father Nand Baba stayed at Nand Mahar while going to Ayodhya. A great fair is being organised on Kartik Poornima day every year.
7. *Loharamau* :– Loharamau is a religious place located adjacent to the Sultanpur District. Big fair is being organised on Shivratri and in the month of Savan to worship Maa Durga.
8. *Pahalwan Bir Baba* :– Famous saint's Mazar known as Pahalwan Bir Baba is located at Payagipur. People use to worship Pahalwan Bir Baba on every Thursday and local fair is also being organised.

9. *Gadha* :– Village Gadha is one of the ten states as mentioned in the Buddhistha religious Book located in Kurwar Block of Sultanpur District. The king of Gadha was Kalam vanshi Kshatriya whose ancient name was Keshiputra, whose extistence was upto thirteenth century.

Conclusion

Population growth in India and the growing demand of fuelwood, fodder, fibre, fruits, fisheries and foodgrain (F^6) has led towards ecological imbalances of the area, over exploitation of natural resources has caused environmental degradation and increase in the wastelands area. Our country has lost 50 per cent of our forest cover which has caused ecological and socio-economic crisis. Out of 75 million hectares which are considered to be forest cover area, about 40 million hectares are considered without sufficient forest/ tree cover. We have also lost 26 to 52 per cent of our grazing lands. Therefore, the reclamation of wastelands have alluded and we have to bring our country into an ecological balance and we have to develop 33 per cent of fun land resources under forest cover while at the moment we have less than 11 per cent forest cover. The wastelands reclamation agencies could not achieve the ear marked target. The Agri-Horti-Afforestation programmes were not implemented as per the requirement, involvement, peoples participation due to which this programme has very poor impact among the society.

The firewood requirement of our country is more than 130 million tonnes per year of which only 39 million tonnes are fetched from the forest. We are authorised to utilize the left out natural resources from our ancestors but not snatching the happiness sources of our future generations.

The justified development should be done through maintaining ecological balances of the area to meet the common minimum needs of the people viz. foodgrain, fodder, fuelwood, fibre, fruits and fisheries (F^6). The natural resources are limited and it should be exploited in an appropriate system. The environmental and ecological, socio-economic crisis emerged on account of excessive exploitation of natural land resources leading towards g:owth of wastelands area.

It is planned to analyse the problems of wastelands at village level and Block level and the factors responsible for development of wastelands. Analysis of policies/planning for Agro-Afforestation management on wastelands, reclamation of wastelands, agro-afforestation management on wastelands and it cost-benefit analysis and suggesting suitable strategies for the reclamation of wastelands for agro-afforestation management to restore the ecological imbalances and improve socio-economic crisis of the area. Inter relationship with different types of wastelands and natural and human factors show a varying trends which is being analysed in this study. The study is based on various sources of data including direct field survey and field work action programmes in five villages viz. Loniapur, Parsanwa, Benipur, Mahmoodpur and Bhaganpur for practical demonstration farmers field for reclamation of wastelands for agro-afforestation management to meet the increasing demand of growing cattle and human population.

In ancient times the headquarters town was known as Kasupura or Kushbhawanpur after the name of its founder Kusha, son of Rama. The town was held by Bhars till the end of thirteenth century when two horse dealers Saiyid Muhammad and Saiyid Ala-ud-Din offered some horses for sale to the chief of Bhars, whose seized the horses and killed the both brothers news of which prompted Ala-ud-Din Khilji to punish the Bhars himself. He attacked the Bhars and powered them. After about one year's unsuccessful seize the old town of Kushbhawanpur was reduced to ashes and a new town called Sultanpur came upto existence which was named from the rank of victor or Sultan.

Geologically the District does not reveal anything striking except the ordinary Gangetic alluvium. The Kankar is only the mineral found along the bed of Gomati River. It lies upto a depth of one meter. Reh and Multani Mitti is also found in some parts of the District. Older alluvium and saline and saline alkali soils are found in the area.

Agro-climatic conditions of the District Sultanpur is appropriate for agro-afforestation programmes.

Sitakund on the bank of river Gomati in Sultanpur city is known for religious importance city is known for religious importance. Dhopap situated in Kadipur Tehsil where Ram Chandra obtained of solution for the sin of killing the demon king Ravana and Visethua Mahaviram temple located in Kadipur, etc. are the religiously important places in District Sultanpur.

Thus the District Sultanpur is full of natural and human resources. Appropriate exploitation of these resources will be helpful in restoring the ecological imbalances and socio-economic crisis of the District.

Keeping the above facts into consideration an attempt is being made to analyse the problems of wastelands at village and Block level in District Sultanpur and factors in wastelands developments, policies and planning of agro-afforestation. Agro-afforested area and reclamation of wastelands for agro-afforestation management and strategies for the agro-afforestation management on wastelands to restore the environmental and ecological degradation and to improve the socio-economic crisis and to meet the increasing demand of growing cattle and human population for fuelwood, fodder, fibre, fruits, fisheries and foodgrain (F^6) for the deprived down trodden people of Amethi Block, Sultanpur District.

Notes

1. Hart, D.R.D. and Sands, M.W. "Sustainable Land use System Research and Development." In *International Workshop on Sustainable Land use System Research*, 1990, Feb. 12-16 p. 3.

2. Swaminathan, M.S., Opening Remarks '*International Workshop on Sustainable Land Use Systems Research, New Delhi*, Feb. 12-16. 1990
3. Tiwari, D.N., "Technology for Sustainable Development National Seminar on Technology for Sustainable Development, March, 17-18 Guru Ghasi Das University, p. 17. 1990.
4. Gedroiz, K.K,. Saline soils and their improvement, *J. exp Agron*, 18, In Russian; translated by Waksman SA).
5. Sharma, H.S, *Ravine erosion in India*, Concept Publishing Co., New Delhi, 1980.
6. Singh, Abha Lakshmi, *Economics and Geography of Agricultural Land Reclamation*, BR Publishing Corp, Vivekanand Nagar, New Delhi, 1978.
7. Yadav, H.R., *Genesis and utilization of wastelands*, Concept Publishing Co., New Delhi, 1986.
8. Dhir, R.P., Concept and definition of wastelands, *Proc ICAR Sponsored Summer Institute*, Central Arid Zone Research Institute, Jodhpur.
9. Sarkar, Vinod, Vegetation of semi-arid wastelands and indicators of degradation, *Proc ICAR Sponsored Summer Institute*, Central Arid Zone Research Institute, Jodhpur.
10. Sen, A.K., Typology of wastelands and mapping procedure in Rajasthan, *Proc ICAR Sponsored Summer Institute*, Central Arid Zone Research Institute, Jodhpur.
11. Saxena, S.K., Economic attributes of some multipurpose plants needed for wasteland development, *Proc ICAR Sponsored Summer Institute*, Central Arid Zone Research Institute, Jodhpur.
12. Chopra, D.P., Promising horticultural plants of economic importance for wastelands, *Proc ICAR Sponsored Summer Institute*, Central Arid Zone Research Institute, Jodhpur, 1986.
13. Shankarnarayan, K.A., Agroforestry, the key of rehabilitation of wasteland, *Proc ICAR Sponsored Summer Institute*, Central Arid Zone Research Institute, Jodhpur, 1986.
14. Mittal, J.P., Role of livestock farming in wasteland development, *Proc ICAR Sponsored Summer Institute*, Central Arid Zone Research Institute, Jodhpur, 1986.
15. Dhir, R.P., Organisations involved or concerned in development of wastelands, *Proc ICAR Sponsored Summer Institute*, (Central Arid Zone Research Institute, Jodhpur, 1986.
16. Verma, Balvir, Principles and practices in gully reclamation, *Proc ICAR Sponsored Summer Institute*, Central Arid Zone Research Institute, Jodhpur, 1986.
17. Chinnamani, S., Forestry, social forestry and agroforestry in ravine reclamation, *Proc ICAR Sponsored Summer Institute*, Central Arid Zone Research Institute, Jodhpur, 1986.
18. Singh, R.P., Dryland agriculture and wasteland development, *Proc*

ICAR Sponsored Summer Institute, Central Arid Zone Research Institute, Jodhpur, 1986.

19. Bhumbla, D.R., Note on reclamation of alkali soils in Uttar Pradesh, *Proc Seminar-cum-Workship on Afforestation of Usar Wastelands,* (Society for Promotion of Wasteland Development, New Delhi) 1985.
20. Pant, S.C., Rols of NABARD in reclamation of usar wasteland, *Proc Seminar-cum-Workshop on Afforestation of Usar Wastelands* Society for Promotion of Wasteland Development, New Delhi, 1985.
21. Aggarwal, V.P., Background note on reclamation of alkali area usar lands of Uttar Pradesh, *Proc. Seminar-cum-Workshop on Afforestation of Usar Wastelands,* Society for Promotion of Wasteland Development, New Delhi 1985.
22. Khanduri, H.C., Reclamation of usar land for agriculture by afforestation, *Proc Seminar-cum-Workshop on Afforestation of Usar Wastelands,* Society for Promotion of Wasteland Development, New Delhi 1985.
23. Shrivastava, K.B., Role of prosopis in wastelands development, *Proc Seminar-cum-Workshop on Afforestation of Usar Wastelands,* Society for Promotion of Wasteland Development, New Delhi 1985.
24. Hegde, N.G., Wasteland development: Alternatives to *Prosopois Juliflora, Proc Sminar-cum-Workshop on Afforestation of Usar Wastelands,* Society for Promotion of Wasteland Development, New Delhi 1985.
25. Sharma, K., Prospects of integrating agroforestry with goat husbandry for economic upliftment of rural poor in wastelands of India, *Proc Seminar-cum-Workshop on Afforestation of Usar Wastelands,* Society for Promotion of Wasteland Development, New Delhi, 1985.
26. Mustafa, K. Tolba, *Rolling back the wasteland,* Lecture delivered at a meet organized by the Society for Promotion of Wasteland Development, India International Centre, New Delhi, 27 December 1982.
27. Bhumbla, D.R., and Khare, Arvind, Estimate of Wastelands in India, in *Wastelands Diagnosis and Treatment,* edited by H.R. Yadav (Concept Publishing Co., New Delhi, 1986.
28. Sen, A.K., Land utilization mapping to estimate the wastelands of arid zone by photo-interpretation technique, in *Wasteland Diagnosis and Treatment,* edited by H.R. Yadav Concept Publishing Co., New Delhi, 1986.
19. Shankarnarayan, K.A., Sen, A.K. and Balakram, Analysis of wastelands in arid zone by remote sensing techniques, in *Wasteland Diagnosis and Treatment,* edited by HR Yadav (Concept Publishing Co., New Delhi) 1980.
30. Banerjee, A.K., Reclamation of wastelands in laterite tracts of Eastern India, In *Wasteland Diagnosis and Treatment,* edited by HR Yadav Concept Publishing Co., New Delhi 1986, 113-22.

31. Abrol, I.P., and Joshi, P.K., Economic viability of reclamation of alkali lands with special reference to agriculture and forestry, in *Wastelands Diagnosis and Treatment*, edited by H.R. Yadav Concept Publishing Co., New Delhi, 1986, 149-68.
32. Mathur, R.K., Economics of agro-forestry for wasteland reclamation, in *Wasteland Diagnosis and Treatment*, edited by H.R. Yadav, Concept Publishing Co., New Delhi, 1986, 175-87.
33. Shah, Parmesh, Economics of wasteland development projects undertaken by Gujarat State Rural Development Corporation, in *Wasteland Diagnosis and Treatment*, edited by H.R. Yadav, Concept Publishing Co., 1986, New Delhi, 189-213.
34. Venkataraman, K.G., Designing, planning and financing of tree plantation projects over state lands, in *Wasteland Diagnosis and Treatment*, edited by H.R. Yadav, Concept Publishing Co., New Delhi, 1986, 221-25.
35. Chowdhary, Kamala, Forestry development: Strategy and structure, in *Wasteland Diagnosis and Treatment*, edited by H.R. Yadav, Concept Publishing Co., New Delhi, 1986, 227-41.
36. Srivastava, Shyam Sundar, "*Agro-forestry*" Published by Central Book House, Sadar Bazar, Raipur, M.P. 1995.
37. Bebarta, K.C. 2002, "*Planning for forest Resources and Bio-Diversity Management Principles Organisation and Methodology*," Published by Concept Publishing Co. Pvt. Ltd., New Delhi.
38. Bhattacharya, A.K., "*Community Participation and Sustainable Forest Development, Global Perspective*," Published by Concept Publishing Company, New Delhi.
39. Singh, A.K, *et al*, 1987, "*Forest Resource Economy and Environment*," Published by Concept Publishing Co., New Delhi, 1987.
40. Tejwani, K.G., "*Agro-Forestry in India*," Published by Concept Publishing Co., New Delhi, 2001.
41. Yadav, H.R., 1x"*Reclaiming Wastelands*," Published by Concept Publishing Co. Pvt. Ltd., New Delhi.
42. *The Imperial Gazette of India*, 33 (1974), 130-37.
43. Singh, M., *Land utilisation in Eastern Uttar Pradesh*, Ph.D. thesis, AMU, Aligarh.
44. Wadia, D.N., *Geology of India* (London), 1953, 385.
45. Krishnan, M.S, *Geology of India and Burma* (Madras), 1960.
46. Glennie, E.A, Gravity anomalies in the structure of earth's crust, *Mem geol Soc India, Prof. Pap. No.* 29, 1932, 22.
47. Blandfor, H .F., Rainfall of India, *Mem Indian met, Dep.*, 33 (1985-86), 130.
48. Clark, K.G.T., The vicissitudes of the summer rainfall of the Indo-Gangetic Plain and the valley, *Geography*, 17 (1932), 288.
49. Shafi, M., *Land utilisation in Eastern Uttar Pradesh*, Ph.D, thesis, Aligarh Muslim University, Aligarh, 1960, 40-41.

2

Problems of Wastelands

Introduction

Man has lived in harmony with nature, from immemorial time, in a symbiotic relationship which had ensured that Nature gave of its bounty to people and was, inreturn, recompensed adequately by the self-regenerating process of eco-development, built into the cultural, socio-economic traditions of human life. Regrettably, in the recent past, man and nature relationship has been shatered, causing in calculable damage to nature and considerable hardship to man. It would be pre-primary task to find out the basic reasons of this collapse, and the remedial measures and effective strategies for reversal of this trend. If we do not succeed, and succeed soon, then the nation will face the prospect of total ecological disaster by the end of this century. For the latest example, Maldive Government organised its cabinet meeting under the sea, to draw the attention of international community to restore the ecological embalances on account of Global warming.

The problems of wastelands has been appropriately documented. The National Commission on Agriculture stated in its report of 1972 that as much as 175 million hectares out of a total of 266 million hectares which are available for agricultural use are wastelands. The explosive increase of population and increasing desire of the people to exploit marginal and sub-marginal lands for a medium of returns, unmindful of the further degradation people causes and pressure from industry for raw material needs, defective land use and cropping patterns and in efficient water management has emerged as the main factors. The result is, multiple and escalating damage to natural resources, due to both by over exploitation and mismanagement.

There has been alarming challange for the loss of our forest cover. The forest land area has been 40 million hectares (totalling 74 million hectares in all), is degraded forest land. Our country is losing 1.5 million hectares of forest land and 12000 million tonnes of top soil is eroded every year due to deforestation and run off. The rehabilitation process will be indeed labourious. It takes anything from 500 to 1000 years to restore one inch of top soil and upto 100 years to re-establish a good natural forest. Therefore, it is imperative that this process be taken up on a war footing by mobilizing every conceivable resource and adopting imaginative strategies. Keeping the above facts into consideration, the former Prime Minister of India Late Sri Rajiv Gandhi established the National Wastelands Development Board in March 1985 with the objectives of afforesting five million hectares of land per annum, with emphasis on fuel and fodder plantations.

The relationship of man with environment, the symbiotic bond between the rural poor and forests, especially among tribals has been closest through the years. The traditional rights of such communities to minor forests produce, to grass and fallen, drywood for fuel have kept the rural communities going through the centuries. It seems the relationship between man and nature now stands threatened. The legal and otherwise, restrictions, increase, it results in an invitation to the rural poor to cause further degradation, simply because they have no alternative. It is observed that afforestation cannot be achieved by government implementing agencies alone. The main object of afforestation targets have to be perceived as the individual's goals and they should act in unison. Therefore, such an endeavour is rendered more difficult because the needs of the community and individual's are at variance with each other. It cannot be reconciled unless poverty amelioration programmes raise the level of living of those below the poverty line. Thus, there has been a slackening of afforestation and absence of support of the local communities for the protection and augmentation of forests.

Various scientific, research and development agencies has also been to direct their energies and skills towards result oriented research on improving the ecology and tackling the problem of afforestation on wastelands. Tissue culture for quick multiplication of seedlings, work on location-specific species like Jojoba on coastal saline wastelands and redeveloping our lost mangrove's system aerial seedlings over areas otherwise inaccessible. These are some of many areas in which not only scientists and experts but each individual need to engage themselves in the integrated sustainable afforestation programme. In this regard a modern poet Kilmer Joice wrote :

> *"I think that I shall never see,*
> *A poem lovely as a Tree*
> *Poems are made by fools like me*
> *But only God can make a tree."*

Therefore, everyone has to strive to create a true conciousness amongst the entire people.

In view of the above observations, the urgency of the problems of wastelands and its reclamation should be taken as a challenge to meet the increasing demand of growing cattle and human population, for fodder, fuelwood, fibre, fruits, fisheries and foodgrains and to restore the ecological and environmental degradation and to improve of socio-economic crisis and ensure eco-friendly sustainable development.

Wastelands

Wastelands are not a new phenomenon. The term wastelands has been used for common lands usually with less fertile soil, which failed to yield and to give any return to the medieval cultivators. Common man may define the wastelands as land lying uninhabited and uncultivated and which is no longer serving any purpose. The adjective waste has disappeared now because in many cases these common lands are much valued as open spaces. The lands which is left out of cultivation to maintain the fertility status of the soil which is termed as follow land and after a year if not cultivated, the left out uncultivated land is termed as old fallow land and after successive years if the same land is not being brought under cultivation such uncultivated land is termed as banjar land. Stamp[1] appropriately defined wastelands as "Land which has been previously used but which has been abandoned and no further use has been found for it."

A broad definition for wastelands would be "Land which is uncultivable or is presently lying unutilized due to different constraints but had been used previously, which is giving very low actual return, i.e., has low economic potential, is ecologically unstable, or whose top soil has completely lost its fertility status, which has developed toxicity and is, therefore, unfit for the growth of crops and trees due to environmental or anthropogenic problems, has been abandoned and no further use has been found for it."

The land which could not produce the Bio-mass as per the soil and water availability, such land may be termed as wastelands.

The land which is lying unuseful due to improper

attention and the land is lying vaccant or due to excessive grazing, soil erosion, land degradation and due to unfertility and in such land in which agricultural cropping expenditure is higher than the profit accrued out of it, such land is termed as wastelands.

The land which is unuseful due to improper care and management or due to over-grazing, land degradation, and due to non-greenery and due to salinity/alkalinity the land is non-profitable and cost of agricultural cropping is higher than the productivity, such land is termed as wastelands.

Such land which is ecologically stayable, which is eroded and its productivity capability provides low productivity, are termed as wastelands.

Any such land whose ecological system is not in accordance with the production capability may be called as wastelands.

The land which has lost it's production capability due to various reasons including improper care, mismanagement and in which the cost of production is higher than the profit accrued out of it, such type of land may be called as wastelands.

Types of Wastelands

The classification of wastelands are being done on the point of view of its utilization, which are useful indifferent forms of application and cultivation of such lands.

The classification of wastelands in this study has been done on the basis of the land use classification proposed by the Directorate of Economics and Statistics, Ministry of Agriculture. The cultivable wastelands of Amethi has been classified into the following broad categories:–

- Waterlogged land
- Usar land
- Banjar land

- Old fallow land
- Fallow land, and
- Other types of wastelands

Fallows other than current fallow land has been further sub-divided into old fallow (2-5 years) land and fallow (1-2 years) land.

Thus in Amethi Block, six types of wastelands have been derived from two important categories of land use, viz., cultivable waste and fallows other than the current fallow. Wastelands of all above types exists in Amethi.

In Sultanpur District two more categories of wastelands are found which are especially:– (i) *Ravine land* — which is found along both sides of river Gomati. The ravine lands are undulated having sandy soil, in which water retaining capacity is very poor and underground water table is found in higher depth. In the ravine land Sarpat, Kash, Munj, and other natural flora and fauna is found, and (ii) *Kankarili land* is found in few patches, in such land due to calcareousness of the soil the hard Kankar pan does not allow the water percolation. The Kankar pan is found at one meter depth. The Kankar land has very low productivity and its reclamation cost is also very high.

The wastelands of Amethi are discussed below :

1. *Waterlogged Land* :– Waterlogged land is that land where water table is at or near the earth's surface and water stands for most of the year and soil pores in the root zones of the crop and get saturated with water which inhibits the growth and activity of plants. As a result such lands are left out uncultivated. and termed as waterlogged land.
2. *Usar Land* :– Those fluffy soils which have a whitish or greyish appearance deposited on the surface and are not easily cultivable. They are commonly known as *reh* or *rehar* or *usar* land.

The lands which have excessive proportions of soluble salts due to which crop production is seriously hampered are known as salt affected soils, locally they are known as usar lands.

3. *Banjar Land* :– These are the lands which has been taken up for cultivation but are presently out of cultivation for a period of not less than five years. Such lands are left uncultivated for along period.
4. *Old Fallow Land* :– Such lands which were under cultivation but presently are left out of cultivation for a period of not less than two years and not more than five years may be termed as old fallow land.
5. *Fallow Land* :– These are the lands which can be taken up for cultivation but temporarily out of cultivation for not less than one year and not more than two years are termed as fallow land.
6. *Other Types of Wastelands* :– Other types of wasteland include such lands which cannot as per definition be put under any other above heads. They are mentioned in the village handbook. The other types of wastelands are those which were under cultivation but are presently left out of cultivation for one reason or the other.

Thus the wastelands have been derived from culturable wasteland and fallows other than current fallow – categories of Land use :

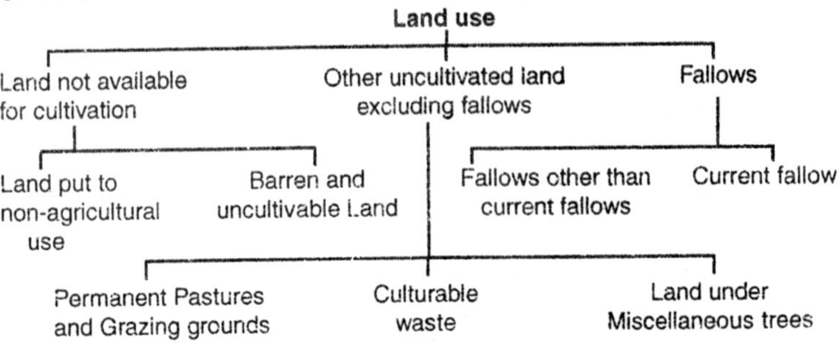

Fig. 2.1. Land use

Thus the above classified culturable wasteland and fallows other than the current fallow land has been sub-classified:

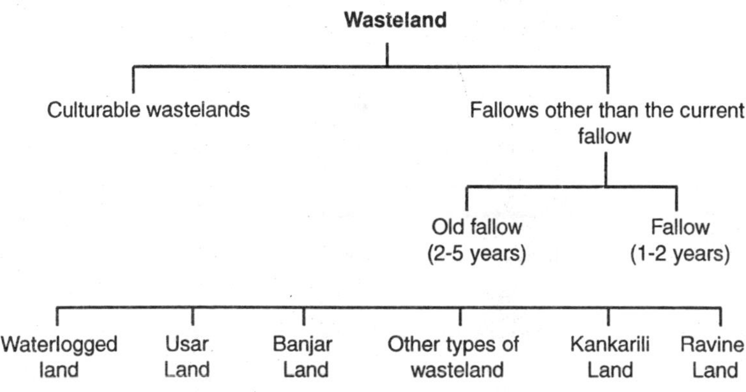

Fig. 2.2 : Wastelands

An attempt is being made to describe the wastelands distribution in Sultanpur District at Block level and special emphasis is being made to analyse the distribution of different types of waste lands at village level i.e., grassroot level in Amethi Block of District Sultanpur with the view to formulate village action plan at grassroot level to develop extensive action plan for the reclamation of wastelands for the agro-afforestation management to fulfil the increasing demand of growing cattle and human population.

Wastelands of Sultanpur

Significant distribution of wastelands are observed in Sultanpur District. Total wastelands in Sultanpur District is found in 1, 03, 608 hectares land. Highest proportion of fallow land covering 41044 hectares land and old fallow land is distributed in 19089 hecatres of land. The old fallow land and fallow land area is comparatively very high because of excessive over cultivation and higher doses of irrigation, fertilizer application and excess use of insecticides and pesticides have reduced the fertility status of the soil. The farmers use to leave the land out of cultivation but due to poor fertility status of the soil non-cultivation has been continued for subsequent year causing to an increase are under old fallow and fallow land in District Sultanpur. The waterlogged land in Sultanpur District is found in 11297 hectares and area under *banjar* wasteland is recorded 9594 hectares. The *banjar* land are such land which are left out of cultivation for subsequent more than five years. The area under different types of wastelands are shown in the Table 2.1. The area under ravine land is also significant because the undulated ravine lands are found along the both sides of river Gomati. The *usar* land in Sultanpur District is observed in 14601 hectares area. While *Kankarili* land is found in 748 hectares area in Sultanpur.

Table 2.1: Wasteland area in Amethi District 2001

Sl. No.	*Types of wastelands*	*Area under wastelands in hectares*
1.	Waterlogged land	11297
2.	Usar land	14601
3.	Banjar land	9594
4.	Old fallow land	19089
5.	Fallow land	41044
6.	Other types of Wasteland	1925
7.	Kankarili land	748
8.	Ravine land	.5310
Total Wastelands		1,03,608

Thus it is evident from the Table 2.1. that waterlogged land is found in the low lying areas and at the tale of canals and due to over irrigation. The usar land is observed more in those areas where calcareousness, alkali or salinity is found at higher extent and at one meter depth hard Kankar pan is found which restricts the water percolation due to which the fertility status of the soil used to be reduced and the farmers are found to leave the land out of cultivation. Similarily, the *banjar* land, old fallow land and fallow lands are observed in most of the villages because the farmers oftenly use to leave the maintain the fertility status of the soil. The *Kankarili* land is found in few areas where calcareousness is found in the soil, while ravine land is found along with the both sides of river Gomati where undulated topography and sandy soils are found. The other types of wastelands are found mostly in all villages of Sultanpur. The category wise distribution of wastelands at Block level in Sultanpur are described in detail.

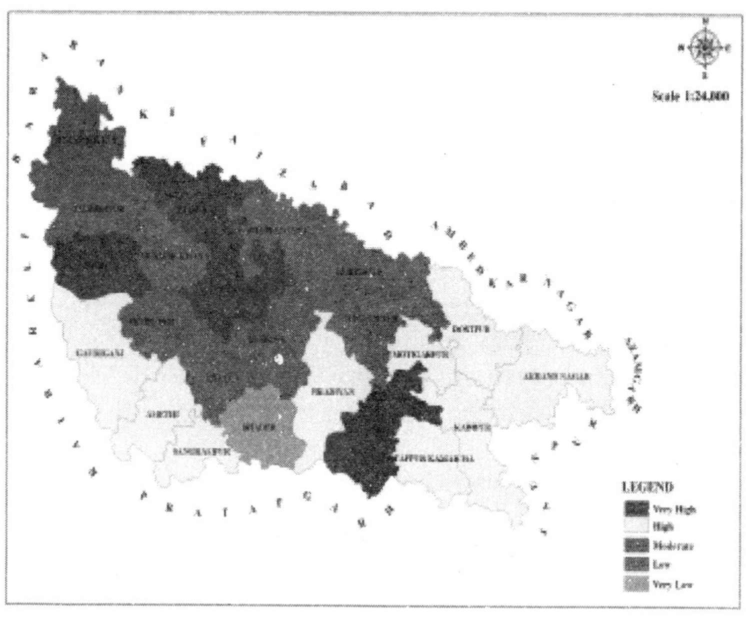

Map-11 : Waterlogged Land in Sultanpur

Waterlogged Land in Sultanpur District

Waterlogged lands are recorded in the low lying areas where

excess natural rainy water or over irrigated water and leftover water from canal gets accumulated in such areas where water table is very close or low to the earth surface. The excess water on the earth surface does not allow the agricultural productivity and due to very poor agricultural productivity due to which the farmers use to leave such lands out of cultivation. Proportionately very high waterlogged land in observed in Jamo and Gauriganj Block which is depicted in the Map - 11. Very low waterlogged land is seen in Pratappur Kamaicha and Sangrampur Blocks because in Pratappur Kumaicha Block undulated uplands are available and in Sangrampur Block. There is no low lying area and no over excess irrigation water areas are found. Proportionately, high waterlogged land is recorded in Dhanpatganj, Kurebhar, followed by Jaisinghpur Blocks where the excess irrigation water is accumulated in the low lying area nearer to the Sharada canal. The excess water is accumulated in the low lying areas which has taken into the form of a Jhil. This Jhil is having much soil silting process, due to which over irrigated water has affected more, the cultivated land leading towards an increase in the area under waterlogged land. Waterlogging has affected maximum areas and in such areas there is no agricultural productivity which is a very serious problem for the farmers because it has not only affected agricultural productivity of the area but it has caused various water born diseases and it has damaged not only the income and wealth of the farmers but also the health of the deprived rural multitudes.

Usar Lands

The usar lands are such areas where calcareousness and alkalinity/salinity is found and pH value of the soil is found more and water percolability used to be very poor and the soil does not have retaining capacity of the plants. Proportionately very high usar land in hectares are found in the Akhannagar Block followed by Kadipur, Dostpur and Dhanpatganj Blocks of District Sultanpur. The distribution of usar land at Block level in Sultanpur District is shown in the Map-12. High usar land area in hectares are observed in Gauriganj, Bhhetua and Dubepur Blocks of District Sultanpur. Very low distribution of usar land in Sultanpur District is seen in Pratappur, Kamaicha Block, Shahgarh, Sangrampur Blocks, and while low usar land area in hectares are recorded in Baldirai, Amethi, Blocks of District Sultanpur. Thus the problem of usar land is an acute adverse situation in Sultanpur District due to poor fertility status of soil and very low agricultural productivity. Thus the restoration of usar land or the reclamation of usar land to maintain the ecological imbalances of the area is very important and to maintain the ecological and improve socio-economic crisis of the area.

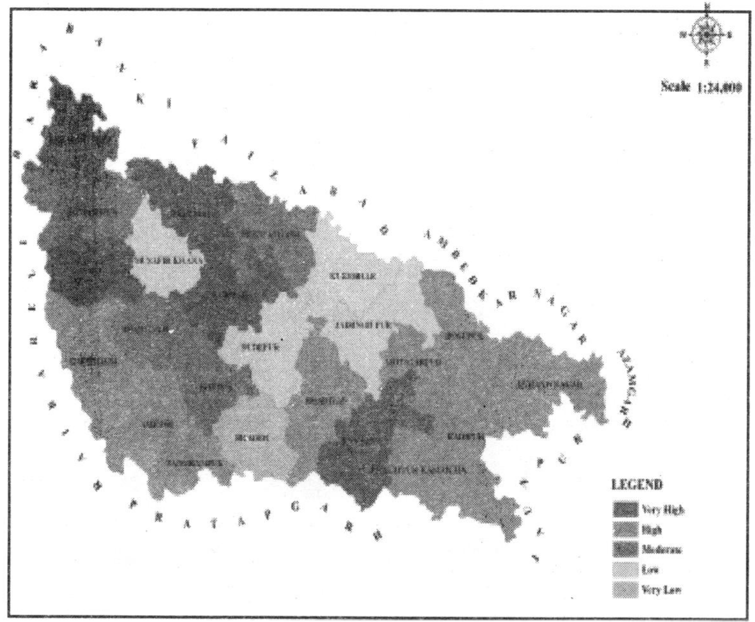

Map-12 : Usar Land in Sultanpur

Banjar Land

The banjar land is found in the 9594 hectares land in Sultanpur District. The Block level distribution of Banjar land in Sultanpur District is shown in the Map-13. Very high banjar land in hectares are found in Baldirai Block of District Sultanpur, because due to very low fertility status of the soil and re-maintain the fertility status of the soil land is left-out of cultivation for more than five years. High banjar land area in hectares are seen in Kurwar Block of Sultanpur District, where due to undulated topography in few villages and salinity problem of soil in some villages have caused an increase under the area of the banjar land. Due to very poor fertility status of the soil, farmers are bound to leave such land out of cultivation from more then five years. Very low area in hectares under banjar land is observed in Shahgarh Block, Sangrampur and Pratappur Kamaicha Blocks of

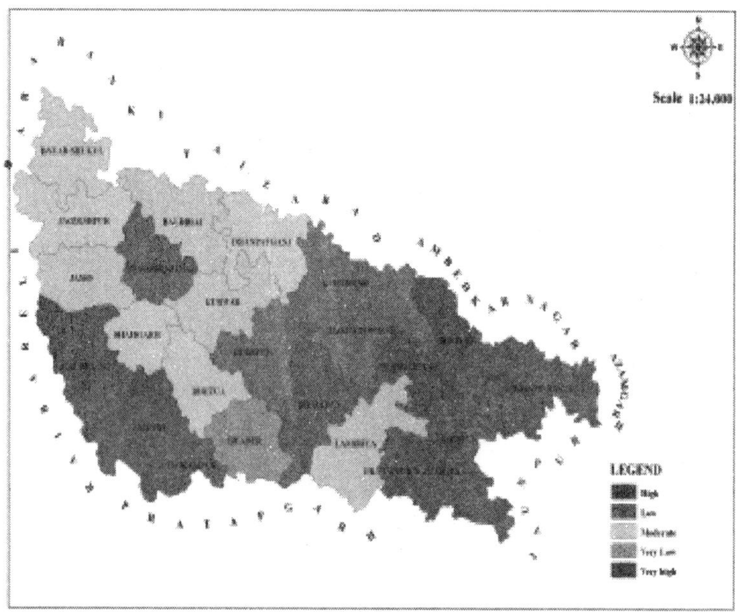

Map-13 : Banjar land in Sultanpur

District Sultanpur. Proportionately low area in hectares under banjar land is found in Musafirkhana, Gauriganj, and Amethi Blocks of the District Sultanpur. The reclamation and restoration of banjar is very important task to improve the ecological imbalance of the area and to improve the socio-economic crisis of the deprived multitudes of the rural poor.

Old Fallow Land

The old fallow land is found in 19089 hectares area in Sultanpur District. Proportionately very high area in hectares of old fallow land is seen in Kurebhar and Jaisinghpur Blocks of Sultanpur District while high old fallow land area in hectares are observed in Kadipur, Akhandnagar, Kurwar, Dhanpatganj, and Shulcul Bazar. The old fallow land is left out of cultivation from two to five years with the view to restore and remaintain the fertility status of the soil. Very low area in hectares under old fallow land is found in Jagdishpur, Musafirkhana and Pratappur Kamaicha Blocks.

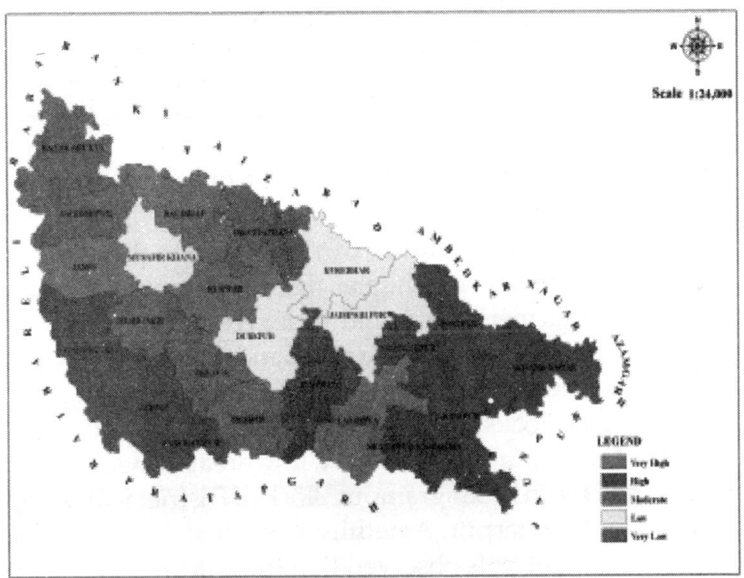

Map-14 : Old fallow land in Sultanpur

It is observed that old fallow land is distributed moderately in Sultanpur District. The distribution of old fallow land in hectares are depicted in the Map-14. The old fallow land has been left out of cultivation to maintain the fertility status of the soil but due to negligence and due to low fertility of the soil and poor economic conditions of the farmers and ignorance of the farmers it had become very difficult to restore the fertility status of the soil from two to five years. The old fallow land can be easily reclaimed for agro-afforestation activities with the view to meet the increasing demand of growing cattle and human population of the District Sultanpur.

Fallow Land

The fallow lands are such lands which has been left out of cultivation from one to two years, with the view to restore and re-maintain the fertility status of the soil. Proportionately, the distribution of fallow land is higher than the other categories of wastelands found in Sultanpur District. The distribution of fallow land in hectares are depicted in the Map-15. There are 41044 hectares fallow land in Sultanpur District. Due to over and excess cropping of land the fertility status of the soil have been reduced, and due to poor agricultural productivity and adoption of traditional agricultural techniques, it had become very difficult to maintain the fertility status of the soil and the cost of agricultural production is higher than the profitability due to which the farmers are found to leave such land out of cultivation and socio-economic imbalances of the area. Very high fallow land in hectares are found in Dhanpathganj, and Akhandnagar Blocks followed by Jagdishpur and Kunbhar Blocks in Sultanpur District. Very low area, in hectares of fallow land is seen in Sangrampur Block of District Sultanpur followed by Motigarpur, Amethi, and Motigarpur Blocks of District Sultanpur. It is observed that the fallow land can be

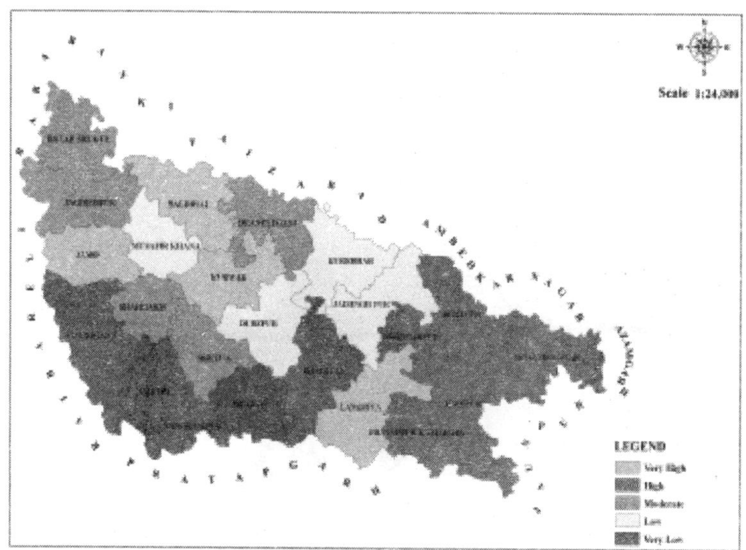

Map-15 : Fallow land in Sultanpur

very easily brought under cultivation through appropriate attention including proper doses of fertilizer, high yielding variety of seeds, improved agricultural cropping pattern and requisite irrigation system as per requirement of the soil and crop.

Other Types of Wastelands

The other types of wastelands are found in 1925 hectares in the District Sultanpur. The distribution of other types of wastelands at Block level is depicted in the Map-16 very high area from 90-99 hectares under other types of wastelands are found in Jagdishpur, Gauriganj, Amethi, Kurwar, Jaisinghpur and Kadipur Blocks of District Sultanpur. The other types of wastelands are such areas which are not specifically categorised as wastelands but are lying waste micellaneously due to various reasons. Very low area under other types of wastelands less than 60 hectares are recorded in Shukul Bazar Block of District Sultanpur. It is obtained

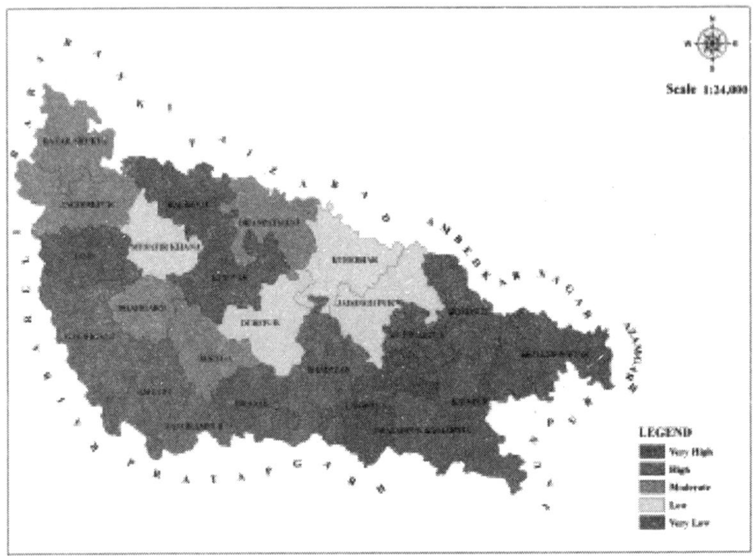

Map-16 : Other types of Wastelands in Sultanpur

that the other types of wasteland distribution in hectares at Block level are very nominal. The other types of wastelands area in hectares varies from 58 to 99 hectares at Block level in District Sultanpur. It has been recorded that the other types of wastelands which are not being utilized miscellaneously can be utilized very easily at least afforestation programmes to restore the ecological and environmental degradation of the area. In the other types of wastelands departmental and community afforestation programme may be implemented with the view to obtain common minimum requirements of the growing population.

Kankarili Land

The Kankarili land is found in 748 hectares area which is mentioned in the Table 2.2. The Kankarili land is found only in 10 Blocks of District Sultanpur. While 13 Blocks are not having Kankarili land. The Kankarili land is not observed in

Table 2.2 : Wastelands District Sultanpur

(Wasteland in Hectares)

Sl. No.	*Name of Block*	*Water-logged*	*Usar*	*Banjar*	*Old Fallow*	*Fallow land*	*Other type of Wasteland*	*Kankarili Land*	*Ravine Land*	*Total Waste-lands*
1.	Shukul Bazar	522	589	622	1014	1445	58	—	340	4590
2.	Jagdishpur	488	613	539	371	2892	99	—	360	5362
3.	Musafirkhana	392	535	256	481	2291	88	—	765	4808
4.	Baldirai	180	377	1075	683	1382	86	—	850	3633
5.	Jamo	1373	423	556	818	2085	79	—	—	5334
6.	Shahgarh	480	280	167	811	1447	74	—	—	3259
7.	Gauriganj	1023	734	213	603	2120	95	—	—	4738
8.	Amethi	131	348	211	712	1128	93	—	—	2623
9.	Bhnetua	142	795	329	603	1673	83	—	—	3625
10.	Bhadar	187	699	310	651	2759	82	—	—	4666
11.	Sangrampur	24	288	199	546	627	72	—	—	1762
12.	Dhanpatganj	889	801	588	1169	3502	78	158	489	7674
13.	Kurebhar	899	506	393	1349	2924	94	135	428	6728
14.	Jaisinghpur	782	514	448	1325	2742	98	95	208	5172
15.	Kurwar	363	451	786	1006	1733	77	180	682	4278
16.	Dubepur	271	706	452	951	2516	86	35	185	5102
17.	Bhadainya	456	621	456	879	2237	87	65	359	5160
18.	Dostpur	424	962	395	859	1655	83	45	188	4611
19.	Akhandnagar	532	1803	382	1191	3008	84	—	—	7000
20.	Lambhua	531	685	370	755	1722	79	—	136	4278
21.	Pratappur Kamaicha	91	278	176	457	1935	71	10	30	3048
22.	Kadipur	114	983	480	1023	2341	99	35	110	1184
23.	Motigarpur	199	613	266	583	1015	81	30	180	2967
	Total	11297	14601	9594	19089	41044	1925	748	5310	103608

the blocks of Musafirkhana, Gauriganj and Amethi Tehsils, followed by Akhandnagar and Lumbhua Blocks of Kadipur and Lambhua Tehsils respectively. Proportionately more than 100 hectares Kankarili land is found in Dhanpatganj, Kurebhar and Kurwar blocks of Sultanpur District. More than 50 hectares to 80 hectares Kankarili land is observed in Jaisinghpur, and Bhadainya Blocks while Dostpur Block has 45 hectares Kankarili land followed by Kadipur and Dubepur Blocks having 35 hectares of Kankarili land and 30 hectares Kankarili land in Motigarpur Block while very low 10 hectares Kankarili land is recorded in Pratappur Kamaicha Block of District Sultanpur. Proportionately, the calcariousness is found very high in Kankarili land and Kankar pan is found in the soil which creates hinderance in the germination of species and plants because of poor percolation of water and due to calcareousness the plants does not grow due to which the Kankarili land is left out of cultivation and such lands are lying waste without any use which has led to ecological and environmental degradation.

Ravine Land

Ravine land has undulated topography and sandy soils which has very poor water retaining capacity due to which agro-afforestation programmes are not successfully implemented. In the ravine land Sarpat, Kash, Munj and Shrubs are grown naturally and the soil erosion in the ravine land is comparatively higher than the other types of land. Due to sandyness and undulated topography and poor water retaining capacity of the soil and poor fertility status of the soil the ravine land is left out of cultivation. The ravine land is found along with the both sides of Gomati river. There are no ravine land in Jamo, Shahgarh, Gauriganj, Amethi, Bhnetua, Bhadar, Sangrampur and Akhandnagar blocks of District Sultanpur. Very high more than 600 hectares ravine land is found in Musafirkhan and Baldirai Blocks and Kurwar

Blocks of Sultanpur District. There are 489 hectares ravine land in Dhanpatganj and 428 hectares ravine land in Kurebhar Blocks followed by 359 hectares in Bhadainya Block and Shukul Bazar - 340 hectares and Jagdishpur having 360 hectares ravine land and 208 hectares ravine land in Jaisinghpur Blocks of District Sultanpur. Low ravine land is observed in Dubepur with 185 hectares and Dootpur with 185 hectares and Lambhua having 136 hectares. Kadipur having 110 hectares ravine land while very low 30 hectares of ravine land is found in Pratappur Kamaicha Block of District Sultanpur. It is very difficult to reclaim the ravine land under cultivation due to very high water table and poor retaining water capacity and undulated topography and sandy soil but ravine land can be easily reclaimed for social forestry programmes to fulfil the increasing demand of fibre, fuelwood, fodder need of the growing cattle and human population and to restore the ecological crisis of the area and improve the socio-economic crisis of people.

Total Wastelands

There are 103608 hectares total wastelands in Sultanpur District. The distribution of total wastelands are depicted in the Map-17. Proportionately very high area under wastelands in hectares are observed in Akhandnagar and Dhanpatganj Block of District Sultanpur followed by Kurebhar Block. Comparatively high area in hectares of wastelands are seen in Jagdishpur, Jamo, Jaisinghpur, Dubepur and Bhadainya Blocks of District Sultanpur, while very low area in hectares under total wastelands are observed Sangrampur and Kadipur Blocks, while low area in hectares of total wastelands are found in Baldirai, Shahgarh, Amethi, Bhnetua, and Pratappur Kamaicha Blocks of the District Sultanpur. The wastelands available in Sultanpur District are lying unutilized due to ignorance and techno-socio-economic backwardness, and such lands can be easily through under

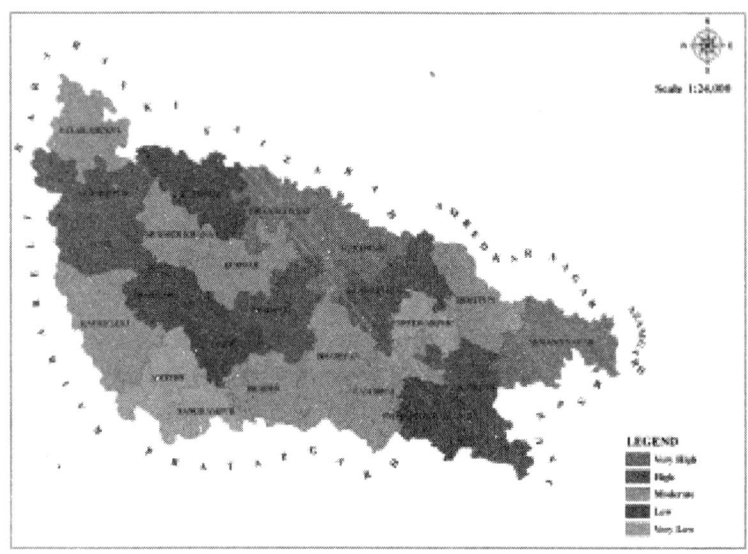

Map-17 : Total Wastelands in Sulpanpur

agro-afforestation activities adopting techno-scientific methods of reclamation. No doubt such reclaimed wastelands can be utilized for agro-afforestation programmes to meet the increasing demand of fuelwood, fodder, fibre, fruits fisheries and foodgrains (F^6) which will be helpful in restoring the ecological and environmental degradation and improving the socio-economic crisis of the deprived multitudes living in the villages of Sultanpur District.

Wastelands in Amethi Block

The wastelands in Sultanpur District are significantly distributed, similarily wastelands in Amethi Block are also distributed significantly except Kankarili and Ravine land are not observed in Amethi due to different soil structure and topographical situations. There are 11.36 per cent total wastelands found in Amethi Block of District Sultanpur. Other types of wastelands are 0.35 per cent followed by 0.47 per cent area under waterlogged land and 1.13 per cent banjar land Table 2.3. Proportionately fallow land has very high percentage (3.87 per cent) area under fallow land followed by 2.56 per cent area under old fallow land in Amethi Block. Thus the wastelands in Amethi Block has significant distribution which has become great concern of the planners. If the control and check for the growth of wastelands are not properly planned and implemented, then, it will have very adverse affect on ecological and environmental conditions of Amethi and subsequently socio-economic crisis among the people living in the area. The proportionate distribution of wastelands categories at village level are described in this study.

Table 2.3 : Wastelands in Amethi

Sl. No.	*Types of wastelands*	*Area in percentage*
1.	Waterlogged land	0.47
2.	Usar Land	1.89
3.	Banjar Land	1.13
4.	Old fallow land	2.56
5.	Fallow land	3.87
6.	Other types of wastelands	0.35
	Total watelands	11.36

Waterlogged land

The waterlogged land at village level in Amethi block is significantly distributed which is less than 1.38 per cent. Proportionately, very high percentage of waterlogged land is observed in Nainha Bartali, Dehra, Saraiya Duban, Chaturbhujpur and Ram Daipur villages of Amethi Block, which is mentioned in the Table 2.4. The detailed distribution of waterlogged land at village level of Amethi Block is depicted in the Map - 18. The moderate waterlogged land from 0.80 per cent to 1.00 per cent is found in Loniapur, Jangal Ram Nagar, Bhaganpur, Mahmadpur, Maharajpur and Gaderi villages of Amethi Block. Very low percentage less than 0.10 per cent

Table 2.4 : Distribution of Wastelands, Amethi-Block, District-Sultanpur

Sl. No.	*Name of village*	*Water-Logged*	*Usar Land*	*Banjar Land*	*Old Fallow Land*	*Fallow Land*	*Other Types of wastelands*	*Total Waste lands*
1	2	3	4	5	6	7	8	9
1.	Kherauna	0.06	0.98	1.23	0.88	2.23	5.71	8.72
2.	Parsanwa	0.03	0.86	3.71	1.75	1.31	6.54	11.61
3.	Benipur	0.74	2.32	3.52	1.24	2.11	5.73	12.34
4.	Katraful Kanwar	0.53	1.63	2.25	0.79	4.64	5.16	13.52
5.	Hathkila	0.11	0.97	3.63	5.15	6.23	2.85	14.32
6.	Dedhpasar	0.31	2.61	2.14	2.64	3.15	5.67	15.34
7.	Mahaso	0.13	1.34	2.18	1.12	3.14	4.23	9.76
8.	Rebha	0.18	2.38	3.16	3.85	2.10	3.78	12.59
9.	Raidaipur	1.21	1.35	2.31	1.67	2.35	3.67	9.88
10.	Loniapur	0.95	0.86	4.25	3.14	3.67	4.28	14.75
11.	Raipur Fulwari	0.46	1.68	4.15	2.34	2.17	3.14	11.28
12.	Ramdaipur	1.24	2.95	2.81	3.59	1.15	2.48	10.54
13.	Mahamodpur	0.62	1.21	2.35	2.67	1.71	3.21	9.84
14.	Sarai Khema	0.15	3.21	1.22	1.85	7.22	1.54	13.35
15.	Jangal Ramnagar	0.88	1.15	2.10	3.15	2.45	4.56	11.72
16.	Katra Maharani	06.2	0.74	1.18	2.85	3.41	2.36	10.13
17.	Trilokpur	0.12	5.61	2.78	1.15	1.44	1.78	9.47
18.	Tala	0.19	1.15	2.54	1.82	1.88	1.25	8.38
19.	Kushi Tali	0.08	0.87	2.78	1.15	2.48	2.51	7.54
20.	Bhaganpur	0.85	1.15	2.14	1.75	1.59	3.43	8.35
21.	Loharta	0.71	2.58	1.78	1.59	1.42	1.35	7.34
22.	Darkha	0.59	1.72	3.54	1.65	3.76	2.15	11.45
23.	Korari Giridharshah	0.35	1.25	2.28	1.45	3.25	4.28	7.92
24.	Nuanwa	0.15	1.43	3.45	1.35	2.54	3.57	6.83

(Contd...)

Table 2.4 : (Contd...)

1	2	3	4	5	6	7	8	9
25.	Umapur Ganapatti	0.38	3.42	2.18	1.34	2.67	4.59	11.78
26.	Dhandhudhar	0.15	1.21	3.38	2.92	3.85	2.54	13.17
27.	Chaturbhujpur	1.35	2.45	3.56	2.48	4.15	3.28	11.78
28.	Mochwa	0.59	1.57	3.78	2.18	1.15	4.78	8.39
29.	Naraini	0.39	0.85	3.18	3.56	2.76	3.15	9.35
30.	Kohra	0.75	1.35	2.58	1.76	3.75	2.87	8.73
31.	Kakawa	0.63	1.56	3.41	1.15	1.39	3.15	5.67
32.	Saidpur	0.35	1.25	2.37	1.78	2.56	2.86	6.74
33.	Saraiya Duban	1.13	0.97	1.73	1.45	3.78	1.71	9.17
34.	Mahmadpur	0.83	1.38	2.78	1.74	1.39	3.25	8.64
35.	Maharajpur	0.95	2.15	1.83	2.38	2.31	2.39	12.35
36.	Agahar	0.15	1.38	1.49	1.68	3.71	2.76	8.74
37.	Purabgaon	0.43	2.34	2.78	1.79	2.68	3.44	7.96
38.	Ramgarh	0.32	1.67	1.23	3.68	1.76	2.37	7.87
39.	Himmatgarh	0.16	0.88	1.85	3.15	1.82	1.65	7.94
40.	Dehara	1.38	1.65	2.48	2.64	2.74	3.85	11.78
41.	Nainaha Bartali	1.16	1.25	3.46	2.85	3.78	4.68	12.76
42.	Bhusahari	0.73	3.18	1.45	1.28	2.19	3.12	9.84
43.	Gaderi	0.82	2.71	1.85	2.18	1.76	2.15	7.87
44.	Gangauli	0.38	1.84	2.74	1.12	2.78	3.56	9.85

waterlogged land is observed in Kherauna, Parsanwa and Kushi Tali villages of Amethi Block while 0.10 per cent to 0.20 per cent waterlogged land is recorded in Himmatgarh, Agahar, Dhandhudhar, Nunwawa, Tala, Trilokpur, Sarai Khema, Rebha Mahso, and Hathkilia villages of Amethi Block very insignificant distribution of waterlogged land is found in the central, northern and eastern villages of the Amethi Block because these villages are less affected by the excessive accumulation of surface water and most of the villages are having appropriate outlet/drainage system for excess accumulated water. The overall proportionate distribution of waterlogged land at village level in Amethi is significantly low. Even this can be checked and waterlogged lands can be reclaimed by constructing proper drainage system as outlets for the accumulated surface natural rain or excess irrigation water and adopting appropriate management of irrigation water and underground water.

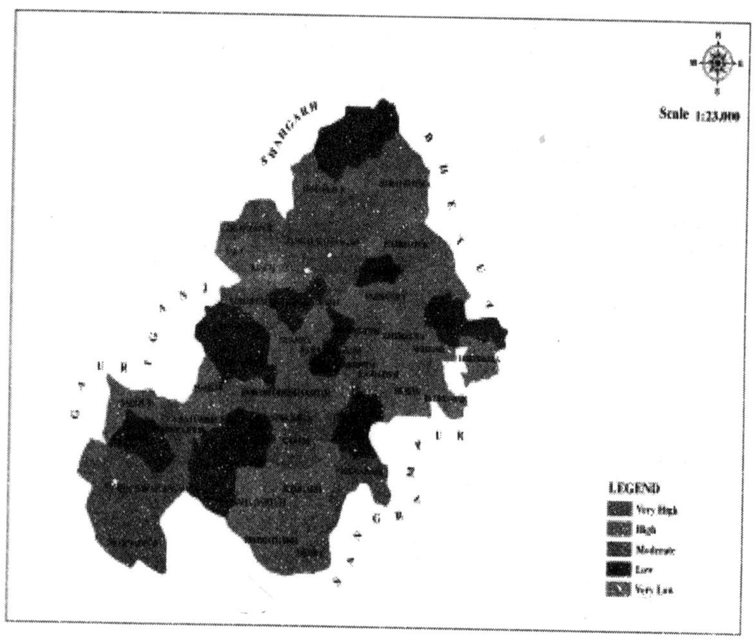

Map-18 : Waterlogged land in Amethi

Usar Land

The usar lands are those soils which have whitish or greyish appearance on the surface of the land and the usar lands are not easily cultivable due to reh or usar. The usar land has excessive proportions of soluble salts due to which cropping of agriculture is seriously hampered such lands are termed as salt affected soils and these soils are locally known as usar land in Amethi area. The distribution of usar land at village level is shown in the Map-19. Proportionately, very high, more than 3 per cent usar land area is found in Trilokpur, Saraikhema, Umapurganapatti and Bhusahari villages of Amethi Block. Moderate usar land area from 2.0 to 3.0 per cent is recorded in Benipur, Dedhpasar, Rebha, Radaipur, Loharta, Chaturbhujpur, Maharajpur, Purabgaon and Gaderi villages of Amethi Block. Very low less than 1.0 per cent of usar land is observed in Kherauna Parsanwa, Hathkila, Loniapur, Katara Maharani, Kushi Tali, Naraini, Saraiya Duban and Himmat garh villages of Amethi Block.

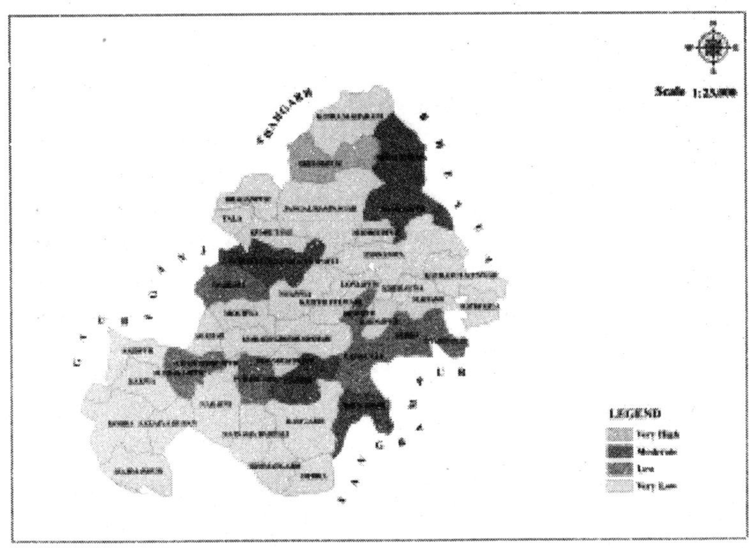

Map-19 : Usar land in Amethi

The usar land of Amethi Block can be easily reclaimed for social forestry especially fuelwood and fodder plants which can survive and sustain in such usar land, but a few decades before the usar land of Amethi had a very negative role in the agricultural economy of the rural poor of Amethi, because in such usar land farmers were not able to grow any crop or plant, due to which the usar land had been left out of cultivation from several years. In view of the non-fertility and agricultural productivity of the usar land, it had been the common pro-verb among the peoples of Amethi that, *"Amethi Na Hot usar, Enha ke Log Hot Daiv Se Dusar"* which means that *"If Amethi had no usar lands then the people of Amethi would have been next after the God."* But at present the usar land of Amethi are being easily reclaimed through latest scientific techniques, and high yielding variety of seeds/ plants and new irrigational system, etc. has made the farmers to reclaim the usar land to meet the increasing demand of growing population and cattle for fuelwood and fodder respectively. Various Government and Non-Government agencies has been involved for the reclamation of usar land but it could not obtained the goals as per the target because there was lack of peoples participation and interest and involvement of the rural poor has been ignored. The involvement of the people and their interest in the planning process of reclamation of usar land agro-afforestation on usar land and its maintenance and management upto distribution of profits accrued out of it may provide a new way to reclaim the usar land to maintain the ecological imbalances and improve the environmental and socio-economic crisis of the people's of Amethi.

Banjar Land

The banjar land in Amethi at village level are significantly distributed which is mentioned in the Table 2.4. The proportionate distribution of banjar land at village level in

Amethi Block is shown in the Map-20. Proportionately, very high percentage of banjar land more than very high percentage of banjar land more than 4 per cent is found in Loniapur and Raipur Fulwari village of Amethi Block. High percentage of Banjar land varying between 3.5 per cent to 4.00 per cent is found in Parsanwa, Benipur, Hathkila, Darkha, Chaturbhujpur, Mochwa, villages of Amethi Block of Sultanpur District. Very low percentage of Banjar land less than 1.50 per cent is recorded in Kherauna, Saraikhema, Katara Maharani, Agahar, Ramgarh and Bhushari villages of Amethi Block. The banjar land are those lands which are left out of cultivation for a period of not less than five years. Thus the banjar lands are left uncultivated for a long period which can be easily brought under cultivation to meet the increasing demand of growing people. The C-2 scientific technology i.e., the system which are available with the farmers and within the villages can be adopted to reclaim the banjar land i.e., application compost/waste materials, proper ploughing, appropriate application of organic and

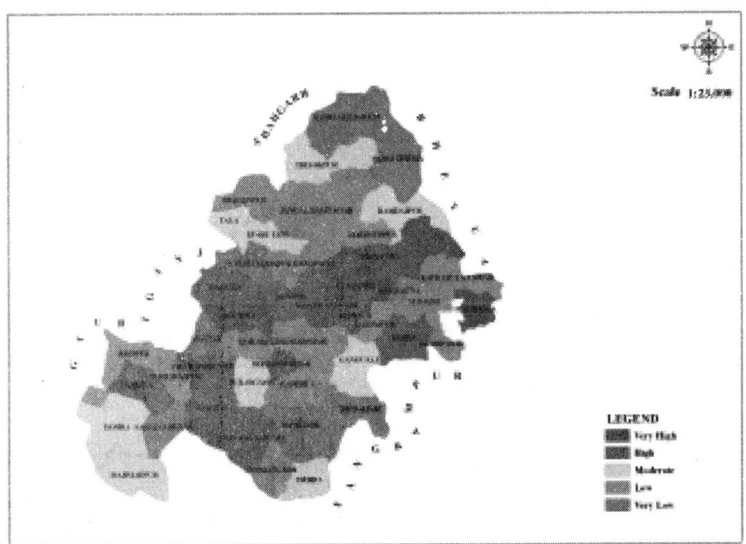

Map-20 : Banjar land in Amethi

inorganic fertilizers, insecticides and pesticides high yielding variety of seeds and plants and proper irrigation system, etc. may be an asset which can be adopted as measures for the reclamation of wastelands for fuelwood, fodder, fibre, fruits and foodgrain production to restore the ecological and environmental degradation and improving the socio-economic crisis of the deprived multitudes of the Amethi people.

Old Fallow Land

The old fallow lands are those lands which are left out of cultivation from two to five years time with the view to re-maintain the fertility status of the soil. The old fallow lands are those degraded lands whose fertility status to grow the crops has been reduced due to some reason or the other including excess or over cropping of the land. The farmers could not adopt the crop rotation cycle and are unable to adopt latest scientific and technical methods of cropping, as

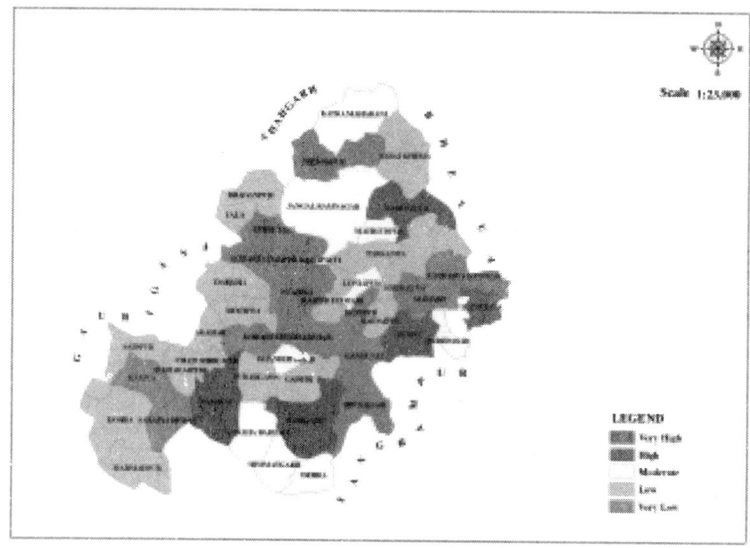

Map-21 : Old fallow land in Amethi

per the ignorance of the farmers the land has lost the fertility status of the soil due to which such lands has been left out of cultivation in anticipation of maintaining the fertility status of the soil. The detailed distribution of old follow land at village level in Amethi Block has been depicted in the Map-21. Proportionately, very high percentage of old fallow land more than 5 per cent is found in Hathkila village. High distribution of old fallow land between 3 per cent to 4 per cent is observed in the Rebha, Loniapur, Ramdaipur, Jangal Ram Nagar, Naraini, Ramgarh and Himmatgarh villages of Amethi Block. While very low percentage of old fallow land is found in Kherauna, Katara Fulkunwar villages of Amethi block. Proportionately, low percentage of old fallow land varying from 1 per cent to 2 per cent is recorded in Parsanwa, Benipùr, Mahso, Raidaipur, Saraikhema, Trilokpur, Tala, Kushi Tali, Bhaganpur, Loharta, Darkha, Koraigirdhar Shah, Nuanwa, Umapur Ganapatti, Kohra, Kakwa, Saidpur, Saraiya Duban, Mahmadpur, Agahar, Purabgaon, Bhusahari and Gänguali villages of the Amethi Block. It is observed that the old fallow land is significantly that the old fallow land is significantly distributed at village level in Amethi Block of the Sultanpur District.

Fallow Land

Fallow land at village level in Amethi are very significantly distributed in Amethi village level distribution of fallow land is shown in the Map-22. Very high percentage of fallow land more than 6 per cent is found in Hethkila, Sarai Khema villages of Amethi Block. Proportionately, high percentage varying between 3 per cent to 4 per cent is recorded in Katara Fulkunwar, Dedhpasar, Mahso, Loniapur, Katara Maharani, Darkha, Korarigirdhar Shah, Dhandhudhar, Kohra, Saraiya Duban, Agahar and Naraini Bartali villages while 4.15 per cent fallow land is observed in Chaturbhujpur village of Amethi Block. Moderate distribution of fallow land from

2 per cent to 3 per cent is observed in Kherauna, Benipur, Rebha, Raidaipur, Raipur Fulwari, Jungal Ramnagar, Kushi Tali, Nuanwa, Naraini, Saidpur, Maharajpur, Purabgaon, Dehra, Bhusahari and Gangauli villages of Amethi Block. Very low percentage of fallow land less than 1.5 per cent is recorded in Mochawa, Kakawa, Mahmadpur, Parsanwa, Ramdaipur, Trilokpur, and Loharta villages of Amethi block of the Sultanpur District. The fallow land can be easily reclaimed for agro-afforestation activities because the fallow land has been left out of cultivation due to poor fertility status of the soil and poor agricultural productivity, in which agricultural cropping expenditure used to be higher than the benefit accrued out of cropping on the fallow land. The fallow land has been left out of cultivation by the farmers to maintain the fertility status of the soil. The fallow land can be easily brought under cultivation on through adopting latest agricultural scientific - techniques reclaiming fallow land. Thus agro-afforestation management on fallow land should be adopted to meet the increasing demand of growing

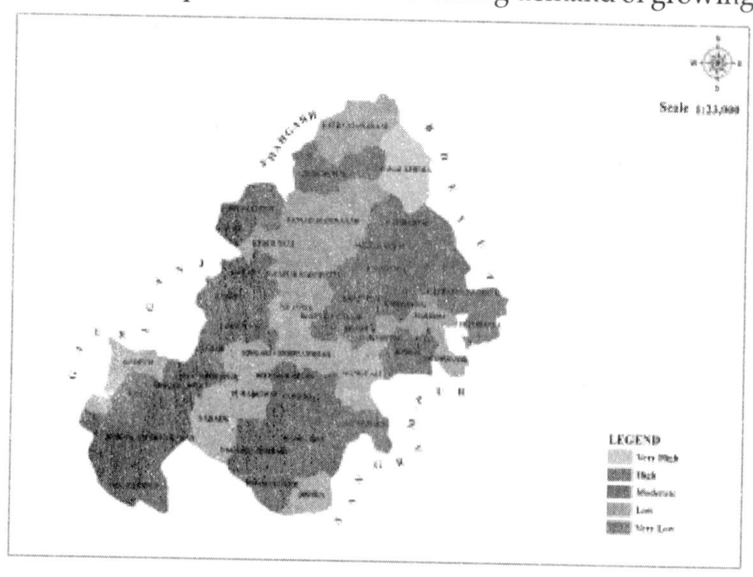

Map-22 : Fallow land in Amethi

cattle and human population for fuelwood, fodder, fibre, fruits, and foodgrain. The awareness of the farmers for adopting proper agricultural cropping pattern, proper attention to maintain the fertility status of the soil. The adoption of appropriate agricultural scientific-technology for reclamation of fallow land, proper doses of organic and inorganic amendments, use of insecticides and pesticides, high yield variety of seeds, proper doses of irrigation and other cropping techniques will be an asset for the restoration of fallow land and to maintain the ecological imbalances of the area.

Other Types of Wastelands

The other types of wastelands are those lands which are lying unutilised miscellanesously but it can be brought under use for some purpose or the other including social-forestry programmes to meet the increasing need of the growing population. The distribution of other types of wastelands at

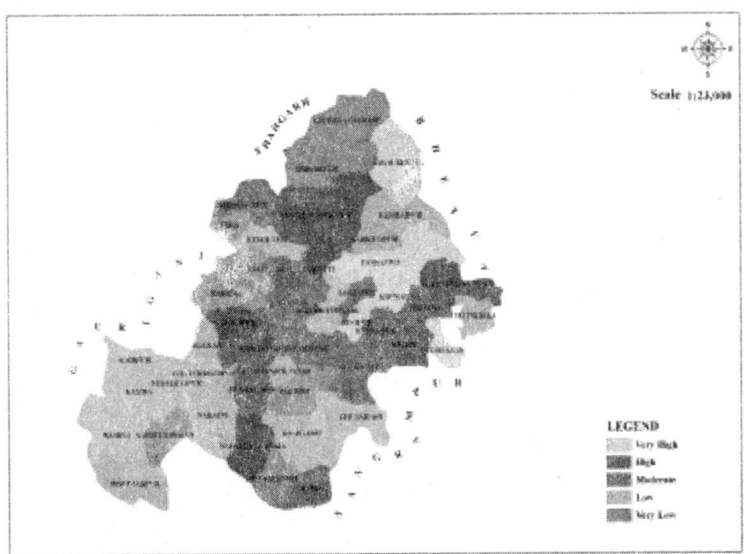

Map-23 : Other type of wasteland in Amethi

village level in Amethi Block has been depicted in the Map-23. Proportionately, very high percentage of other types of wastelands more than 5 per cent is found in Kherauna. Parsanwa, Benipur, Kataraful Kunwar and Dedhpasar villages of Amethi Block, while high percentage of other types of wastelands between 4 per cent to 5 per cent is observed in Mahso, Loniapur, Jangal Ram Nagar, Korarigirdhar Shah, Umapur Gana Patti, Mochwa, and Nainaha Bartali Villages of Amethi Block. Very low percentage between 1 per cent to 2 per cent other types of wastelands are found in Saraikhema, Trilokpur, Tala, Loharta, Saraiya Duban and Himmatgarh villages of Amethi Block of the Sultanpur District. The other types of wastlands are not under use for various miscellaneous reasons which can be easily brought under social-forestry programmes for maintenance of ecological and environmental imbalances of the area. The reclamation of other types of wastelands will be helpful in restoring the ecological and environmental crisis of the area. The other types of wastelands can be reclaimed for social-forestry programmes to obtain especially fuelwood and fodder needs of the growing human and cattle population respectively.

Wastelands in Amethi Block

The wastelands in Amethi Block at village level are significantly distributed. The proportionate distribution of wastelands at village level in Amethi Block has been shown in the Map-24. Very high percentage of wastelands more than 14 per cent has been recorded in Hathkila, Dedhpasar, Loniapur villages of Amethi Block while high percentage of wastelands between 12 per cent to 14 per cent are observed in Benipur, Katarafulkunwar, Rebha, Saraikhema, Dhandhudhar, Maharajpur and Nainha Bartali villages of Amethi Block very low percentage of wastelands less than 8 per cent has been found in Kushitali, Loharata, Kosarigirdhar

Shah, Nunwawa, Kakwa, Saidpur, Purabgaon, Ramgarh, Himmatgarh and Goderi villages of the Amethi Block. While low percentage of wastelands varying between 8 per cent to 12 per cent are seen in the Gangauli, Bhusahari, Agahar, Mahmadpur, Saraiya Duban, Mochwa, Naraini, Kohra, Tala, Bhaganpur, Trilokpur, Mahmadpur, Raidaipur, Mahso and Kherauna villages of the Amethi Block of the District Sultanpur. The wastelands of Amethi Block can be reclaimed through adopting scientific-techniques and latest techniques of agro-afforestation system to meet the fuelwood, fodder, fibre, fruits, fisheries, and foodgrain (F^6) requirements of the increasing cattle and human population and maintaining the ecological and environmental degradation in crisis of the area.

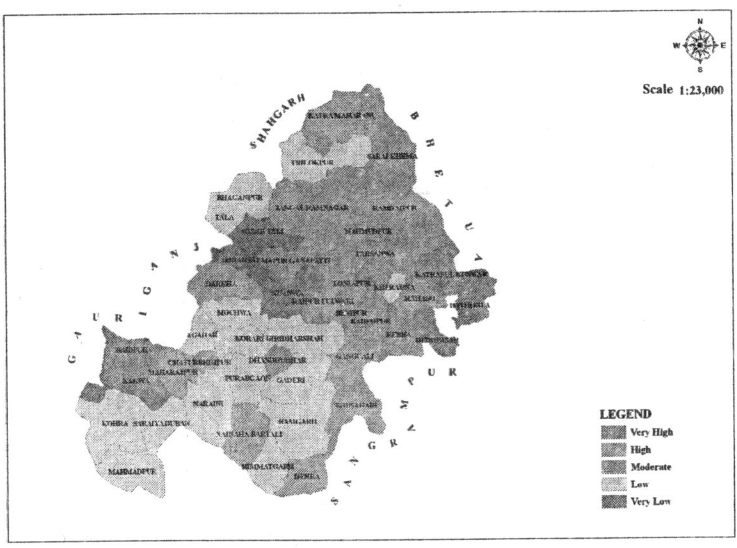

Map-24 : Total wasteland in Amethi

Conclusion

Symbiotic relationship between man and nature is continued

from immemorial time. In the past man and nature relationship has been shattered causing in calculable damage to nature which has caused hardship to man. The remedial measures and effectitve strategies for reversal of this trend has to be searched. The problem of wastelands has been appropriately documented. There has been alarming challenge for lost of our agricultural land which is 175 million hectares and 40 million hectares of forest land which is degraded forest land. Thus our country is loosing 1.5 million hectares of forest land and about 12000 million tonnes of top soil is eroded every year. The rural poor depends on the forest resources.

Thus the problems of wastelands and its reclamation should be taken a challenge to meet the increasing demand of growing cattle and human population in the form of fuel wood, fodder, fibre, fruits, fisheries, and foodgrains, etc. with the view to restore ecological and environmental degradation and the improve socio-economic crisis of the area.

The wastelands are those lands which are uncultivable or is presently lying unutilized due to different constraints but it had been used previously, which is giving very low actual return, i.e., it has low economic potential and it is ecologically unstable or whose top soil has completely lost it's fertility status, which has developed toxicity and is therefore unfit for the growth of crops and trees due to environmental or anthropogenic problems, has been advanced and no further use has been found for it.

The classification of wastelands have been derived from land use categories taking culturable waste and fallow land, the culturable wasteland have been sub-divided into—waterlogged, usar, banjar, kankarili ravine and other types of wastelands while fallow land other than the current fallow land has been sub-divided into old fallow land and fallow land excluding current fallow land. These eight categories of wastelands are available in Sultanpur District. While only six categories of wastelands viz. waterlogged, usar land, banjar land, old fallow land, fallow land and other types of wastelands are found in Amethi Block of Sultanpur District.

Wastelands are significantly distributed in Sultanpur District. There are 10, 3608 hectares of waste lands in Sultanpur District. The fallow lands are found comparatively very high, covering 41044 hectares land followed by old fallow land having 19089 hectares land and usar land 14601 hectares land. The water logged land is found in 11291 hectares area and banjar land in 9594 hectares area. Similarily, significant area under ravine land along with the Gomati River is found which spread in 5110 hectares area and the miscellaneous other types of wastelands are found in 1925 hectares land while very low area covering 748 hectares Kankarili land is observed in Sultanpur District.

Proportionately, the wastelands are very significantly distributed in Amethi Block at village level. There are 11.36 per cent total wastelands found in Amethi Block. Comparatively fallow land area is very high which is 3.87 per cent to the total area of the Block. The old fallow land is found in 2.56 per cent area while usar land is observed in 1.89 per cent area. The other types of wastelands in Amethi Block are recorded 0.35 per cent and waterlogged land covering 0.47 per cent area in Amethi Block of District Sultanpur.

At village level waterlogged land is found very high in Chaturbhujpur Dehra and Ramdaipur villages while very low waterlogged lands is observed in Kherauna, Parsanwa, Kushi Tali villages of Amethi Block.

The usar lands are comparatively very high more than 3 per cent in Bhusahari and Umpanganapatti, Tirlokpur, and Sarai Khema villages while very low percentage less than 1.0 per cent usar land is observed in Kherauna, Parsanwa, Hathkila, Loniapur, Katara Maharani, Kushi Tali, Naraini, Saraiya Duban and Himmatgarh villages of Amethi Block of District Sultanpur.

Banjar lands are significant by distributed in Amethi at village level. Very high percentage of banjar land more than 4 per cent is found in Loniapur, Raipur Fulwari villages while very low percentage of banjar land less than two per cent is observed in Gaderi, Bhusahari, Ramgarh, Himmatgarh, Agavar, Maharajpur, Saraiya Duban, Loharta, Katara Maharani, Sarai Khema, and Kherauna villages of Amethi Block.

Porportionately more than 5 per cent old fallow land is seen in Hathkilla village and very low percentage old fallow land less than one per cent is observed in Kherauna, Katarfulkanwar villages of Amethi Block.

Comparatively very high percentage more than 5 per cent of fallow land is seen in Hathkilla, Saraikhema, villages of Amethi Block while very low percentage less than 1.5 per cent fallow land is observed in Parsanwa, Benipur, Ramdaipur, Trilokpur, Loharta, Mochwa, Kakwa, Mahmoodpur villages of Amethi Block of Sultanpur District.

Other types of wastelands are found very high more than 5 per cent in Kherauna, Parsanwa, Benipur, Katarafulkunwar villages while very low less than two percent while very low less than two in Sarai Khema, Trilokpur, Tala, Loharta, Saraiya Duban and Himmatgarh village of Amethi Block.

The total wastelands are very significantly distributed in Amethi Block. Very high percentage of wastelands more than 15 per cent is seen in Dedhpasar village followed by Hathkila (14.32 Per cent), Loniapur (14.75 Per cent) villages while very low percentage of wastelands less than 8 per cent are recorded in Kushi Tali, Loharata, Korarigirdharshah, Nuanwa, Kakwa, Saidpur, Purabgaon, Ramgarh, Himmatgarh, and Goderi villages of Amethi Block of Sultanpur District.

Thus it is observed that the wastelands are significantly distributed at village level not only in Amethi Block but Sultanpur District as whole, which has become a challenging problem to the planners and developmental agencies engaged at Sultanpur.

It has been recorded during the field survey and action field work programme that the wastelands of Sultanpur and Amethi Block has been left out of cultivation for very smaller reasons and ignorance of the cultivators. Such wastelands can be easily reclaimed adopting latest scientific and technical methods and applying C-2 scientific technology i.e., the scientific system available within the village or household itself. The adoption of scientific cropping system/pattern, proper ploughing techniques appropriate doses of organic and inorganic amendments in form of fertilizers and application of insecticides and pesticides, appropriate high yielding variety of seeds and plants, proper management system including irrigation and post-harvest technology will be helpful in bringing out the wastelands under proper use to grow–fuelwood, fodder, fibre, fruits, fisheries and foodgrains to meet the increasing demand of growing cattle and human population on the one hand and restoring the ecological and environmental degradation and imbalances of the area and improving socio-economic crisis of the people's of Amethi in Sultanpur District of Uttar Pradesh.

Reference

1. Stamb, L.D., "*Land of Britain, It's use and Misuse*" vol. xv and No. v, 1968, AMU, G.S., Aligarh.

3

Factors in Wastelands

Introduction

The spatial distribution of wastelands and the marked changes in the areas of wastelands in Amethi and Sultanpur District necessiates to probe into the cause and effect phenomenon of wastelands. Various causative factors responsible for the development of wastelands are numerous but the predominant ones can be identified and understood easily.

The development and formation of wastelands as a type of landuse system can be attributed to a complex processes interacting at varying levels. Therefore, it has become necessary to investigate the factors affecting wastelands of Amethi Block at village level and also at the block level in Sultanpur in general. It is assumed that the development of wastelands occurs through unhealthy interaction of a triangle of agencies viz. *Man* → *Nature* → *Technology*. In other words where the environment is severe, man's ability to interact with nature to his advantage is curtailed and man fails to fully avail himself of the land resources. On the other hand the combined impact of interaction between man and nature, when technology as a tool is very low, wastelands development grows. On the whole, the combined impact of interaction between man and nature and varying levels of technological inputs are considered to be the main factors involved in the formation of wastelands. Through the natural factors assume primary importance, man's varying levels of ability to utilize land through technological innovations also accelerate wasteland formation. Therefore, it is necessary to clearly identify and investigate all determinants of wasteland formation.

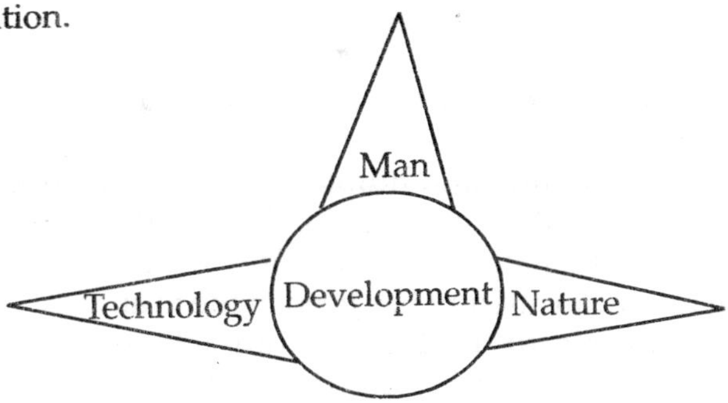

Man

Technology Development Nature

In view of the above assumptions, various natural (morphometric, hydrologenic, pedogenic) and human or anthropological factors have been selected for analysing each wasteland type separately, because generation and changes cannot be made for all the wasteland types taken together for the reason that different factors have varying impact on them. The major factors have been grouped into two main heads and sub-divided as follows :

I. *Natural factors*

(a) *Morphometric*

(i) Slope

(ii) Ruggedness Number

(b) *Hydrologic*

(iii) Drainage Density

(iv) Quality of water in pH

(v) Behaviour of water table

(c) *Pedogenic*

(vi) NPK of the soil

(vii) pH value of the soil

II. *Human Factors*

(viii) Land concentration (Gini's Co-efficient Ratio)
(ix) Percentage of scheduled caste population
(x) Population Growth
(xi) Growth of Fertilizer
(xii) Growth in Gross Irrigated area
(xiii) Agricultural workers.

Thus the causative factors responsible for the development of wastelands are numerous but the major and predominent natural and human factors can be identified and analysed with the view to check and control such factors for further strategies. Keeping, the above facts into consideration, an attempt has been made to analyse various human factor's to analyse its impact on wastelands development, in general so that the block level development of wastelands can be analysed for the formulation of planning strategies to reclaim the wastelands for agro-afforestation.

Factors of Wastelands in Sultanpur

The relationship between man and nature has been shattered. The nature has given bounty to man but in return man could not do anything for restoration and sustainence to nature. Man exploited the nature excessively due to which ecological and environmental crisis has taken place, which has caused socio-economic crisis. The combined impact of interaction between human and nature and varying levels of technological inputs are considered to be the predominant factors responsible for the development of wastelands at different levels. Out of numerous causative factors some of the important anthropogenic or human factors are explained at Block level variation of indicators in Sultanpur District.

Population Growth

The explosive population growth is one of the predominant

factors in the development of wastelands. The natural land resources are limited and man or population is totally dependent on natural/land resources. The over exploitation of natural land resources to meet the increasing demand of fuelwood, fodder, fibre, fruits, fisheries and foodgrains, etc. has caused the land degradation causing ecological and environmental crisis.

The population growth in Sultanpur District has been recorded 25.27 per cent from 1991 to 2001 which is illustrated in the Table 3.1. The population growth during 1991 to 2001 has been observed very high in Jagdishpur Block having 47.03 per cent population growth. This population growth has been recorded very high due industrialization in Jagdishpur area and peoples immigration. The excess/explosive population growth and industrialization has caused development of wastelands in the study area. High population growth between 25 per cent to 30 per cent has been found in Shukul Bazar, Amethi, Kurebhar, Dubepur, Bhadainya, Lambhua, Pratappur Kamaicha, Kadipur Block of Sultanpur District. The population growth in these blocks have positive growth due to urbanisation and small scale secondary and tertiary workers concentration which has caused

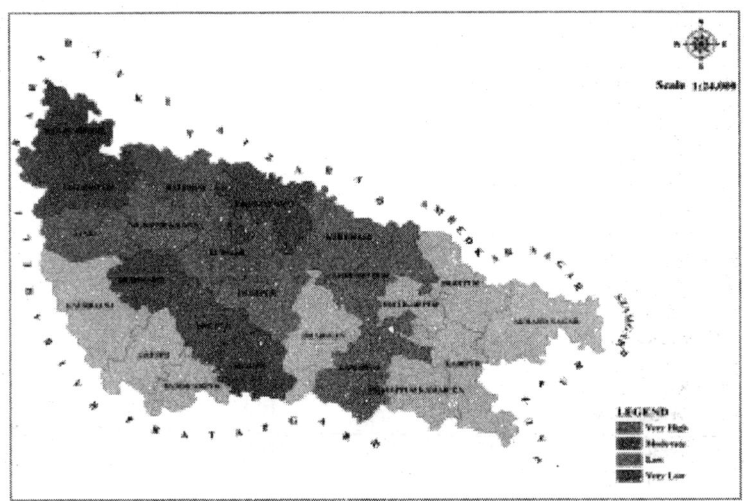

Map-25 : Population Growth in Sultanpur

positive change in the development of wastelands. Very low percentage population growth less than 20 per cent has been recorded in Bhnetua, Sangrampur and Dhanpatganj Blocks which is shown in the Map-25.

Thus it has been noticed that the excessive population growth play an important role in the development of wastelands because the infrastructural, institutional and people's need based development programmes are one of the major factors in the development of wastelands.

Table 3.1 : Factors in Wastelands, Sultanpur

Sl. No.	*Name of Block*	*Population Growth*	*S.C. % to total population*	*% Growth of Fertilizer 1991-2001*	*% Growth in Gross Irrigated Area 1991 to 2001*	*% agri-culture workers*
1.	Shukul Bazar	25.25	27.3	30.1	17.2	79.6
2.	Jagdishpur	47.03	24.3	35.8	29.3	62.7
3.	Musafirkhana	22.8	26.2	36.0	36.6	76.1
4.	Baldairai	24.9	21.7	24.0	14.6	73.6
5.	Jamo	22.1	30.1	26.0	11.00	83.6
6.	Shahgarh	23.4	22.3	44.7	20.6	83.0
7.	Gauriganj	21.7	25.4	26.0	21.3	78.5
8.	Amethi	27.0	19.9	29.7	12.3	71.5
9.	Bhnetua	17.5	20.9	34.3	10.8	78.6
10.	Bhadar	23.5	21.2	38.0	11.2	74.3
11.	Sangrampur	19.6	16.9	42.3	9.6	72.8
12.	Dhanpatganj	19.5	21.3	14.0	18.6	76.9
13.	Kurebhar	26.3	20.2	34.0	16.3	63.8
14.	Jai Singh Pur	22.1	22.6	34.8	19.3	77.7
15.	Kurwar	21.0	15.2	38.3	13.2	64.4
16.	Dubepur	28.8	17.2	12.7	17.7	55.8
17.	Bhadainya	25.0	23.0	11.3	11.1	64.6
18.	Dostpur	24.7	23.9	41.3	14.2	83.6
19.	Akhandnagar	24.2	27.4	19.7	14.0	85.2
20.	Lambhua	28.1	24.1	32.3	17.5	77.3
21.	Pratappur Kamaicha	25.2	22.8	39.5	12.4	76.6
22.	Kadipur	25.3	27.0	47.8	16.00	76.3
23.	Motigarpur	24.6	25.7	31.3	10.2	77.6
	Total	25.27	22.9	37.8	15.2	73.7

Scheduled Caste Population

The proportionate distribution of scheduled caste population also plays an important role in the development of wastelands. The scheduled caste population has positive impact on wastelands development because the scheduled caste population is mainly dependent on natural land resources and the over exploitation of natural land resources causes land degradation and wastelands development. The scheduled caste population in Sultanpur District is observed 22.9 per cent to the total population of the district. The distribution of scheduled caste population in the Geographic Information System (GIS) has been depicted in the Map - 26 and scheduled caste population data is illustrated in the Table 3.1. It has been observed that very high percentage of scheduled caste population to total population is found in Jamo Block having 30.1 per cent scheduled caste population. High percentage scheduled caste population between 25 to 30 per cent is found in Shukul Bazar, Musafirkhana, Gauriganj, Akhandnagar, Kadipur and Motigarpur blocks of the

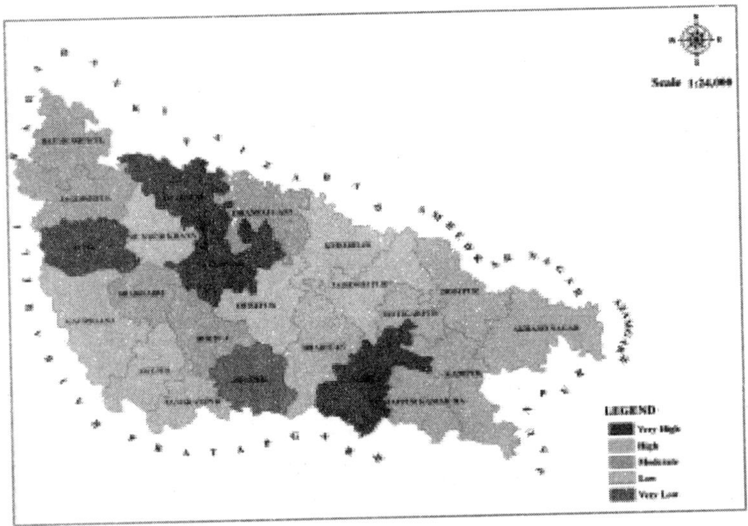

Map-26 : Scheduled Caste Population in Sultanpur

Sultanpur District. Very low percentage of scheduled caste population less than 20 per cent is recorded in Amethi, Sangrampur, Kurwar and Dubepur Blocks of Sultanpur District.

In view of the above it has been observed that the scheduled caste population has positive impact on wastelands formation, because there scheduled caste population in the remote rural areas are mainly dependant on natural land resources in the form of fuelwood, fodder, fibre, fruits, vegetables, fisheries, wood, foodgrains, etc. The over exploitation of the land resources in an un-organised manner to fulfil the increasing demand of the growing people had led to land degradation and wastelands development.

Fertilizer Growth

The application of fertilizer plays an important role in the formation of wastelands. The cultivators have common feeling that high doses of fertlizer application will increase the agricultural production of the field. In anticipation of increasing agricultural productivity, the cultivators are applying fertilizers in a multiple system, which at a certain stage inspite of increasing agricultural productivity, it reduces the fertility status of the soil. Thus expenditure in agricultural production is higher than the profit accrued out of agricultural farming. In view of the low profit than high expenditure farmers have left the land uncultivated, and such land is lying as wasteland. The higher doses of fertilizer application or growth in fertilizer use has positive impact on wastelands development. The percentage growth of fertilizer application has been computed from 1991 to 2001. The percentage growth of fertilizer application has been depicted in the Map-27. The fertilizer growth in Sultanpur District has been noticed as 37.8 Per cent. Very high percentage fertilizer growth i.e., 47.8 per cent has been observed in Kadipur Block while high percentage fertilizer growth between 40 to 45 per cent has been recorded in Shahgarh, Sangrampur, Dospur Blocks of District Sultanpur. Very low percentage fertilizer growth less than 15 per cent is found in Dhanpatganj, Dubepur, and Bhadainya Blocks while low percentage fertilizer growth between 15 to 20 per cent is noticed in Akhandnagar block of Sultanpur District. Thus it is observed that fertilizer application growth is very significantly distributed at Block level in Sultanpur District. It is noticed that the high doses of fertilizer application has positive impact on wastelands development. Therefore, it is necessary that before application of fertilizer the soil status should be tested and as per the soil requirements the organic and inorganic amendments should be applied for various crops in different cropping pattern.

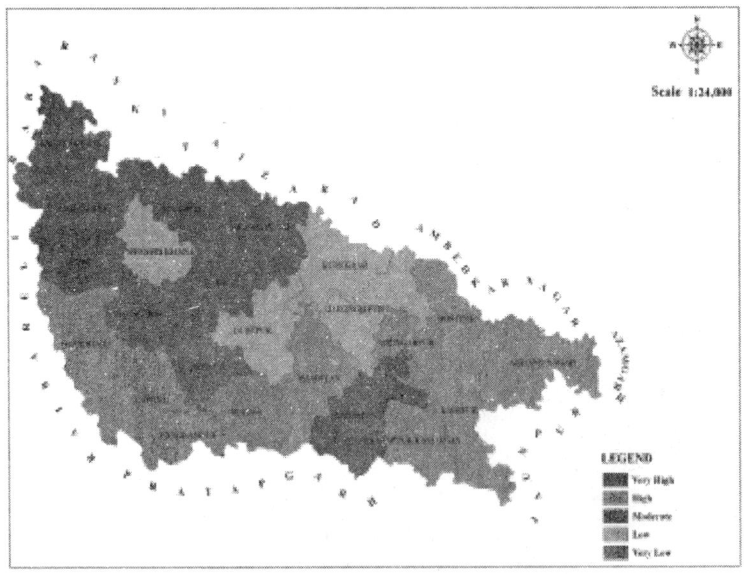

Map-27 : Growth of Fertilizer in Sultanpur

Growth of Gross Irrigated Areas

High doses of irrigation water is injurious to the soil because it disturbs the water table and fertility status of the soil

percolates with underground water and it creates problem of waterlogging. Thus it is assumed that high doses of irrigation water and percentage growth in gross irrigated area has positive impact with wastlands development. The percentage growth in gross irrigated area from 1991 to 2001 at Block level in Sultanpur District has been shown in the Map-28. There is 15.2 per cent growth in Gross Irrigated Area from 1991 to 2001. Very high percentage of growth in gross irrigated area is found in Musafirkhana Block which is 36.6 per cent from 1991 to 2001. High percentage growth in gross irrigated area between 20 to 30 per cent is observed in Jagdishpur, Shahgarh, and Gauriganj Blocks of District Sultanpur. Very low percentage of growth in gross irrigated area less than 10 per cent is recorded in the Sangrampur Block while low percentage growth in gross irrigated area is noticed in Baldirai, Jamo, Amethi, Bhnetua, Bhadar, Kurwar, Bhadainya, Dostpur, Akhandnagar, Pratappur Kamaicha and Motigarpur Blocks of District Sultanpur. Thus high doses of irrigation and growth in gross irrigated area has positive relationship with wastelands development in District Sultanpur.

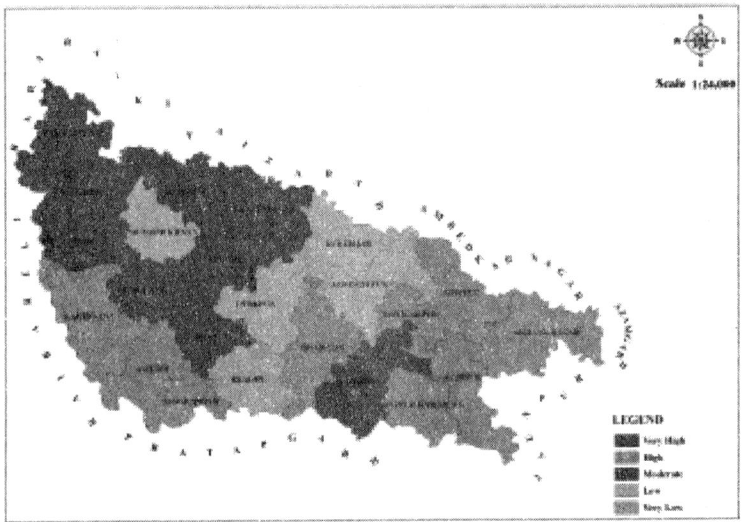

Map-28 : Growth in Gross Irrigated Area in Sultanpur

Agricultural Workers

Proportionate distribution of agricultural workers have positive impact with the wastelands development. The percentage of agricultural workers at Block level in District Sultanpur has been depicted in the Map-29. Very high percentage of agricultural workers more than 85 per cent is found in Akhandnagar Block while high percentage between 80 to 85 per cent agricultural workers are recorded in the Jamo Shahgarh and Dostpur Blocks of District Sultanpur. Very low percentage of agricultural workers less than 60 per cent is found in the Dubepur Block with low percentage agricultural workers between 60 to 70 per cent are observed in Jagdishpur, Kurebhar, Kurwar and Dubepur Blocks of District Sultanpur. Thus, there is positive relationship between agricultural workers and wastelands development at Block level in Sultanpur District.

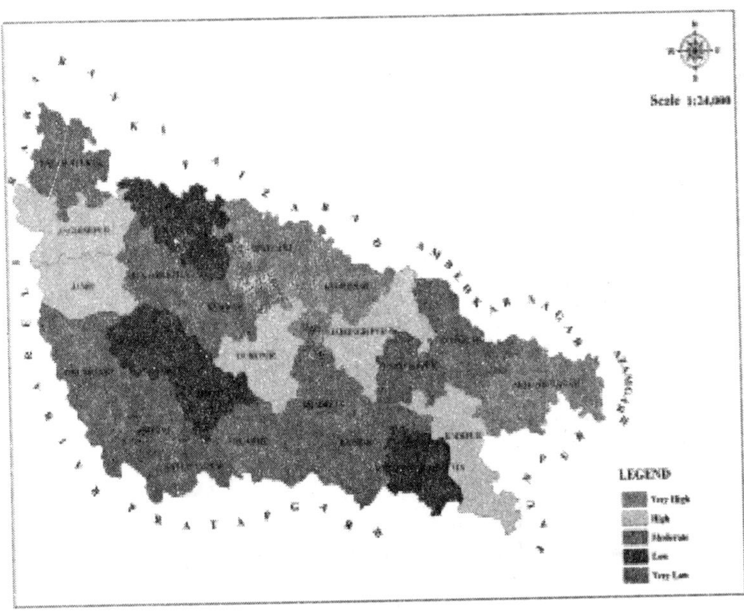

Map-29 : Agricultural workers in Sultanpur

Population in Sultanpur

The total population of District Sultanpur is 31,90,926 persons comprising of 16,11,936 males and 15,78,990 females. The 4.77 per cent urban population while rest of them are the rural population. The details of the occupational structures comparatively in circle diagram and dot distribution system is depicted in the Map-30. The circle diagram indicates agricultural workers, household industry workers, other workers and marginal workers are very insignificant while very high percentage of non-workers are observed in Sultanpur District. In the urban areas other workers and marginal workers are significantly found while more than 75 per cent non-workers are found in rural and urban and rurban areas as well. The population distribution in Sultanpur District indicates that there is positive relationship with the wastelands development in Sultanpur District.

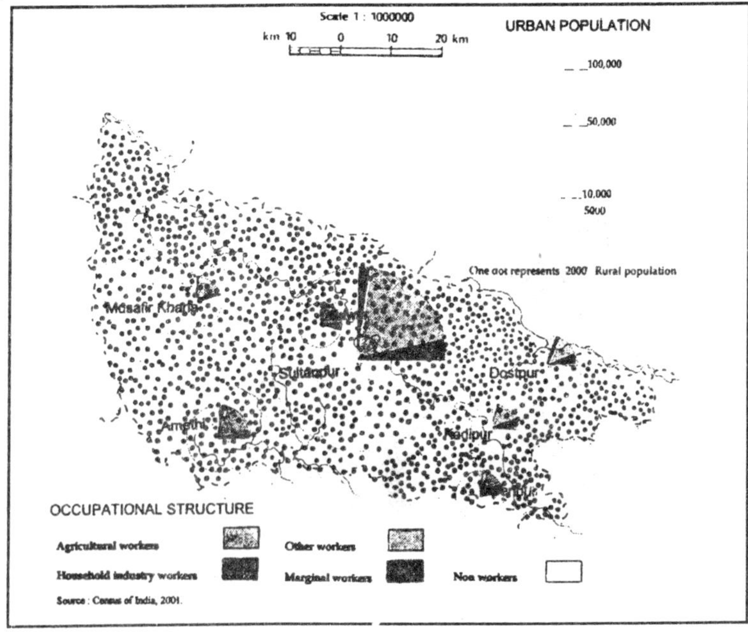

Map-30 : Population in Sultanpur

Industries

It has been observed that Industries have positive impact on wastelands. The distribution of industries has been depicted in the Map-31. The agricultural, metalurgical (iron and steel), Heavy engineering, light engineering, cement, sugar, handicraft, handloom industries, paper and paper board industries are depicted in the map. The Sultanpur district has many favourable indicators for industrial development. There are 11 major and medium industries like paper, cement, sugar, plastic, fertilizer, iron, and aeronautical have been established mainly in Jagdishpur, Tikaria, Munshiganj, Industrial areas of the District Sultanpur. Brassware, textile, agricultural implements, wood and steel furniture, oil and floor, soap, footwear, stings and ropes, pottery, jaggery, and card board boxes are the small and household industries existing in different areas of District Sultanpur. It is has been observed that there is positive relationship between industrial development and wastelands development in District Sultanpur.

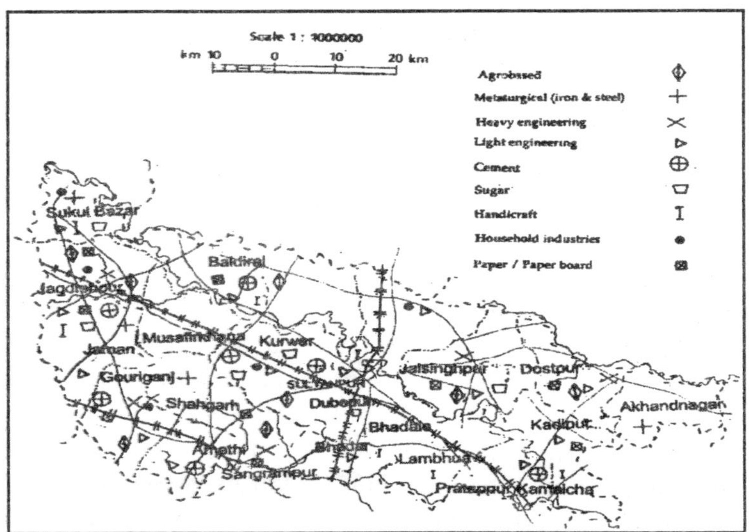

Map-31 : Development of Industries in Sultanpur

Factors of Wastelands in Amethi

The factors for wastelands development at village level has been analysed through natural and human indicators. The natural factors at grassroot level really play an important role in the formation of wastelands. Various morphometric, hydrologic and pedogenic factors and anthropogenic indicators have been analysed to explain the relationship between wastelands formation and natural and human factors. Attempt has been made in this study to analyse the relationship between dependent and independent variable adopting statistical methods i.e., correlation matrix and step-wise regression analysis. The accumulated information has been digitised and mapped through Geographical Information System (GIS) at village level for Amethi Block.

Slope

The average slope at village level in Amethi block has been shown in the Map-32. Very high slope more than 1.50° has been observed in Naraini, Mochawa, Kohra, Bhusahari and Gaderi villages of Amethi Block, while high slope between 1.00° to 1.50° is recorded in Kakawa Hathkila and Ramgarh villages of the Amethi Block. Very low slope less than 0.60° has been found in Kataraful Kurwar, Mahso, Rebha, Mahmudpur, Saraikhema, Katara Maharani, Trilokpur, Tala, Kushi Tali, Korari Girdharshah, Nuanwa, Umapur Ganapatti, Dhandhudhar, Mochwa, Agahar, Himmatgarh, Nainaha Bartali and Goderi villages of the Amethi Block of Sultanpur District. It has been observed that the slope has positive relationship with the wastelands development, because higher degree of slope causes more soil erosion which leads to the deterioration of the fertility status of the soil and at a later stage the cultivators oftenly use to live the land uncultivated and the such land is left as wastelands. The soil erosion and deterioration of fertility status of the soil is responsible for the ecological and environmental degradation.

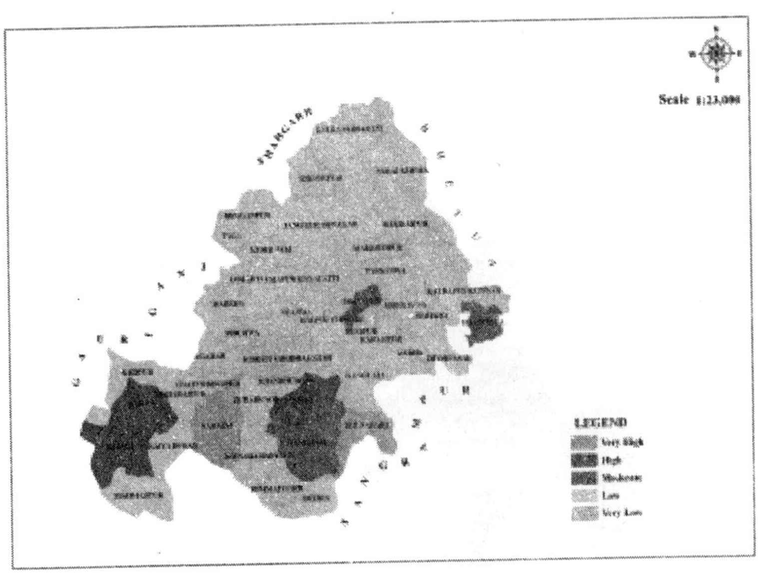

Map-32 : Slope in Amethi

Ruggedness Number

Ruggedness number at village level in Amethi Block has been depicted in the Map-33. Very high ruggedness number more than 0.38 is found in Naraini and Ramdaipur villages, while high ruggedness number between 0.25 to 0.30 has been seen in Benipur, Hathkila, Raidaipur, Loniapur, Kohra, Maharajpur and Ramgarh villages of Amethi Block. Very low ruggedness number has been found in Rebha, Tala, Himmatgarh, Nainha Bartali and Gangauli villages of Amethi Block. Low ruggedness number has been observed in Khesauna, Parsanwa, Kataraful Kunwar, Dedhpasas Mahso, Raipurfulwari, Mahmudpur, Sarai Khema, Katara Maharani, Trilokpur, Kushitali, Korari girdharshah, Nunawa, Umapur Ganapatti, Dhandhudhar, Mochwa, Mahmadpur, Agahar and Dehra villages of Amethi Block. It has been observed that there is positive relationship between ruggedness number and wastlands development. Proportionately, high ruggedness number will lead towards high wastelands development.

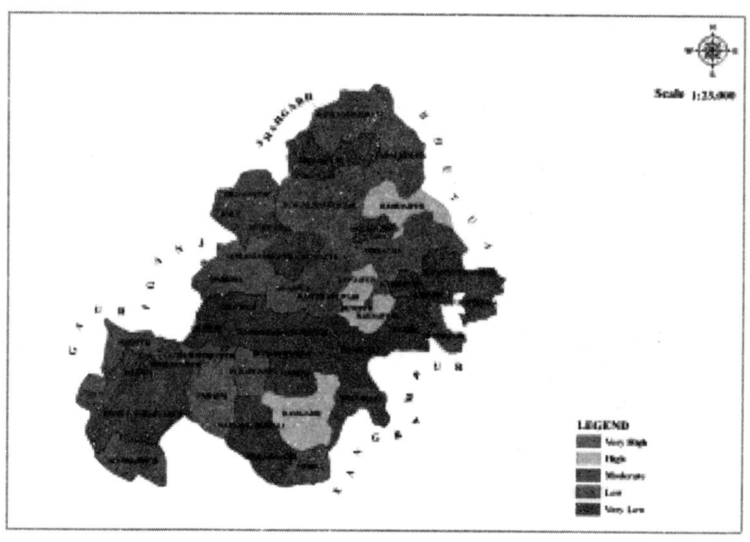

Map-33 : Ruggedness Number in Amethi

Drainage Density

Statistically calculated artificial and natural drain's drainage density have been depicted in the Map-34. Very high drainage density more than 4.50 per sq. km. has been seen in the Loniapur Dedhpasar, Saraikhema, Saraiya Duban and Saraikhema, Mahrajpur, villages of Amethi Block. High drainage density from 4.00 to 4.50 per sq. km. has been recorded in Parsanwa, Benipur, Hathkila, Dedhpasar, Rebha, Loniapur, Raipur fulwari, Mahmudpur, Jangal Ram Nagar, Darkha, Dhandhudhar, Chaturbhujpur, Mochwa, Kakwa, Dehra, Nainha Bartali, Bhusahari and Gangauli villages of the Amethi Block. Very low drainage density below 3.00 per sq.

km. has been found in Mahmadpur and Himmatgarh villages of the Amethi Block. It has been observed that there is positive relationship between drainage density with wastelands development. The high number of drainage system causes soil erosion and water accumulation which develops the wastelands formation in the area.

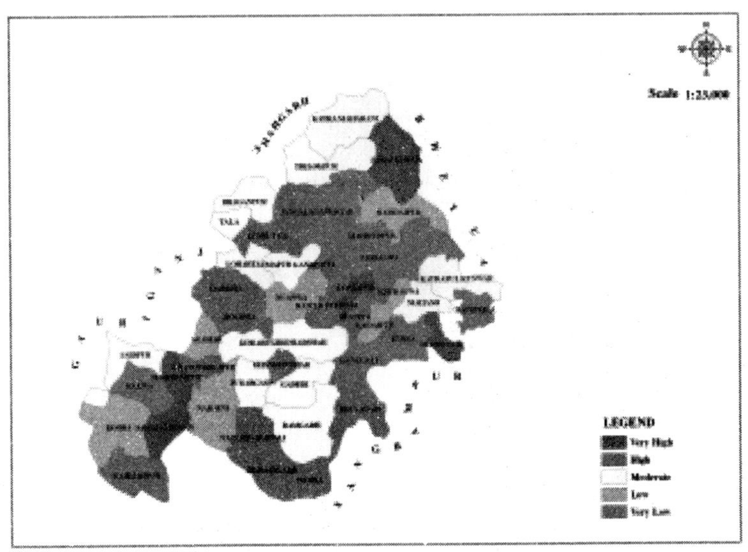

Map-34 : Drainage Density–Amethi

Quality of Water in pH

There is positive relationship between quality of water in pH and wastelands development. High pH value in the quality of water leads towards salinity and it develops usarisation in the soil hence develops the area in wastelands. The proportionate distribution of quality of water pH has been depicted in the Map-35. Very high quality of water in pH more than 9.0 has been seen in the Hathkila village and high quality of water in pH between 8.5 to 9.0 has been recorded in the Dedhpasar, Loniapur, Mahmudpur, Saraikhema, Jangal Ram Nagar, and Dhandhudhar, Saraiya

Duban villages of the Amethi Block. Very low quality of water in pH less than 7.75 has been observed in the Raidaipur, Ramdaipur, Bhaganpur, Korarigirdharshah, Nuanwa, Mochwa, Kohra, Mahmadpur, Purabgaon, Himmatgarh, Dehra and Gaderi villages of the Amethi Block.

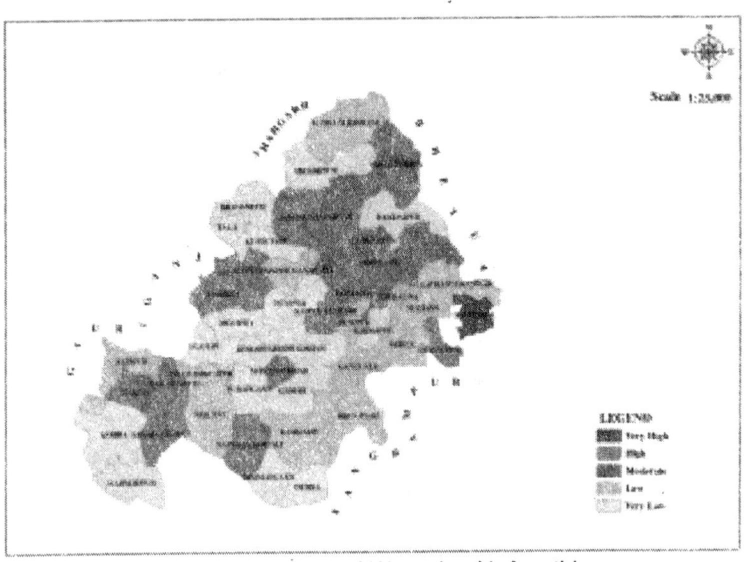

Map-35 : Quality of Water in pH–Amethi

Behaviour of Water Table

The behaviour of water table in feet has been shown in the Map-36 at village level in Amethi Block. The high water table in feet between 22 to 24 been seen in the Hathkila, Dhandhudhar, Saraiya Duban, Maharajpur and Nainaha Bartali villages while very high behaviour of water table more than 24 feet has been observed in the Gedhpasar, Loniapur, Saraikhema villages of the Amethi Block. Very low behaviour of water table less than 14 feet has been found in the Raidaipur, Tala, Bhaganpur, Nunawa, Himmatgarh and Dehra villages of the Amethi Block. It has been assumed that there is positive relationship between behaviour of water table and wastelands development.

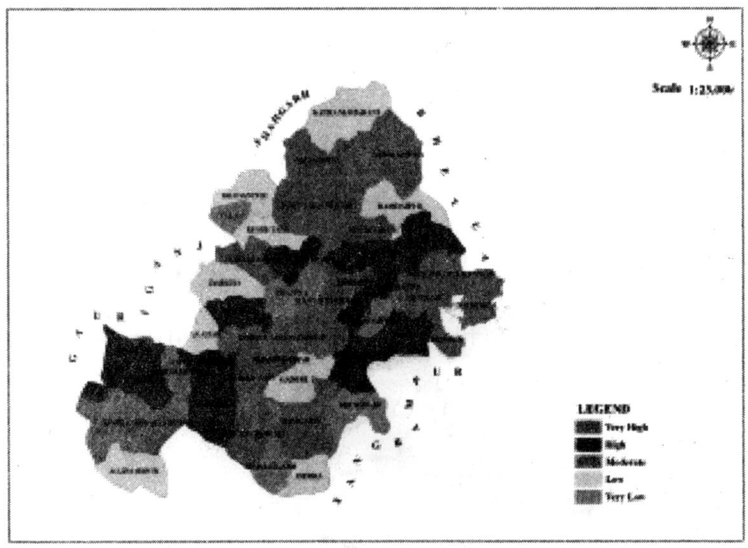

Map-36 : Behaviour of Water Table in Amethi

NPK of the Soil

The proportionate distribution of NPK of the soil in percentage has been shown in the Map-37 at village level in Amethi Block. It has been assumed that there is negative relationship between NPK of the soil and wastelands development, because the low NPK percentage of the soil will cause the low agricultural productivity and increase the expenditure/cost of the production due to which the cultivators are forced to lease the land uncultivated. Very high NPK of the soil more than 3.00 per cent has been observed in the Kherauna, Benipur, Mahmodpur, Sarai Khema and Nunawa villages while high (2.5 to 3.0) NPK of the soil has been found in the Dedhpasar, Mahso, Raidaipur, Ramdaipur, Jangal Ram Nagar, Katara Maharani Kushitali, Loharata, Korarigirdharshah, Loharta, Kohara, Saidpur, Mahmadpur, Himmatgarh, Dehra, Bhusahari villages of the Amethi Block. Very low NPK of the soil less than 2.10 per cent has been observed in the Agarhar, Maharajpur villages of the Amethi Block of Sultanpur District.

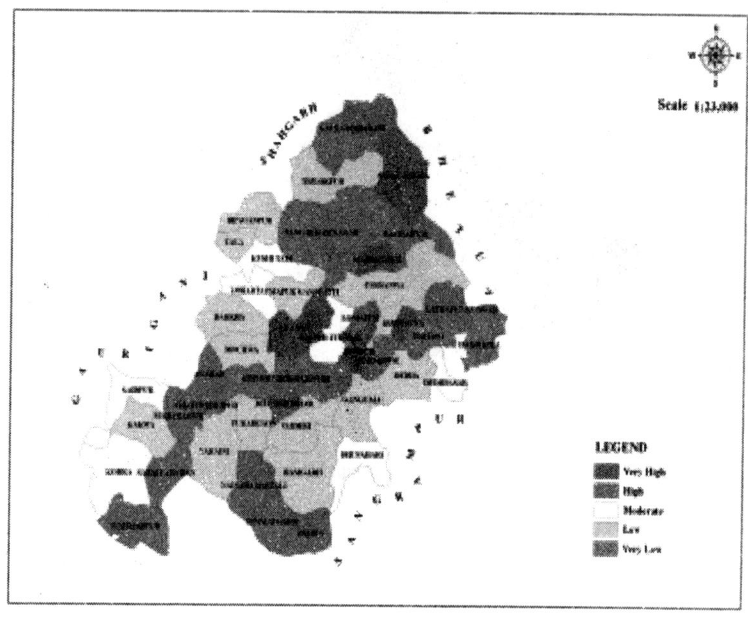

Map-37 : NPK Soil in Amethi

pH Value of Soil

There is positive relationship between pH value of the soil and wastelands development. The very high pH value of the soil will lead to usarisation of the soil which leads towards much formation of wastelands development. The distribution of the pH value of the soil has been depicted in the Map-38. Very high pH value of the soil more than 8.5 has been recorded in the Hathkila, Loniapur, Saraikhema, Umapurganapatti and Saraiya Duban villages of the Amethi Block. Very low pH value of the soil less than 7.6 has been found in the Raidaipur, Tala, Kushitali villages of the Amethi Block.

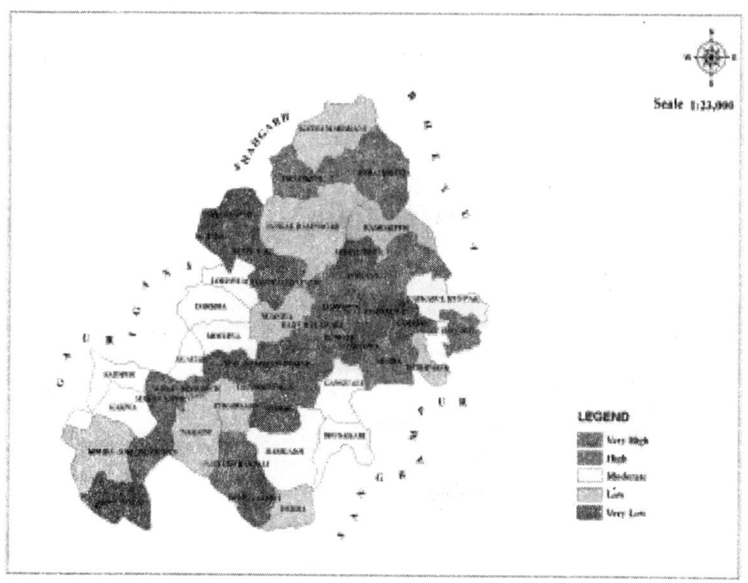

Map-38 : pH Value of Soil in Amethi

Land Concentration

The size of land holding has been computed adopting Gini's co-efficient ratio formula to find out the concentration of size of land holding. The land concentration has positive relationship with wastelands development because high size land holders and land concentrated cultivators do not care much attention for low productive land due to which the area under wastelands has been increased. The value of the land concentration has been shown in the Map-39 at village level in Amethi Block. Very high land concentration more than 0.8 has been found in the Jangal Ram Nagar, Saidpur, Agahar, Himmatgarh and Bhusahari villages of the Amethi Block. Very low land concentration less than 0.5 has been recorded in the Benipur, Rebha, Ramdaipur, Nunawa and Dehra villages of the Amethi Block of the District Sultanpur.

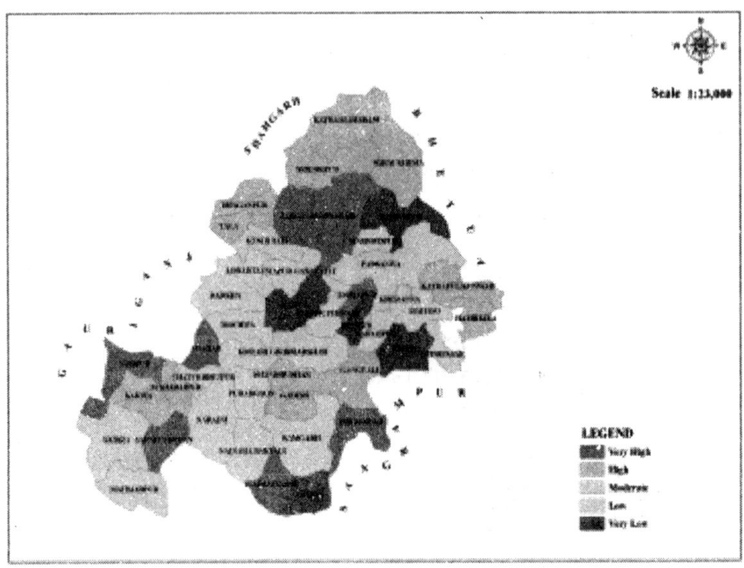

Map-39 : Land Concentration in Amethi

Scheduled Caste Population

The scheduled caste population has positive relationship with the wastelands development, the scheduled caste population are oftenly the landless population in area is high then the land will be concentrated among the limited housholds. The household having concentration of land oftenly do not pay attention for the less productive land or less fertile land which causes an increase in the area under wastelands. The proportionate distribution of scheduled caste population has been depicted in the Map-40. The very high percentage of scheduled caste population more than 35 per cent has been observed in the Kushi Tali, Ramdaipur villages while high percentage of scheduled caste population between 30 to 35 per cent has been found Saidpur and Gaderi villages of the Amethi Block. Very low percentage of scheduled caste population less than 10 per cent has been recorded in the Dedhpasar, Bhaganpur, and Dehra villages of the Amethi. It has been observed that the scheduled caste population in Amethi Block at village level has been significantly distributed.

Thus it has been observed that the NPK of the soil has negative relationship with the wastelands development, while slope in degree, ruggedness number, drainage density per sq. km. quality of water in pH, behaviour of water table in feet, pH value of the soil, land concentration and scheduled caste population has positive relationship with wastelands development in the selected area of the study.

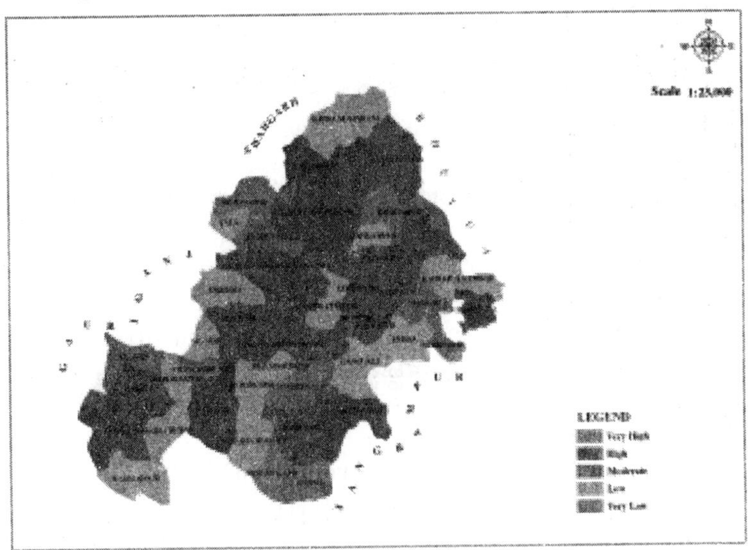

Map-40 : Scheduled Caste Population in Amethi

Analysis of the Relationship between Natural and Human Factor with Wastelands Development

The relationship among the dependent and independent variables has been analysis through the *Correlation Matrix* and *Stepwise Regression* analysis. The correlation matrix has been computed to see the trend of the correlation among the different independent variables for various types of

Table 3.2 : Factors in Wastelands Amethi

Sl. No.	Name of Villages	Land concentration	Per cent S.C. Population	Slope in Degree	Rugged-ness number	Drainage Density. per sq. km	Quality of water in pH	Behaviour of Water table in pt.	NPK of soil per cent	pH value of soil
1	2	3	4	5	6	7	8	9	10	11
1.	Kherauna	0.64	18.6	0.64	0.17	3.27	7.95	17	3.15	7.65
2.	Parsanwa	0.52	17.9	0.62	0.18	4.31	8.35	21	2.32	8.40
3.	Benipur	0.35	21.1	0.74	0.28	4.38	8.17	20	3.16	8.48
4.	Katraful Kunwar	0.75	15.2	0.51	0.16	3.86	8.14	18	2.15	8.10
5.	Hathkila	0.68	27.4	1.21	0.26	4.32	9.18	22	2.12	8.82
6.	Dedhpasar	0.59	9.5	0.91	0.19	4.73	8.72	24	2.71	7.85
7.	Mahaso	0.65	10.4	0.58	0.17	3.71	7.97	17	2.85	7.75
8.	Rebha	0.42	12.3	0.52	0.14	4.28	8.23	21	2.28	8.36
9.	Raidaipur	0.59	28.4	0.83	0.28	3.24	7.63	12	2.73	7.55
10.	Loniapur	0.78	19.5	1.18	0.29	4.67	8.67	24	2.14	8.83
11.	Raipur fulwari	0.63	13.9	0.67	0.19	4.03	8.37	18	2.48	8.35
12.	Ramdaipur	0.45	36.3	0.73	0.38	3.36	7.65	14	2.85	7.88
13.	Mahmudpur	0.61	17.5	0.52	0.17	4.21	8.54	17	3.14	7.80
14.	Sarai Khema	0.73	19.2	0.56	0.18	4.82	8.63	24	3.15	8.82
15.	Jangal Ram Nagar	0.81	18.1	0.96	0.20	4.19	8.61	18	2.84	7.85
16.	Katra Maharani	0.67	14.8	0.57	0.19	3.19	7.95	15	2.85	7.83
17.	Trilokpur	0.71	28.6	0.55	0.17	3.85	7.85	18	2.27	8.42
18.	Tala	0.68	12.4	0.52	0.14	3.73	7.78	11	2.38	7.52
19.	Kushi Tali	0.51	37.5	0.54	0.17	3.98	7.85	16	2.63	7.59
20.	Bhaganpur	0.68	7.8	0.74	0.24	3.87	7.71	14	2.25	7.63
21.	Loharta	0.56	18.1	0.87	0.21	3.64	8.36	17	2.57	8.15
22.	Darkha	0.64	15.6	0.73	0.20	4.35	8.17	16	2.32	8.17

Contd...

(**Table 3.2** : *Contd...*)

1	2	3	4	5	6	7	8	9	10	11
23.	Korari Giridharshah	0.53	22.7	0.57	0.17	3.64	7.68	17	2.86	7.67
24.	Nunwa	0.41	19.7	0.55	0.18	3.17	7.68	13	3.10	7.82
25.	Umapur Ganapatti	0.58	28.9	0.54	0.17	3.86	7.98	21	2.32	8.65
26.	Dhandhudhar	0.73	16.3	0.58	0.16	4.27	8.54	22	2.15	8.42
27.	Chaturbhujpur	0.65	4.4	0.69	0.21	4.25	8.07	20	2.24	8.36
28.	Mochwa	0.52	21.6	0.57	0.17	4.13	7.68	19	2.35	8.22
29.	Naraini	0.61	28.5	1.92	0.39	3.18	8.15	19	2.35	7.99
30.	Kohra	0.54	22.8	1.63	0.25	3.13	7.77	18	2.62	7.98
31.	Kakawa	0.68	21.7	1.41	0.24	4.08	8.33	21	2.45	8.23
32.	Saidpur	0.81	33.5	0.92	0.21	3.83	8.16	20	2.67	8.12
33.	Saraiya Duban	0.78	13.6	0.86	0.22	4.54	8.74	23	2.12	8.78
34.	Mahmadpur	0.63	11.7	0.62	0.18	2.96	7.67	15	2.85	7.68
35.	Maharajpur	0.75	13.1	0.61	0.25	4.78	8.28	23	2.02	8.82
36.	Agahar	0.82	13.8	0.57	0.16	3.59	7.86	16	2.10	8.22
37.	Purabgaon	0.59	14.7	0.61	0.18	3.73	7.72	17	2.30	7.81
38.	Ramgarh	0.66	22.8	1.36	0.28	3.85	8.16	18	2.32	8.35
39.	Himmatgarh	0.87	11.1	0.54	0.14	2.62	7.68	12	2.82	7.71
40.	Dehara	0.45	6.1	0.92	0.19	4.16	7.72	14	2.73	7.83
41.	Nainaha Bartali	0.59	16.1	0.52	0.14	4.17	8.38	22	2.21	8.42
42.	Bhusahari	0.81	24.6	1.79	0.23	4.14	8.19	13	2.67	8.18
43.	Gaderi	0.68	31.2	1.54	0.24	3.89	7.69	15	2.25	7.62
44.	Gangauli	0.72	13.8	0.52	0.14	4.12	8.14	20	2.43	8.14

wastelands development. Stepwise regression analysis has been computed to see as how the parameters change when new variables are added one by one.

Waterlogged Land

The correlationship of waterlogged land with various natural and human factors computed data has been mentioned in the Table 3.3. The correlation matrix indicates that there is significant positive correlation between drainage density (X_3) independent variable and proportion of waterlogged land (Y) dependent variable which is significant at 1 per cent level of significance, because high drainage density helps in accumulation of surface water in the low lying areas, which is helpful in the rise of water table of the area.

The positive correlation between slope (X_1) and ruggedness number (X_2) which is significant at 5 per cent and 10 per cent levels of significance respectively. High values of ruggedness number and slope creates positive conditions for maximum surface waterflow and accumulation of water in the low lying areas. Behaviour of water table (X_5) has positive correlation with the waterlogged land but this relationship is significant at 5 per cent level of significance. There is negative correlation between NPK of the soil which is significant at 10 per cent level of significance because low NPK of the soil means low fertility status of the soil. The other variables viz. pH value of the soil (X_8); land concentration (X_7), scheduled caste population (X_9) and quality of water repressed in pH value (X_4) has positive correlation with the waterlogged land but these relationships are insignificant. Therefore, these variables fail to provide explanation for variation in the proportion of waterlogged land at village level in the Amethi Block of the Sultanpur District.

The stepwise regression analysis has been computed to study the correlation of various dependant variables with

Table 3.3 : Correlation Matrix for Waterlogged Land

Symbol	Variable	*Y*	X_1	X_2	X_3	X_4	X_5	X_6	X_7	X_8	X_9
Y	per cent of waterlogged land		1.000								
X_1	Slope, deg	0.548**	1.000								
X_2	Ruggedness No.	0.317*	0.247	1.000							
X_3	Drainage density per sq. km.	0.639***	0.053	-0.199	1.000						
X_4	Quality of water (pH)	0.152	0.072	-0.064	0.697***	1.000					
X_5	Behaviour of water table	0.421**	0.126	-0.0120	0.721***	0.734***	1.000				
X_6	NPK of soil,%	-0.343*	0.144	-0.014	0.514**	-0.364*	-0.435*	1.000			
X_7	Land conc.	0.136	0.101	-0.120	0.720***	0.703***	0.825***	0.522**	1.000		
X_8	pH of soil	0.243	0.076	-0.083	0.597***	0.670***	0.776***	-0.305*	0.714***	1.000	
X_9	Scheduled caste	0.312	0.135	-0.012	0.613***	0.689***	0.781***	-0.416*	0.785***	0.816***	1.000

*** Significant at 1 per cent level of significance

** Significant at 5 per cent level of significance

* Significant at 10 per cent level of significance

the proportion of waterlogged land as the independent variable. The waterlogged land intercorrelation matrix obtained is mentioned in the Table 3.4. The most predominant variable in explaining the variability in waterlogged land is found to be the slope (X_1) which explains 29.9 per cent variation in the waterlogged land at village level in the Amethi Block. It is also interesting to note that in the subsequent step, the variable drainage density (X_3) enters and jointly with variable X_1 explains 32.7 per cent total variation in the proportionate distribution of waterlogged land.

In the stepwise regression analysis the other variables could not enter in this system of analysis. It indicates that these variables fail to explain the variation fail to explain the variation in the proportionate distribution of waterlogged land at village level in the Amethi Block of the District Sultanpur.

Usar Land

It has been observed that there is a positive correlation between usar land and pH value of the soil (X_7) which is significant at 1 per cent level of significance. It indicates that the villages having proportionately high percentage of usar land have high pH value of the soil because of excessive concentration of neutral salts mainly chlorides and sulphates of sodium in usar soils. The relationship between dependent and independent variables has been illustrated in the Table 3.5. It has been observed that there is positive correlation between land concentration (X_8) and scheduled caste population (X_9) with the distribution of usar land at village level in Amethi Block which are significant at 5 per cent level of significance because the farmers having large size of land holdings are unable to remaintain the fertility status of the soil, while such cultivator pay much attention for cropping in the fertile land because the farmers are quite certain to

Table 3.4 : Stepwise Regression Analysis of Waterlogged Land

Variables		*Intercept*	*Regression coeff.*	*SE*	*T*	R^2	*Increase*	*R*	R^2	*F*
Step (1)	(1)	0.092632	0.635	0.107	5.96***	0.299	—	0.547	0.291	35.55***
Step (2)	(3)	0.255998	0.607	0.106	5.72***	0.327	0.028	0.572	0.311	19.98***

*** Significant at 1 per cent level of significance.

Table 3.5 : Correlation Matrix for Usar Land

Symbol	*Variable*	*Y*	X_1	X_2	X_3	X_4	X_5	X_6	X_7	X_8	X_9
Y	Per cent of usar Land	1.000									
X_1	Slope, deg	0.295	1.000								
X_2	Ruggedness No.	0.168	0.247	1.000							
X_3	Drainage density per sq. km.	0.208	0.53	-0.699	1.000						
X_4	Quality of water	(pH)	0.191	0.072	-0.064	0.697***	1.000				
X_5	Behaviour of water table	0.317*	0.126	-0.120	0.721***	0.734***	1.000				
X_6	NPK of soil	-0.385*	-0.144	-0.014	-0.514*	-0.364*	-0.435*	1.000			
X_7	pH of soil	0.762***	-0.101	-0.120	0.720***	0.703***	0.825***	-0.522**	1.000		
X_8	Land conc.	0.478**	0.076	-0.083	0.597**	0.670***	0.776***	-0.305*	0.714***	1.000	
X_9	Scheduled caste Per cent	0.513**	0.093	-0.095	0.613***	0.695***	0.854***	-0.437*	0.846***	0.734***	1.000

*** Significant at 1 per cent level of significance
** Significant at 5 per cent level of significance.
* Significant at 10 per cent level of significance.

achieve due benefit from such cropping system and the scheduled caste farmers in most of the areas are landless but some of the scheduled caste people have been allotted wastelands on *patta* basis but such usar land is not yet reclaimed by the scheduled caste farmers due to ignorance and socio-economic backwardness due to which the usar lands are still left out of cultivation. The behaviour of water table (X_5) has positive correlation with the usar land which is significant at 10 per cent level of significance. In the usar land water table is low land at a certain strata, the soil profile is not very preamble due to the presence of Kankar pan. Due to this the water table rises and water gets enriched through soluble salts. It has been recorded that there is negative correlation between the NPK of the soil (X_6) and usar land but this relationship is not strong because it is significant at 10 per cent level of significance. The other variables viz. slope (X_1), ruggedness number (X_2), drainage density (X_3) and quality of water in pH (X_4) have positive correlation with the distribution of usar land in Amethi, but these variables fail to explain the variation in the usar land because their relationship is in significant.

The stepwise regression analysis with usar land has been tabled in the Table 3.6. The values of the different in dependent variables (X) for usar land (Y) indicates a high degree of multi-collinearity among these variables. To remote inconsistancies arising from the multicollinearity, stepwise regression analysis has been attempted. In this exercise percentage of usar land is considered as the dependent variable (Y) and other natural and human factors as independent variables (X). The intercorrelation matrix has been obtained from stepwise regression analysis. The most dominant variable in stepwise regression analysis in explaining the variability of usar land, is the pH value of the soil and scheduled caste population. The stepwise regression analysis indicates that 14.4 per cent variation in the proporitionate distribution of usar land at village level in

Table 3.6 : Stepwise Regression Analysis of Usar Land

Variables	*Intercept*	*Regression coeff.*	*SE*		*T*	R^2	*Increase in* R^2	*R*	R^2	*F*
Step (1)	(7)	2.413898	1.107	0.296	3.73***	0.144	—	0.379	0.134	13.95***
Step (2)	(9)	2.388459	2.187	1.013	2.16	0.189	0.045	0.436	0.170	9.61***
		1.183	o.292	4.05**						

*** Significant at 1 per cent level of significance

Table 3.7 : Correlation Matrix for Banjar Land

Symbol	*Variable*	*Y*	X_1	X_2	X_3	X_4	X_5	X_6	X_7	X_8	X_9
Y	Per cent of banjar land	1.000									
X_1	Slope, deg	-0.089	1.000								
X_2	Ruggedness No.	-0.168	0.247	1.000							
X_3	Drainage density	0.352*	0.053	-0.199	1.000						
X_4	Quality of water (pH)	0.429*	0.072	-0.064	0.697***	1.000					
X_5	Behaviour of Water table	0.215	0.126	-0.120	0.721***	0.734***	1.000				
X_6	NPK of soil	0.346*	-0.144	-0.014	-0.514**	-0.364*	-0.435	1.000			
X_7	pH of soil	0.623**	-0.101	-0.120	0.720	0.730***	0.825***	-0.522**	1.000		
X_8	Land conc.	0.403*	0.076	-0.083	0.597**	0.670***	0.776***	-0.395*	0.714***	1.000	
X_9	Scheduled Caste %	0.514**	0.082	-0.134	0.614***	0.774***	0.872***	-0.481*	0.816***	0.712***	1.000

*** Significant at 1 per cent level of significance.
** Significant at 5 per cent level of significance.
* Significant at 10 per cent level of significance.

Amethi. In the subsequent step variable (X_9) scheduled caste population enters and jointly with the variables (X_7) pH value of the soil explains 18.9 per cent total variation in the proportionate distribution of usar land at village level in Amethi. The other variables could not enter in the stepwise regression analysis which indicates that there are other factors that these variables which are responsible for the proportionate distribution of usar land. Thus, among the selected variables pH value of the soil and percentage distribution of scheduled caste population are the important variables in explaining the variations in usar land at village level in Amethi Block of Sultanpur District.

Banjar Land

It has been observed that there is positive correlation between the percentage distribution of banjar land (Y) and pH value of the soil (X_7) which is significant at 5 per cent level of significance. The analysis of correlation matrix for banjar land has been depicted in the Table 3.7. The high pH value of the soil has high concentrations of salts, which hampers the crop production. The variable (X_9) scheduled caste population has positive correlation with the banjar land which is significant at 5 per cent level of significance and the variable (X_8) land concentration has positive correlation with the banjar land. The relationship between banjar land and land concentration is significant at 5 per cent level of significance. The variable quality of water in pH (X_4) and variable (X_3) drainage density have positive correlation with banjar land and their relationships are significant at 10 per cent level of significance. Therefore, these variables are not of much importance in this study because their relationship with the variable (Y) banjar land is significant at 10 per cent level of significance. It has been recorded that there is positive correlation between the behaviour of water table (X_5) with banjar land which is insignificant. There is positive correlation with the NPK of the soil (X_6) and banjar land which is significant at 10 per cent level of significance. The slope (X_1) and ruggedness number (X_2) have negative correlation with banjar land but their relationships are insignificant.

The correlation matrix for the various independent and independent variables shows positive correlations of the some of variables with the proportionate distribution of banjar land. Stepwise regression analysis has been attempted to see as how many of these variables can explain the variables in the distribution of banjar land has been mentioned in the Table 3.8. The variable (X_7) pH value of the soil has been found to be dominant variable in explaining the variation in the banjar land. Stepwise regression analysis explains 23.9 per cent variation of banjar land. The other natural and human factors could not enter in the stepwise regression analysis indicating that these variables fail to explain the variation in the proportionate distribution of banjar land at village level in Amethi Block.

Old Fallow Land

It has been observed that there is a positive correlation between pH value of the soil (X_7) and porportionate distribution of old fallow land. The relationship between these variables are significant at 10 per cent level of significance. The correlation matrix between old fallow land (Y) and natural and human factors (X) variables has been shown in the Table 3.9. Variable slope (X_1), ruggedness number (X_2), drainage density (X_3), quality of water in pH (X_4) and behaviour of water table (X_5) have insignificant correlationship with the percentage distribution of old fallow land at village level in Amethi Block.

The calculated correlation matrix indicates the multicollinearity among the independent indicators. Stepwise regression analysis of old fallow land has been illustrated in the Table 3.10. To remove the inconsistancies,

Table 3.8 : Stepwise Regression Analysis of Banjar Land

Variables		*Intercept*	*Regression coeff.*	*SE*	*T*	R^2	*Increase in* R^2	*R*	R^2	*F*
Step (1)	(7)	2.009181	0.913	0.247	2.08***	0.239	—	0.323	0.646	14.3

*** Significant at 1 per cent level of significance.

Table 3.9 : Correlation Matrix–Old Fallow Land

Symbol	*Variable*	*Y*	X_1	X_2	X_3	X_4	X_5	X_6	X_7	X_8	X_9
Y	Per cent of old fallow land	1.000									
X_1	Slope, deg	0.176	1.000								
X_2	Ruggedness No.	-0.045	0.247	1.000							
X_3	Drainage density	0.286	0.053	-0.199	1.000						
X_4	Quality of water (pH)	0.294	0.092	-0.064	0.697***	1.000					
X_5	Behaviour of Water table	0.246	0.126	-0.120	0.721	0.734***	1.000				
X_6	NPK of soil	-0.375*	-0.144	-0.014**	-0.514*	-0.364	-0.435*	1.000			
X_7	pH of soil	0.436*	-0.101	-0.120	0.720***	0.703***	0.825***	-0.522**	1.000		
X_8	Land conc.	0.425*	-0.076	-0.083	0.0597**	0.670***	0.776***	-0.305*	0.7147***	1.000	
X_9	Scheduled Caste Per cent	0.483*	0.098	-0.095	0.0615**	0.782***	0.845***	-0.417*	0.785***	0.734***	1.000

*** Significant at 1 per cent level of significance.

** Significant at 5 per cent level of significance.

* Significant at 10 per cent level of significance.

the stepwise regression analysis has been done. In the first step of regression analysis variable (X_7) pH value of the soil enters, it explains 11.3 per cent variation in the proportionate distribution of old fallow land. The other variables do not get incorporated in this analysis which indicates that other natural and human factor's indicators are in capable of the explaining the variations in the proportionate distribution of old fallow land. Inspite of these indicators there are few other factors which are responsible for the uneven distribution of old fallow land at village level in Amethi Block.

Fallow Land

The correlation matrix for fallow land with the various natural and human factors has been depicted in the Table 3.11. A significant positive correlationship has been found between the fallow land and drainage density (X_3). The relationship between these two variables is significant at 5 per cent level of significance. The variable quality of water in pH (X_4) has positive correlation with the proportionate distribution of fallow land which is significant at 5 per cent level of significance. The behaviour of water table (X_5) has positive correlation with the fallow land which is significant at 10 per cent level of significance. The relationship between the NPK of the soil (X_6) and fallow land is recorded negative and this relationship is significant at 10 per cent level of significance. The pH value of the soil (X_7) and land concentration (X_8) and scheduled caste population (X_9) has positive correlation with the proportionate distribution of fallow land. The correlationship between X and Y variables are not of much importance their relationships are significant at 10 per cent level of significance. Slope (X_1) and ruggedness number (X_2) have negative correlation with the fallow land which is insignificant.

Stepwise regression analysis has been done adopting

Table 3.10 : Stepwise Regression Analysis of Old fallow land

Variables		*Intercept*	*Regression coeff.*	*SE*	*T*	*R^2*	*Increase in R^2*	*R*	*$\bar{R}^2$*	*F*
Step (1)	(7)	2.296997	0.917	0.282	3.25***	0.113	—	0.336	0.102	10.5***

*** Significant at 1 per cent level of significance.

Table 3.11 : Correlation Matrix for Fallow land

Symbol	*Variable*	*Y*	*X_1*	*X_2*	*X_3*	*X_4*	*X_5*	*X_6*	*X_7*	*X_8*	*X_9*
Y	Per cent of banjar land	1.000									
X_1	Slope, deg	-0.160	1.000								
X_2	Ruggedness No.	-0.176	0.247	1.000							
X_3	Drainage density	0.544**	0.053	-0.199	1.000						
X_4	Quality of water (pH)	0.479**	0.072	-0.064	0.697***	1.000					
X_5	Behaviour of Water table	0.427*	0.126	-0.120	0.721***	0.734***	1.000				
X_6	NPK of soil	-0.372*	-0.144	-0.014	-0.514***	-0.364	-0.435	1.000			
X_7	pH of soil	0.418*	-0.101	-0.120	0.720	0.703***	0.825	-0.522	1.000		
X_8	Land conc.	0.382*	0.079	-0.083	0.597	0.670***	0.776	-0.305	0.714	1.000	
X_9	Scheduled Caste Per cent	0.316*	0.084	-0.095	0.635***	0.785***	0.816***	-0.381	0.793***	0.785***	1.000

*** Significant at 1 per cent level of significance.
** Significant at 5 per cent level of significance.
* Significant at 10 per cent level of significance.

fallow land as dependent variable (Y) and other natural and human factors as independent variables (X) are mentioned in the Table 3.12. The stepwise regression analysis indicates that in the first step variable pH value of the soil (X_7) enters and explains 22.9 per cent variations in the distribution of fallow land. In the second step variable (X_3) drainage density enters jointly with the variable X_7 explains 25.3 per cent total variations in the proportionate distribution of fallow land at village level in Amethi Block. The other variables do not get incorporated in the stepwise regression analysis which indicates that these variables could not explains the variation in the proportionate distribution of fallow land at village level in the Amethi Block.

Other types of Wastelands

It has been observed hat there is positive correlation between NPK of the soil (X_6) and the proportionate distribution of other types of wastelands, which is depicted in the Table 3.13. The relationship among these two variables is significant at 10 per cent level of significance. The variable land concentration (X_8) and scheduled caste population (X_9) has significant positive correlation with other types of wastelands. The relationship between these variables are significant at 10 per cent level of significance, because the large size land holder do not pay much attention for the other wasteland's reclamation and the scheduled caste population are oftenly the landless and they have been allotted the other types of wastelands on *patta,* which is not yet reclaimed because of the ignorance and socio-economic backwardness of such *patta* land allottee scheduled caste population, that is why such lands are still lying uncultivated and demarcated as other types of wastelands. The cultivators are engaged in cultivating such lands which are profitable and do not pay attention in the cropping of any such land which is expensive in cropping and benefits accrued from the cultivation is lower

Table 3.12 : Stepwise Regression Analysis of Fallow Land

Variables		*Intercept*	*Regression coeff.*	*SE*	*T*	R^2	*Increase in* R^2	*R*	R^2	*F*
Step (1)	(7)	4.292062	2.630	0.529	4.97***	0.229	—	0.479	0.219	24.67***
Step (2)	(3)	6.266952	0.839	0.519	1.62***	0.253	0.034	0.503	0.235	13.88***
			1.807	0.731	2.47***					

*** Significant at 1 per cent level of significance.

Table 3.13 : Correlation Matrix for Other Types of Wastelands

Symbol	*Variable*	*Y*	X_1	X_2	X_3	X_4	X_5	X_6	X_7	X_8	X_9
Y	Per cent of other types of Wastelands	1.000									
X_1	Slope, deg	-0.023	1.000								
X_2	Ruggedness No.	-0.067	0.247	1.000							
X_3	Drainage density	0.212	0.053	-0.199	1.000						
X_4	Quality of water (pH)	0.123	0.072	-0.064	0.697***	1.000					
X_5	Behaviour of Water table	0.087	0.126	0.128	-0.721***	0.734***	1.000				
X_6	NPK of soil	0.333*	-0.144	-0.014	-0.514**	-0.364*	-0.435*	1.000			
X_7	pH of soil	0.095	0.101	-0.120	0.720***	0.703***	0.825***	-0.522**	1.000		
X_8	Land conc.	0.412*	0.076	-0.083	0.097**	0.670	0.776***	-0.305*	0.714***	1.000	
X_9	Scheduled Caste Per cent	0.516*	0.082	0.095	0.185**	0.875	0.795***	-0.413*	0.785***	0.719***	1.000

*** Significant at 1 per cent level of significance.
** Significant at 5 per cent level of significance.
* Significant at 10 per cent level of significance.

than the expenditure of cropping. Thus due to low fertility and productivity of the lands such other types of wastelands are left uncultivated and the cultivators are having tradition farming system and within the limited input cultivators are unable to cultivate the other types of wastelands. The other variables viz. slope (X_1), ruggedness number (X_2) drainage density (X_3), quality of water in pH (X_4) behaviour of water table (X_5) and pH value of the soil (X_7) have not much importance in explaining the correlationship between the proportionate distribution of other types of wastelands their relationships are insignificant. The system of explaining with endogenic variables discussed with the above variables shows the existence of a high degree of multi-collinearity among each other.

The intercorrelation matrix obtained through stepwise regression analysis is illustrated in the Table 3.14. The most dominant variable in the first step of regression analysis is (X_8) land concentration which explains 16.9 per cent variations in the proportionate distribution of other types of wastelands at village level in Amethi Block. The other variables could not come in the optimal regression line, indicating their failure to explain the variations in the proportionate distribution of other types of wastelands at village level in Amethi Block.

Wastelands

The correlation matrix for wastelands has been depicted in the Table 3.15. It has been observed that excess drainage density (X_3) causes much soil erosion, which leads towards land degradation and accumulation of water in the low lying areas. Thus high drainage density is associated with high proportionate distribution of wastelands. The correlation matrix for wastelands (Y) and with other natural and human factors are illustrated in the Table 3.15. There is positive correlation between drainage density and the proportion of

Table 3.14 : Stepwise Regression Analysis of Other Types of Wastelands

Variables		*Intercept*	*Regression coeff.*	*SE*	*T*	R^2	*Increase in* R^2	*R*	R^2	*F*
Step (1)	(8)	1.025384	3.787	1.524	2.48***	0.169	—	0.263	0.058	6.17***

*** Significant at 1 per cent level of significance.

Table 3.15 : Correlation Matrix for Wastelands

Symbol	*Variable*	*Y*	X_1	X_2	X_3	X_4	X_5	X_6	X_7	X_8	X_9
Y	Per cent of wastelands	1.000									
X_1	Slope, deg	0.113	1.000								
X_2	Ruggedness No.	-0.095	0.247	1.000							
X_3	Drainage density	0.750***	0.053	-0.199	1.000						
X_4	Quality of water (pH)	0.741***	0.072	-0.064	0.697***	1.000					
X_5	Behaviour of Water table	0.839***	0.126	-0.120	0.721***	0.734***	1.000				
X_6	NPK of soil	-0.465***	-0.144	-0.014	-0.514**	-0.364**	-0.435	1.000			
X_7	pH of soil	0.848***	0.101	-0.120	0.720***	0.703***	0.825***	-0.522**	1.000		
X_8	Land conc.	0.797***	0.076	-0.083	0.597**	0.670***	-0.305*	0.714***	1.000	1.000	
X_9	Scheduled Caste Per cent	0.843***	0.092	-0.141	0.635**	0.786***	0.852***	-0.416*	0.842***	0.851***	1.000

*** Significant at 1 per cent level of significance.
** Significant at 5 per cent level of significance.
* Significant at 10 per cent level of significance.

wastelands which is significant at 1 per cent level of significance. High pH value of the soil has high salinity which causes hindrance in crop production and responsible for the formation of wastelands. It has been proved statistically that the relationship between these variables is significant at 1 per cent level of significance.

The land concentration is found to be high in those villages where percentage distribution of wastelands are also high. It indicates that there is positive correlation between land concentration (X_8) and the proportionate distribution of wastelands. The farmers having large size of land holdings are least interested in maintaining the fertility status of the soil due to high expenditure and very low output from such lands. The cultivators concentrate on good quality of lands from which they are sure to obtain good returns. The positive correlation between land concentration and wastelands is significant at 1 per cent level of significance. There is positive correlation between scheduled caste population and the wastelands distribution at village level in Amethi Block because the scheduled castes are oftenly the land less and as per the government policy the landless scheduled caste people are allotted land on *patta* which is normally the wastelands. The *patta* allotted wastelands are mostly lying uncultivated due to ignorance and socio-economic backwardness of the scheduled caste population because the scheduled caste people are resourceless and within the limited resource they are interested for their livelihood and survival of life but not to expend their resources in the cultivation/reclamation of such *patta* allotted wastelands which required high expenditure and very low productivity and least benefit, due to which such patta allotted waste lands are lying wastelands. The high percentage of scheduled caste which are mostly landless also indicates the land concentration among very few people. The concentration of land with limited people also proves that the large size land holders are interested to maintain the productive and fertile land but not to invest the finance in such land which requires high expenditure and very low out put, due to which high percentage scheduled caste population dominated villages are also having very high percentage of waste lands. The positive relationship between scheduled caste population (X_9) with wastelands (Y) is significant at the 1 per cent level of significance. The variables slope (X_1) and ruggedness number (X_2) are not important in explaining the variations in the proportionate distribution of wastelands because their relationship among these variables with wastelands are insignificant.

Stepwise regression analysis has been depicted in the Table 3.16. It is observed from the stepwise regression analysis that (X_9) pH value of the soil enters in the first step and explains 72.0 per cent variation in the proportionate distribution of wastelands at village level in Amethi Block. In the second step variable (X_8) land concentration jointly with variable (X_7) pH value of the soil explains 79.5 per cent variation in the proportionate distribution of wastelands at village level in Amethi Block. In the third step variable (X_9) scheduled caste enters along with pH value of the soil (X_7) and land concentration (X_8) and explains 80.9 per cent total variations in the distribution of wastelands. Lastly in the fourth step variable (X_5) behaviour of water table enters jointly with (X_7) pH value of the soil, (X_8) land concentration (X_9) and scheduled caste population, which explains 82.8 per cent variations in the proportionate distribution of wastelands at village level in Amethi Block of the District Sultanpur. Thus the total variations in the proportionate distribution of wastelands explained by selected natural and human factors has been recorded 82.8 per cent. However, the interaction between the set of natural and human factors and the proportionate distribution of wastelands provides a great clue of great significance at 1 per cent level of significance, while the main variables explaining the percentage of wastelands are pH value of the soil, land

Tab le 3.16 : Stepwise Regression Analysis for Total Wastelands

Variables		Intercept	Regression coeff.	SE	T	R^2	Increase in R^2	R	R^2	F
Step (1)	(7)	3.065437	5.506	0.376	14.62***	0.720	—	0.849	0.717	213.76***
Step (2)	(8)	3.928026	3.693	0.463	7.98***	0.795	0.075	0.892	0.790	159.45***
Step (3)	(9)	4.537645	1.194	0.361	3.31***	0.809	0.024	0.905	0.813	122.82***
			2.803	0.513	5.46***					
			8.365	1.620	5.16*					
Step (4)	(5)	5.171252	0.988	0.369	2.68***	0.828	0.009	0.910	0.819	96.51***
			0.141	0.071	2.00*					
			2.261	0.572	3.95**					
			6.763	1.782	3.79**					

*** Significant at 1 per cent level of significance.
** Significant at 5 per cent level of significance.
* Significant at 10 per cent level of significance.

concentration, scheduled caste population and behaviour of water table.

Thus it has been observed that man and nature relationship has been shattered because most of the environmental indicators are positively responding to the growth in the wastelands area. The scheduled caste population which are mostly landless population are completely dependent of the nature for fuelwood, fodder and foodgrain, etc. are responsible for the wastelands. The increasing population has the major role in the exploitation of natural resources especially the land resources, which causing natural, ecological, environmental land degradation and crisis in the eco-system of the area. The severe ecological imbalances has also caused socio-economic crisis in the rural areas.

Conclusion

The relationship between man and nature is symbiotic. The combination of human and natural factors plays an important role in the spatial distribution of wastelands and its various categories. The correlation matrix and stepwise regression analysis statistically proves that slope and drainage density are the dominant variables in explaining the variations in waterlogged land at village level in Amethi. The main important variables in explaining the proportionate distribution of usar land are the pH value of the soil and scheduled caste population followed by land concentration. The important variable in explaining the distribution of banjar land are the pH value of the soil, followed by scheduled caste population. The pH value of the soil, followed by the scheduled caste population and land concentration are the major dominant variables in explaining the variations of old fallow land at village level in Amethi Block. The pH value of the soil and drainage density are the main dominant variables in explaining the proportionate distribution of fallow land at village level in Amethi. The land concentration one of the main dominant variable followed by the scheduled caste population and pH value of the soil in explaining the distribution of other types of wastelands.

The main dominant variables in explaining the proportionate distribution of wastelands at village level in Amethi Block are the pH value of the soil, land concentration, scheduled caste population and behaviour of water table. Thus the variables which features dominating in explaining the variations in wastelands are the natural factors which are pH value of the soil, drainage density, behaviour of the water table and human factors which comprises mainly the land concentration and scheduled caste population. Thus, lastly it can be said that the natural and human factors including some of the other variables directly or indirectly responsible for the proportionate distribution of wastelands at village level in Amethi Block, District Sultanpur.

4

Agro-Afforestation System

Introduction

The magnitude of the problem of wastelands has been fairly well documented. The National Commission on Agriculture described in its report of 1992 that as much as 175 million hectares out of a total of 266 million hectares which are available for agricultural use are wastelands, due to degradation of land of some form or the other. The explosive increase of the population, increasing desire of man to exploit marginal and sub-marginal lands for a modicum of return, unmindful of the further land degradation, man causes defective land use and cropping patterns and efficient water management have emerged as one of the main factors.

In particular, the loss of forest cover, has been alarming, as much as 40 million hectares forest land out of 74 million hectares is degraded forest land. It has also been estimated that our country is lossing 1.5 million hectares of forests and 12,000 million tonnes of top soil every year due to deforestation and run-off. The process of rehabilitation may take anything from 500 to 1, 000 years to restore one inch of top soil and upto 100 years to re-establish a good natural forest cover.

The relationship of man and nature, the symbiotic bond

between the rural poor and forests expecially among scheduled castes, has been closest through the years. The traditional rights of such scheduled caste communities to minor forest produce, to grass and fallen dry wood for fuel have kept the rural communities going through the centuries. The man and nature relationship now stands threatened. Afforestation efforts, an endeavour, is rendered more difficult since the needs of the community and those of the individual are at variance with each other and cannot be reconciled unless poverty amelioration programmes raise the level of living of those surviving below the poverty line. So far there has been a slackening of afforestation on the one hand and absence of support of the local communities for the protection and augmentation of forests on the other.

Agro-Afforestation programme must be initiated as a peoples movement. The agro-afforestation programme must be implemented by the people and for the people, through leasing of forest and non-forest land and wastelands to the deprived rural poor, the *Tree Ṗatta Schemes* must be reformulated and procedures should be simplified tree grows co-operatives must be promoted and farmers should be encouraged to undertake tree plantation on their own farms and agricultural field boundaries. So far as the idea of leasing of wastelands is concerned it has been observed at the field level that individual must have a vested interest ingrowing trees thereon. If our programmes on agro-forestry and social-forestry and under poverty alleviation schemes, confine themselves to providing wage employment to the rural poor, the land less and the unemployed, in on going agro-afforestation programmes and such programmes are foredoomed preciously because they fail to create such a vested interest among the people to plant trees, and to look after and maintain them with a view to enjoy the usufruct obtained from the agro-afforestation programmes.

Agro-Afforestation Systems

Agro-afforestaton is a system of land use along with combined growing of agricultural crops with social forestry animal husbandaries including foodgrain, fodder, fuelwood, fibre, fruits, fisheries and vegetables. Common cultivators has been engaged in cultivating agricultural crops along with social-forestry, and the domestication of livestock-wood trees, fuelwood-fodder- fibre- fruits and vegetables, etc. to fulfil their day-to-day requirements, and the farmers have stopped using the trees. In response to agro-ecological conditions of the area, in about 700 B.C. man changed from hunting and food-gathering to agricultural crop-food production.

The promotion and development of agro-forestry – aims, potential and positive interaction between ecological and economic agricultural and forestry activities – can be emphasized when proved scientifically. The increased production and productivity, sustainable land management and ecological conservation are some of the important objectives of the agro-afforestation system.

The restoration of ecological and environmental degradation and to improve the socio-economic and ecological crisis sustainable development of land resources have to be managed and maintained. The sustainable development comprises of the preservation of environmental, equitable development Scientific technological change is a dire necessity for obtaining self-sufficiency in foodgrains, fodder, fuelwood, fibre, fruits, fisheries, vegetables and other produce. An unbroken symbiotic relationship with man and nature has to be re-established. Development should aim at improving the eco-system and the environment for living cattle and human people providing them water, shelter, reclaiming the wastelands for greening and interior rural areas habitable. The higher standard of living and increased agro-afforestation productivity must be achieved with despoiling environmental and nature of its beauty, freshness and purity of nature are so essential for the survival of down trodden people surviving in the remote rural areas.

It has been observed that there has been a shift in the policy during the recent past from sustained productivity to sustained development. The ecological, socio-economic, scientific and technological inputs are important for determining sustainable management systems. In the present scenario, it is required to link the eco-system processes with the multifaceted socio-economic activities centered for the sustainable development of a region.

There are different opinions and views regarding Agro-forestry systems like Agro-forestry is not a perfect system because there has been both success and failure with the various agro-forestry systems adopted. No doubt, agro-forestry has provided viable alternative of land use system with a suitable environment, and compatible social conditions, agro-forestry system should be helpful in providing sustantial output. A good agro-forestry system should be able to solve ecological, land and enviromental degradation crisis and socio-economic crisis and problem and it should be helpful in over coming the physiological, ecological and environmental protection constraints that causes hinderance in the agro-forestry development and adoption of the agro-forestry system for the sustainable development of the area.

Thus there is tremendous pressure of the human population which has resulted in deforestation and degradation of land and degradation of valuable forest resources. It is now an established fact that unless there is stabilization of population participatory management for the reclamation of wastelands and agro-afforestation management for sustainable development to meet the increasing demand of growing cattle and human population for fuel wood, fodder, fibre, fruits, fisheries, and foodgrains, etc.

Afforestation in Uttar Pradesh

The cultural systems of our country has symbiotic relationship with the forest. Forests are the land's largest and most important eco-system of the area. Forests have profound influence on the structure and functions of the human habitat. The forest is one of the prestigious propoerty for the human being. Man is dependent on forest from pre-historical period. Explosive population growth and increasing demand of cattle and human population has caused deforestation and land degradation. Awareness for the afforestation is the need of the hour. As per the National Forest Policy one third land of the total geographical area must be afforested from good quality forest cover. The total geographical area of the Uttar Pradesh is 240, 928 sq. km, Forest Survey of India, Dehradun Report-2003 indicated that there are only 14,118 sq. km. land which is afforested and it is only 5.86 per cent forest area to the total geographical area of the Uttar Pradesh.

Central Afforestation Council has been established in 1948 to strengthen the forest conservation and development programmes. *Van Mahotsava* programme had been launched during the year 1950 with the objective of the popularisation of afforestation programme among the people. New forest Policy of India was launched during the year 1952 with the objective of planning and implementation of different afforestation programme. National Forest Policy was launched during 1988 to increase the afforestation area and the Government of Uttar Pradesh also implementled "Uttar Pradesh State Forest Policy 1998."

(i) ***Highly Dense Forest*** :— There are 1297 sq. km. area under policy dense forest in Uttar Pradesh. (Table 4.1.) District Shrawasti has 210 sq. km. and Balrampur - 144 sq. km. highly dense forest, Bijnor District has 42 sq. km., Chandauli District - 2 sq. km. and Gonda District has only one sq. km. highly dense forest cover.

Table 4.1 : Districtwise Afforestation in Uttar Pradesh

(Area in sq km)

Sl. No.	*District Name*	*Geographical Area*	*Afforested Area*			
			Highly Dense Forest	*Dense forest*	*Open forest*	*Total*
1.	Agra	4027	—	74	199	273
2.	Aligarh	3650	—	6	49	55
3.	Allahabad	5137	—	28	69	97
4.	Ambedkar Nagar	2337	—	2	32	34
5.	Azamgarh	4234	—	1	30	31
6.	Bagpat	1321	—	4	11	15
7.	Bahraich and					
8.	Shrawasti	6878	210	294	347	851
9.	Balrampur	3349	144	253	135	532
10.	Ballia	2981	—	—	23	23
11.	Banda	4532	—	27	76	103
12.	Barabanki	4402	—	4	82	86
13.	Bareilly	4120	—	7	36	43
14.	Basti	2688	—	6	12	18
15.	Bijnor	4561	42	252	129	423
16.	Badanu	5168	—	16	26	42
17.	Bulandshahar	2910	—	35	81	116
18.	Chandauli	2549	2	190	327	519
19.	Chitrakut	3092	—	346	208	554
20.	Deoria	2538	—	1	16	17
21.	Etah	4446	—	8	81	89
22.	Etawa	2311	—	46	139	185
23.	Faizabad	2174	—	5	51	56
24.	Farukhabad	2181	—	13	32	45
25.	Fatehpur	4152	—	6	36	42
26.	Ferozabad	2361	—	5	39	44
27.	Gautam Budh Nagar	1442	—	12	23	35
28.	Ghaziabad	2590	—	17	26	43
29.	Ghazipur	3377	—	4	43	47
30.	Gonda	4003	1	59	47	107
31.	Gorakhpur	3321	—	40	25	65
32.	Hamirpur	4282	—	67	111	178
33.	Hardoi	5986	—	7	118	125
34.	Hathras	1840	—	1	24	25
35.	Jyotibaphule Nagar	2249	—	30	52	82
36.	Jalaun	4565	—	68	179	247
37.	Jaunpur	4038	—	13	42	55
38.	Jhansi	5024	—	34	168	202
39.	Kannuj	5024	—	34	168	202
40.	Kanpur Nagar and					
41.	Kanpur Dehat	6176	—	19	97	113

(Contd...)

Table 4.1 : (Contd...)

42.	Kaushambi	2124	—	9	22	31
43.	Kheri	7680	366	502	446	1314
44.	Kushinagar	2906	—	4	30	34
45.	Lalitpur	5039	—	146	426	572
46.	Lucknow	2528	—	115	183	298
47.	Mahrajganj	2952	202	141	118	461
48.	Mahoba	2884	—	20	74	94
49.	Mainpuri	2760	—	1	15	16
50.	Mathura	3340	—	7	54	61
51.	Mau	1713	—	1	17	18
52.	Merut	2590	—	30	32	62
53.	Mirzapur	4521	—	316	466	782
54.	Moradabad	3718	—	4	21	25
55.	Muzaffarnagar	4008	—	13	27	40
56.	Auraya	2015	—	10	59	69
57.	Pilibhit	3499	290	204	203	697
58.	Pratapgarh	3717	—	28	67	95
59.	Raibarelli	4609	—	6	91	97
60.	Rampur	2367	3	20	49	72
61.	Saharanpur	3689	—	147	224	371
62.	Sant Kabir Nagar	1646	—	—	2	2
63.	Sant Rabi Das Nagar	1015	—	—	1	1
64.	Shahjahanpur	4575	20	54	44	118
65.	Siddhartha Nagar	2895	—	10	29	39
66.	Sitapur	5743	—	15	201	216
67.	Sonbhadra	6788	17	846	1606	2469
68.	Sultanpur	4436	—	18	157	175
69.	Unnao	4558	—	34	197	231
70.	Varanasi	1528	—	1	11	12
	Total	240928	1297	4699	8122	14118

Source : Forest Survey of India Repot, 2003.

The Kheri District is having 366 sq. km. Maharajganj District - 202 sq. km. Pilibhit 290 sq. km., Rampur-3 sq. km., Sahjahanpur - 20 sq. km., and Sonbhadra District is having 17 sq. km., highly dense forest in Uttar Pradesh. Thus the highly dense forest area in Uttar Pradesh is very insignificant.

(ii) ***Dense Forest*** :— Uttar Pradesh is having 4699 sq. km., dense forest area which is depicted in the Table 4.1. Dense forest area is found very high (846 sq. km.) in Sonbhadra District, Kheri (502 sq. km.) Mirzapur (316 sq. km.) and Chitrakut (346 sq. km.) in Uttar Pradesh. Dense forest area between 200 to 230 sq. km. is found in Pilibhit, Shrawasti, Balrampur, and Bijnor Districts of Uttar Pradesh. Dense forest between 100 to 200 sq. km. is recorded in Lalipur, Maharajganj, Lucknow Saharanpur and Chandauli District, while dense forest between 50 to 100 sq. km. area is observed in Agara, Gonda, Hamirpur, Jalaun, and Shahjahanpur District of Uttar Pradesh. District Kannauj, Sant Kabir Nagar, Sant Ravi Das Nagar, Ballia district are without dense forest and other district are having less than 50 sq. km., dense forest area in Uttar Pradesh.

(iii) ***Open Forest*** :— There are 8122 sq. km., open forest area in Uttar Pradesh. Very high open forest area 1606 sq. km., is found in Sonbhadra District, followed by Kheri - 446 sq. km., Lalitpur- 426 sq. km., Mirzapur- 466 sq. km., Shrawasti District - 347 sq. km., Chandauli - 327 sq. km., open forest area. District Agara is having 199 sq. km., open forest area, followed by Bijnore (129 sq. km.), Etawa (139 sq. km.), Hamirpur (111 sq. km.), Hardoi (118 sq. km.), Jalaun (179 sq. km.), Jhansi (168 sq. km.), Lucknow (183 sq. km.), Maharajganj (118 sq. km.), Pilibhit (203 sq. km.), Saharanpur (224 sq. km.), Sitapur (201 sq. km.), Sultanpur (157 sq. km.) and Unnao District 197 sq. km. open forest area, while other district are having less than 100 sq. km. open forest area which is insignificant. The open forest areas are found more along with the foot steps of Himalayas, along with the Chambal and Gomati Rivers and Vindhyan range.

(iv) ***Total Afforestation*** :— Total afforestation area of Uttar Pradesh is 14,118 sq. km. which is 5.86 per cent to the total geographical area of the state and it is very insignificant than the 33 per cent earmarked forest cover for normal survival of the common people and restoration of ecological and environmental crisis of the state. Very high afforested area 2,469 sq. km., is seen in Sonbhadra District, followed by Kheri - 1314 sq. km., while Shrawasti District has 811 sq. km., forest, Mirzapur- 782 sq. km., Pilibhit- 697 sq. km., Balrampur - 532 sq. km., Bijnor - 423 sq. km., Chandauli - 519 sq. km., and Chitrakut- 554 sq. km., forest area while other Districts of Uttar Pradesh are having very nominal forest area.

It has been observed that there had been 4.46 per cent forest cover to the total geographical area of Uttar Pradesh during 1977. During 1999 the forest area percentage was 4.464 per cent to the total geographical area having 0.002 per cent growth from 1977 to 1999. The percentage of forest area was found 5.705 per cent during the year 2001, which was 1.241 per cent growth in the forest area from 1999 to 2001. It has been observed that there is 5.86 per cent forest area during 2003, to the total geographical area of the Uttar Pradesh. There is 1.398 per cent growth in the forest area during 1977-2003 in Uttar Pradesh.

Thus the percentage area under forest to the total geographical area of Uttar Pradesh is very insignificant as per the National Forest Policy and Uttar Pradesh State Forest Policy, while percentage growth in the forest area is also very nominal which is a great concern to the common people and the State of Uttar Pradesh as well. The forest degradation and ecological and environmental crisis of Uttar Pradesh is a great challenge to the Government Departments/ implementing agencies/planners and the policy-makers of the State of Uttar Pradesh.

The most of our rural population is completely dependent on the forest resources to obtain fuelwood, fodder, etc. There is explosive population growth in Uttar Pradesh alongwith the growth of cattle population on the one hand and very insignificant growth in the forest area which is only 1.398 per cent from 1977 to 2003. The forest area of the Uttar Pradesh is only 5.86 per cent to the total geographical area in comparison to the 33 per cent forest cover earmarked by the

National Forest Policy 1988 and Uttar Pradesh State Forest Policy 1998. The deforestation and land degradation crisis has to be controlled through peoples movement to meet the increasing demand of growing cattle and human population and also to restore the ecological and environmental crisis and also to improve the socio-economic crisis of the deprived rural multitudes.

Agro-Afforestation in Sultanpur

Agro-afforestation programme in Sultanpur is not planned appropriately because it has no peoples participation and need of the local people has not been given due importance for successful implementation, maintenance and management of the agro-afforestation activities in Sultanpur District. Various government departments/implementing agencies viz. Agri-culture-Horticulture-Forestry departments of the District Sultanpur are engaged in the implementation of various programmes. Therefore, it is imperative to explain the departmentwise agricutural - horticultural-afforestation programmes being implemented in Sultanpur district for sustainable development of the District Sultanpur.

Agricultural System

The agriculture is the main occupation of the people. Agriculture provides 74 per cent occupation to the people out of the total main workers in the District Sultanpur. The area under cultivation is 73.86 per cent followed by forest 0.44 per cent, non-agricultural uses of the land 11.35 per cent. About 58 per cent of the agricultural land is irrigated through 2044 km. long canals, 774 Government tubewells and other sources of irrigation. Wheat and rice are the major crops and pulses and sugarcane are the minor crops grown in the District Sultanpur.

Agricultural production plays an important role in the economic development of our country. Department of Agriculture is contributing in the various agricultural practices and agricultural investment programmes. Presently Rs. 6.68 lakhs expenditure has been sanctioned under the District Plan out of which Rs. 4.24 lakh expenditure has been allocated for high yielding variety of seeds, agricultural implements, irrigation pipes, insecticides and pesticides and also the field demonstrations through subsidy on agriculture to the farmers. Latest agricultural implements and agricultural techniques are being demonstrated to the interested farmers of the District Sultanpur.

Inspite of the above 4691.20 mt. tonnes seed and 5432.25 mt. tonnes fertilizer has been distributed among the farmers and a sum of Rs. 2873.35 lakhs cropping loan and 59340 farmers credit cards has been made available to the farmers. Thus, the department of agriculture is playing an important role for increasing the agricultural productivity and economic development of the District Sultanpur. Crop protection programmes plays an important role in cropping system. Approximately 25 to 30 per cent loss in the agricultural production is due to the insecticides starting from cultivation-crop cultivation, crop-harvesting and storage of the grain. The check and control of the loss in the cropping can be managed through insecticides and pesticides. The farmers are being technically trained and awareness training camps are being organised. Integrated Plant Protection Management demonstration and training programme is being demonstrated in the farmers field. On an average 22,5000 kg./litre insecticides and pesticides and chemicals and 4500 kg. bio-pesticides are being utilized for treating 52,5000 hectares area agricultural crops. Thus, it is observed that to increase the agricultural production various scientific and technical support system and application of insecticides and pesticides are being made available to farmers of the District Sultanpur.

There are 65.8 per cent net sown area to the total area of the District Sultanpur which is mentioned in the Table 4.2. Proportionately very high percentage net sown area 70.5 per cent in Baldirai Block and 70.1 per cent in Lambhua Block to the total area is recorded in the Baldirai Block of District Sultanpur which is indicated in the Map-41. High percentage net sown area between 65 to 70 per cent has been observed in the Jamo, Gauriganj, Amethi, Kurwar, Bhadainya, Dostpur, Akhandnagar, Pratappur Kamaicha, Kadipur and Motigarpur Blocks of the District Sultanpur. Very low net sown area 55.1 per cent has been recorded in the Bhadar Block of the District Sultanpur.

Table 4.2 : Agro-Afforestation, Sultanpur

Sl. No.	*Name of Block*	*% of forest land to total area*	*% of Horticultural land to total area*	*% of Net sown area to total area*
1.	Shukul Bazar	4.62	2.52	64.2
2.	Jagdishpur	0.29	3.41	62.9
3.	Musafirkhana	2.43	1.82	60.4
4.	Baldirai	0.17	2.39	70.5
5.	Jamo	00	1.78	68.1
6.	Shahgarh	0.05	2.15	63.1
7.	Gauriganj	0.04	1.55	66.7
8.	Amethi	0.05	3.41	67.2
9.	Bhnetua	00	4.28	61.5
10.	Bhadar	0.44	3.58	55.1
11.	Sangrampur	00	6.29	64.5
12.	Dhanpatganj	0.11	0.83	60.7
13.	Kurebhar	0.66	0.49	60.4
14.	Jai Singh Pur	0.19	0.61	60.2
15.	Kurwar	0.0	0.93	67.5
16.	Dubepur	0.06	1.67	60.4
17.	Bhadainya	0.58	0.83	65.6
18.	Dostpur	0.12	0.52	66.9
19.	Akhandnagar	00	0.33	65.6
20.	Lambhua	0.01	0.75	70.1
21.	Pratappur Kamaicha	1.33	0.69	66.4
22.	Kadipur	00	0.57	67.1
23.	Motigarpur	0.09	0.57	66.6
	Total	3.97	1.67	65.8

Thus it is observed that the agriculture is one of the main predominant occupation in the District Sultanpur because agricultural cropping systems covers two-third area out of the total geographical area of the Sultanpur, but it requires agricultural, scientific and technical support system to increase the agricultural production through multiple cropping system for optimum utilization of available land resources to meet the increasing demand of growing cattle and human population in the form of fuelwood, wood, fodder, fibre, fruits, fisheries, vegetables, and foodgrains, etc. for sustainable development of the District Sultanpur.

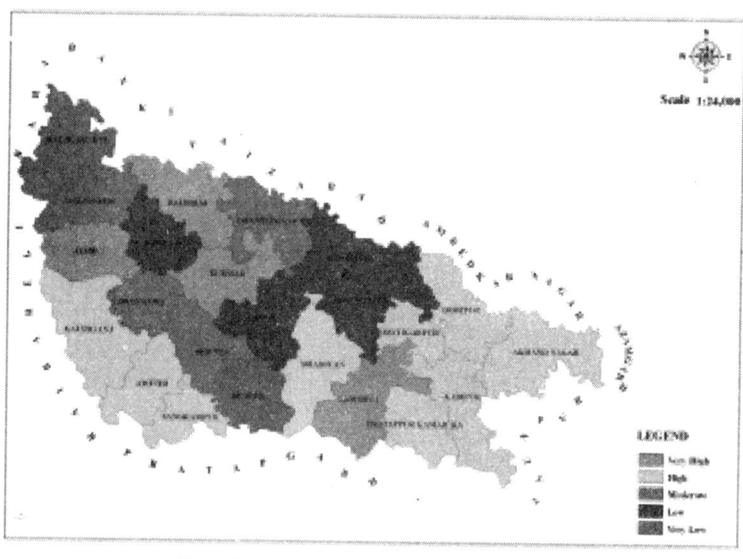

Map-41 : Net Sown Area in Sultanpur

Horticultural System

Horticultural cropping system of the District Sultanpur has been strengthen through newly horticultural plantation system. It has been planned to cover 1000 hectares area under horticultural plantation programmes and one lakh fruit plants has been distributed among the horticultural growers of the District Sultanpur. Potato cultivation area has been covered in 5107 hectares and 305 quintals potato seeds has been distributed among the horticultural growers. Intensive potato cultivation techniques have been demonstrated in the 520 hectares land of the farmers.

Vegetables development programmes has been implemented in the 26,500 hectares farmers land. The vegetables production target has been obtained 38,5002 mt. tonnes. High yielding varieties seeds distribution obtained 52.42 quintals in the 1800 hectares hybrid seeds and horticultural techniques extension programmes has been implemented in the horticultural growers field. Under the special component plan fruits, vegetables 4.5 hectares and new horticultural plantation 20 hectares scheduled caste field has been practically demonstrated and special fruits developments scheme has been launched in 110 hectares land of general cultivators and 20 hectares land of the scheduled caste farmers and scheme has been lanuched in Amethi,

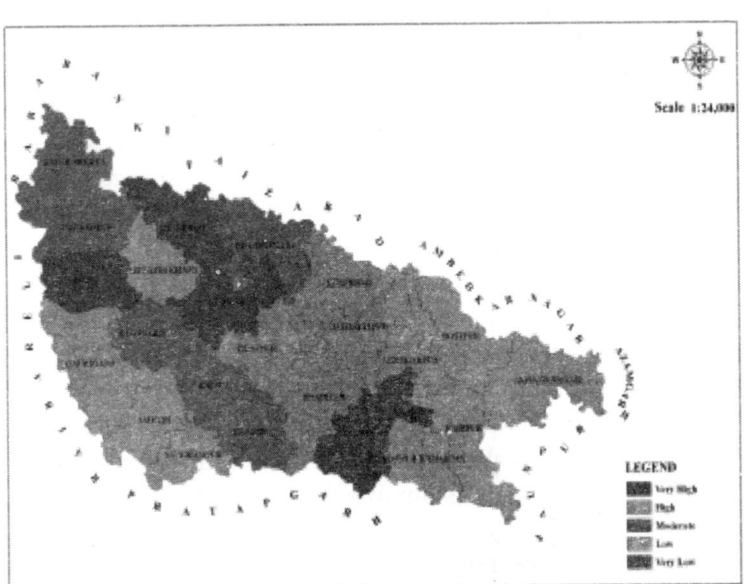

Map-42 : Horticultural Land in Sultanpur

Kurwar, Lambhua, Bhadainya, development blocks of the District Sultanpur. Two horticultural nurseries has been established in Kadipur and Bhadar Blocks. In Kadipur Nursery 6640 grafted plants and 34,640 seedlings and in Bhadar Nursery - 10, 000 grafted plants and 32,000 seedlings nursery plants has been developed for the horticultural growers. In the Government vegetables field – located at Dikhauli 5 hectares potato seed production has been ensured. Thus it is recorded that horticutural cropping system in Sultanpur District has significant role in the sustainable development of the District Sultanpur.

It is noticed from the Table 4.2. that there are 1.67 per cent horticultural land to the total area of the District Sultanpur. Very high percentage of horticultural land 6.29 per cent has been recorded in the Sangrampur Block of the District Sultanpur. The proportionate distribution of the horticultural land to the total area at Block level has been depicted in the Map-42. High percentage of horticultural land between 3.9 to 5.0 per cent has been seen in the Jagdishpur, Amethi, Bhnetua, and Bhadar Blocks of the District Sultanpur. Medium percentage of horticutural land betwen 2 to 3 per cent has been observed in Shukul Bazar, Baldirai Shahgarh Blocks of the District-Sultanpur while very low less than one percentage of horticultural land has been recorded in Dhanpatganj, Kurebhar, Jaisinghpur, Kurwar, Bhadainya, Dostpur, Akhandnagar, Lambhua, Pratappur Kamaicha, Kadipur and Motigarpur Blocks of the District Sultanpur. It is observed that area under horticultural programmes in District-Sultanpur is very insignificant. It requires integrated cropping system of Agri-Horti-Forestry programme of multi cropping techniques for optimum utilization of available natural resources and human resources for sustainable development.

Afforestation System

The exploitation and destruction of forests in the District goes back to the British period where forest wealth were consumed for commercial gains. The trend for deforestation continued even after independence and the forests were used not for imperative economic growth but for other various reasons. The denudation of forest land, however, had now showed down in the recent years despite human, cattle and commercial pressure growing cattle and human population, one of the main fact-ors for deforestation, increases the need of the land for more food production to feed the growing number of people causes environmental degradation.

Afforestation land in District Sultanpur is only 3.97 per cent to the total area of the District, which is very insignificant in comparision to the forest land earmarked by the National Forest Policy, 1988. The proportionate distribution of forest land area is illustrated in the Table 4.3. The percentage distribution of forest land to the total geographical area at the Block level in the District Sultanpur has been depicted in the Map-43. Very high percentage of forest land area which is 4.62 per cent to the total area has been found in the Shukul Bazar followed by Musafirkhana 2.43 per cent forest land to the total area of the Block. Pratappur Kamaicha Block has 1.33 per cent forest land to the total geographical area of the block. It has been observed that there are 0.66 per cent forest land in Kurebhar Block, 0.58 per cent forest land in Bhadainya block, 0.29 per cent forest land in Jagdishpur Block Dostpur 0.12 per cent and 0.17 per cent forest land in the Baldirai Block and 0.19 per cent forest land in the Jaisinghpur Block and Bhadar 0.44 per cent to the total area of the Block in the District Sultanpur. The Shahgarh, Gauriganj Amethi. Dubepur. Lambhua and Motigarpur Blocks are having less than 0.09 per cent forest land to the total area of the Block, while Jamo, Bhnetua, Sangrampur, Kurwar, Akhandnagar and Kadipur Blocks are without forest land. The insignificant forest land in Sultanpur District is a great concern to the development workers, planners and administrators of the District Sultanpur. An integrated afforestation programme

Table 4.3 : Afforestation in Sultanpur, 1996-1998

Sl. No.	*Name of Block*	*BSA (Gomti)*		*D.F.O.*		*D.H.O.*		*I.F.F.D.C.*		*U.P.L.D.C.*		*Total*
		No.	*Hect.*	*No.*	*Hect.*	*No.*	*Hect.*	*No.*	*Hect.*	*No.*	*Hect.*	*No.*
1.	Shukul Bazar	0	0.00	86400	53.25	0	0.00	109081	79.55	0	0.00	195481
2.	Jagdishpur	10550	167.50	154080	95.55	0	0.00	498502	335.45	0	0.00	29570
3.	Musafirkhana	15000	214.00	13500	10.00	1070	12.50	0	0.00	0	0.00	29570
4.	Baldirai	0	0.00	0	0.00	0	0.00	299287	248.27	0	0.00	299287
5.	Shahgarh	0	0.00	17400	11.50	1000	10.00	181465	139.75	16464	26.51	216329
6.	Jamo	0	0.00	0	0.00	0	0.00	0	0.00	0	0.00	0
7.	Gauriganj	0	0.00	36350	28.50	0	0.00	0	0.00	0	0.00	36350
8.	Amethi	0	0.00	8000	5.00	1200	12.00	0	0.00	0	0.00	9200
9.	Bhetua	0	0.00	0	0.00	0	0.00	0	0.00	31450	49.52	31450
10.	Bhadar	0	0.00	99600	55.25	0	0.00	133922	68.10	1560	2.55	235082
11.	Sangrampur	0	0.00	104700	60.00	0	0.00	0	0.00	0	0.00	104700
12.	Dhanpatganj	0	0.00	16000	10.00	850	10.00	0	0.00	0	0.00	16850
13.	Kurebhar	0	0.00	0	0.00	0	0.00	0	0.00	0	0.00	0
14.	Jaisinghpur	0	0.00	78400	43.25	0	0.00	75512	83.04	0	0.00	153912
15.	Kurwar	29100	453.00	95600	53.26	0	0.00	133134	93.62	0	0.00	257834
16.	Dubepur	0	0.00	132200	80.50	0	0.00	102145	74.20	555	0.89	234900
17.	Bhadaiyya	10900	154.00	0	0.00	700	7.00	81933	57.25	5340	8.55	98873
18.	Dostpur	0	0.00	20000	12.50	1350	13.50	0	0.00	0	0.00	21350
19.	Akhandnagar	0	0.00	0	0.00	850	8.50	0	0.00	0	0.00	850
20.	Lambhua	0	0.00	32000	70.00	630	9.00	297627	270.80	4140	7.20	334397
21.	P.P. Kamaicha	0	0.00	0	0.00	525	7.50	0	0.00	0	0.00	525
22.	Kadipur	5325	67.00	9200	5.00	940	10.00	0	0.00	0	0.00	15465
	Total value	70875	1055.50	903430	593.55	9115	100.00	1912608	1450.03	59509	95.22	2955537

Abbreviations : BSA: Bhumi Sanrakshan Adhikari, DFO: District Forest Office, DHO: District Horticulture Office, IFFDC: Indian Farms and Forestry Development Corporation, UPLDC: Uttar Pradesh Land Development Corporation.

Source : NIC, Sultanpur.

has to be launched in the district through peoples participation and as per the local need.

In view of the above and other facts Government of India and other agencies have launched various promotional schemes all over the country for afforestation and fress tree plantation to increase the forest cover in which the participation of local people is also taking place. However, due to lack of centralised database, the agencies are sometimes not in a position to plain their projects in an efficient way. The National Informations Centre (NIC) Sultanpur has taken initiative to resolve their problem, though partially, by undertaking in the District Sultanpur. The report deals with the consolidation of the plantation work of various kinds of trees done by different agencies in different years geographically.

Social forestry division, Sultanpur planted 2.53 lakhs plants in 118.50 hectares land, and 261.0 hectares area of the village community land has been planted, in which advance soil work, forest block and road side afforestation programme

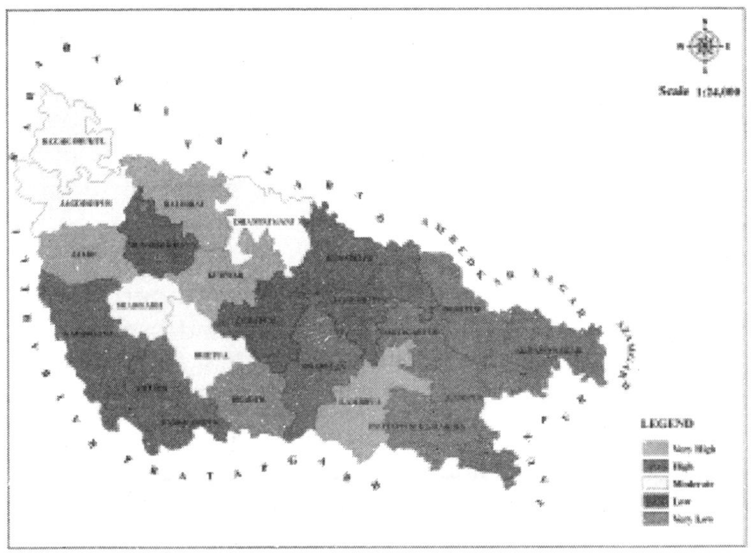

Map-43 : Forest land in Sultanpur

has been implemented and 1170 new Vikramgaurd has been constructed and trees has been planted.

There are 13 nurseries established by the Social Forestry Division, Sultanpur. Various varities useful plants has been developed in these nurseries. The developed plants of these nurseries are utilized for departmental plantation and larger afforestation programme. Out of the 13 nurseries one nursery has been established in Amethi nearer to Railway Station. In the larger plantation programme 52.69 lakh plants has been planted. The farmers of Sultanpur District have established 61 farmer's nurseries, in which approximately 60 lakh plants has been developed. The available plants from farmers nurseries are being purchased for the plantation programme by the individuals and plantation agencies.

The detailed plantation programme and planted area in hectares by different implementating agencies during the year 1996-1998 at block level in the District Sultanpur has been illustrated in the Table 4.3.

Bhumi Sanrakshan Adhikari, Gomati (BSA) Sultanpur planted 70,875 covering 1055.50 hectares area in the District. The BSA Gomati Planted 10550 plants in 167.50 hectares land in Jagdishpur Block and 1,500 plants has been planted in 214.0 hectares land in the Musafirkhana Block while 29,100 plants has been planted covering 453.0 hectares land. BSA Gomati also planted 10,900 plants in the 154.0 hectares land in the Bhadainya Block while 5,325 plants has been planted covering 67.0 hectares land in the Kadipur Block of the District Sultanpur.

The District Forest Officer (DFO) Sultanpur, planted 90,3430 plants covering 593.55 hectares land in Sultanpur which is depicted in the Table 4.3. DFO Sultanpur has planted 86,400 plants in 53.25 hectares land in Shukul Bazar Block and 154,080 plants has been planted in 95.55 hectares land in Jagdishpur Block and 13,500 plants has been planted in the 10.0 hectare land in Musafirkhana Block of the Sultanpur District. There has been plantation of 17,400 plants covering

11.50 hectares land in Shahgarh Block and plantation of 36,350 plants in 28-50 hecatres land in Gauriganj Block and 8000 plants plantation in 5.0 hectares land in Amethi Block and 99,600 plants plantation covering 55.25 hectares land in Bhadar Block. There has been 16,000 plants plantation in 10.00 hectares land in Dhanpatganj Block and 78,400 plant plantation covering 43,25 hectares land in Jaisinghpur Block and 95,600 plant plantation in 53.25 hectares land in Kurwar Block and 132,200 plants plantation in 80.50 hectares land in the Dubepur Block and 20,000 plants plantation in 12.50 hectares land in Dostpur Block in the District Sultanpur. The District Forest Officer, Sultanpur planted 32,000 plants covering 70.0 hectares land in the Lambhua Block and 9200 plants has been planted covering 5.0 hectares land in the Kadipur Block of the District Sultanpur.

The Indian Farms and Forestry Development Corporation (IFFDC) has planted 19,12,608 plants covering 1450.03 hectares land in Sultanpur District. It has planted 109,081 plants covering 79.55 hectares land in Shukul Bazar Block and 498,502 plants has been planted in 335.45 hectares land in the Jagdishpur Block while 299,287 plants has been planted in 248.27 hectares land in Baldirai Block and 181,465 number of plants has been planted in 139.75 hectares land in Shahgarh Block, while 133,922 plants has been planted covering 68.10 hectares land in the Bhadar Block. Thus IFFDC Sultanpur has planted 75,512 plants covering 83.04 hectares land and 133,134 plants has been planted in 93.62 hectares land in Kurwar Block and 102,145 plants has been planted covering 74.20 hectares land in Dubepur Block and 81,933 plants has been planted covering 57.25 hectares land in Bhadainya Block while 297,627 plants has been planted covering 270.80 hectares land in Lambhua Block of the District Sultanpur. Thus Indian Farms and Forestry Development Corporation has planted 19,12,608 plants covering 10 Blocks of the District Sultanpur.

The District Horticulture Officer (DHO) Sultanpur has

ensured plantation of 9115 plants covering 100.0 hectares land in Sultanpur District. District Horticulture Officer Sultanpur has ensured the plantation of 1070 plants in 12.50 hectares land in Musafirkhana Block and 1000 plants plantation has been done in 10.0 hectares land in Shahgarh Block and 1200 plants plantation has been carried out covering 12.0 hectares land in Amethi Block and 850 plants plantation has been done in 10.0 hectares land in Dhanpatganj Block and 700 plants plantation has been carried out in 7.0 hectares land in Bhadainya Block of the District Sultanpur. The District Horticulture Officer, Sultanpur ensured the plantation of 1350 plants covering 13.50 hectares land in Dostpur Block and 850 plants plantation has been done in 9.50 hectares land in Akhandnagar Block and 630 plants has been planted in 9.0 hectares land in Lambhua Block and 525 plants has been planted in 7.50 hectares land in Pratappur Kamaicha Block while 940 number plants has been planted covering 10.0 hectares land in Kadipur Block of the District Sultanpur.

The Uttar Pradesh Land Development Corporation (UPLDC) has carried out plantation of 59,509 plants covering 95.22 hectares land in Sultanpur District which is depicted in the Table 4.3. It has planted 16,464 plants in 26.51 hectares land in Shahgarh Block and 31,450 plants has been planted in 40.52 hectares land in Bhnetua Block and 156 plants has been planted in 2.55 hectares land in Bhadar Block and 555 plants has been planted covering 0.89 hectares land in Dubepur Block and 5,340 plants has been planted in 8.55 hectares land in Bhadainya Block while 4,140 plants has been planted covering 7.20 hectares land in Lambhua Block of the District Sultanpur. Thus Uttar Pradesh Land Development Corporation has planted 59,509 plants in 6 Blocks of the District Sultanpur. The plantation programme in Sultanpur District has been very insignificant in comparision to the total geographical area of the Block.

Thus Bhumi Sansrakshan Adhikari, Sultanpur, District Forest Officer, Sultanpur, District Horticulture Officer,

Sultanpur, Indian Farms and Forestry Development Corporation and Uttar Pradesh Land Development Corporation jointly planted 29.56 lakhs plants in the District Sultanpur very high 6.63 lakh plantation was done in Jagdishpur Block followed by 3.35 lakh plantation in Lambhua Block followed by 2.58 lakh plants in Kurwar Block, 2.35 lakhs plants in Bhadar Block 1.95 lakh plants in Shukul Bazar and 2.16 plants in Shahgarh Block and 2.99 lakh plants in Baldirai Block and 2.34 lakh plants in the Dubepur Block, has been planted in Sultanpur District. Thus, there has been 1.05 lakh plants plantation in Sangrampur Block and 1.59 lakhs plants plantation has been ensured in Jaisinghpur Block of the District Sultanpur. There has been 0.30 lakh plants plantation in Musafirkhana, 0.37 lakh plants in Gauriganj, 0.311 lakh plants in Bhnetua and 0.17 lakh plants in Dhanpatganj, 0.99 lakh plants in Bhadainya, 6.21 lakh plants in Dostpur and 0.15 lakh plants in Kadipur Block has been planted. Very insignificant plantation has been carried out in Pratappur Kamaicha Block (525 plants), Akhand Nagar Block (850 plants) and Amethi Block (9200 plants) of the District Sultanpur, while no plantation has been carried out in Jamo Block and Kurebhar Block of the District Sultanpur. It is observed that there has been very least plantation has been done in the various Blocks of the District Sultanpur which is very insignificant incomparision to the National Forest Policy 1988 and Uttar Pradesh State Forest Policy 1998.

Eco-system of Sultanpur

(i) ***Flora*** :— The major part of the District Sultanpur was covered with the forests of Dhak and Thorny bushes forming a valuable site of refuge in trouble times of the Nawabi rules during former historical days. During the beginning of the 19th century it is stated that one large tract of dense forest extended in an unbroken stretch near Ram Nagar in Tehsil Amethi.

The Jungles of Bhadainya covered an area of more than 404 hectares even after the freedom struggle of 1857 when portions of Jungle Tract were cleared off by the British forces. During the Second World War period and thereafter, in furtherance of the Grow More Food Compaign, the jungles were recklessly cut down. Presently, small patches of jungles are seen near Unchagaon and to the west of Musafirkhana in the western part of the District Sultanpur. In the eastern part of the district the remnants of extensive wood are found near the village of Kathaura, Rampur, Baragaon, Navgavan, Mahadeo and between Dulhapur and Bhavanpur. Small portions of land between Bhumi and Tikarmafi and the south of the Islampur, all in Tehsil Amethi are covered with natural vegetation growth. Small tract of jungle are also seen on the ravine lands of the banks of the Gomati River and Kadu Nala.

The areas covered with timber and other trees and shrubs, which comes under the control of Forest Department is about 1600 hectares of which an area of about 1253 hectares lies in Tehsil Musafirkhana and 347 hectares in Tehsil Sadar Sultanpur. In addition to the above, road side avenues, controlled by the Forest Department are about 74 kms in Tehsil Musafikhana, 80 kms. in Tehsil Kadipur, 132 kms. in Tehsil Sadar Sultanpur and 60 kms. in Tehsil Amethi. The Jungle area under the control of Gram Sabha is about 3847 hectares of which 1852 hectares are covered with timber trees and the remaining with other species of trees and shrubs of the Timber Jungles Tehsil. Amethi contains 740 hectares, Tehsil Sadar Sultanpur contains 680 hectares, Tehsil Musafirkhana 394 hectares and Tehsil Kadipur 38 hectares. The forest areas under other trees and shrubs cover 917 hectares in Tehsil Sadar Sultanpur, 527 hectares in Tehsil Musafirkhana, 325 hectares in Tehsil. Amethi and 226 hectares in Tehsil Kadipur. However, these cannot be called forests of which they lack the stateliness and density, seen in the twilight at the season of the year their leaves are gathered for fuel; their crooked trunks and branches present the appearance of a number of gaunt, weired figures in all sorts of grotesgue and fantastic shapes.

The main species of the trees found in these jungles are Dhak, Shisham, Neem, Babool, Bel, Pipal, Bargad, Goobar, Rakar, and Mahua. Among these species which have been introduced recently *Mango,* Khair, Safed Siris, Kala Siris, Kachnar, Amaltas, Jamun, Sagaun, Semah, Arjun, Bahera and Zezyphus are commonly seen in the area under the forest department along the road sides in the District Sultanpur.

(ii) ***Fish*** :— Fish are found in the rivers, lakes, ponds, canals and artificial reserviours of the District Sultanpur. The main species of the fish found are Bata, Rehu, Karuanch, Singhi, Nain, Raia, Bhakur and Belgagra.

As per the policy of the government lowlying or the wastelands or common village Panchayat land is being allotted to the interested needy people on *Patta* for fisheries. To improve the village pond for fisheries a sum of Rs. 60,000 per hectares and a sum of Rs. 30,000 per hectares is being made available on loan to the fisherman for the initial investments of the fishing. Out of the sanctioned loan 20 per cent grants for general person and 25 per cent subsidy for the scheduled caste person is being provided to the fisherman.

For the construction of pond on the individual land Rs. 2.00 lakh per hectare and for the initial investment of fishing Rs. 30,000 per hectare bank loan is being made available, while 20 per cent for the general and 25 per cent for the scheduled caste person subsidy is being provided to the above loan.

The animal husbandry programme viz. cow, buffallow, duck, hen and pig along with fisheries can be managed and along with the funds of the pond fruits and vegetables cultivation can be implemented to increase the income of the fisherman and to ensure optimum utilization of the pond land. For the integrated fisheries programme a sum of Rs.

80, 000 per hectare is also being provided by the bank out of which 20 per cent subsidy for general person and 25 per cent subsidy for the scheduled caste person is being made available by the Fisheries Development Agency, Sultanpur.

As per the government order, individual land owners who has constructed pond in their own land and engaged in the fisheries programme, general person 20 per cent and scheduled caste person 25 per cent subsidy is being made available to the total cost estimated for the construction of pond and fisheries initial investment during the first year of the fishing work.

Scientific training cum demonstration programme for fish cultivation for 10 day short duration is being provided by the Fisheries Development Agency and during the such training period Rs. 100 as training expense and Rs. 100 as tour expense at once is also being provided to the fishermen.

For the individual fish hatchury programme upto the 1.5 hectare pond for mini-hatchury construction for 10 million fry capacity fish hatchury a sum of Rs. 8.0 lakh loan is being provided and at the rate of 10 per cent subsidy upto Rs. 80, 000 maximum is also provided to the fishermen.

As per the demand of the fishermen Rohu, Bhakur, Nain, Kamal corp, silver corp and grass corp high tech fish seedlings are being made available to the hatchuries fishermen from the fisheries department's pond by the Uttar Pradesh Fish Development Corporation at the nominal government's rates.

The soil and water testing is being ensured free of cost for the ponds of the fishermen by the Fisheries Development Agency.

The scientific technological advice is being made available time to time to the fishermen as per growth of the fish.

For the integrated development of fishermen. Fishermen

Co-operative Socieites are formed for the self-sustenance of the fishermen.

Under the scheme of Fishermen Accident Insurance, the registered Fishermen Co-operative Socieities are able to get the insured amount ratio by the Government of India and the Government of Uttar Pradesh, in this programme Fishermen Co-operative Societies members during the accidental conditions Rs. 50,000 in case of death and Rs. 25, 000 in case of handicapness insurance amount is being made available by the Fisheries Development Agency.

In the fishermen dense populated areas the below poverty line fishermen are being provided Rs. 25,000 for housing and for 10 houses jointly Rs. 20, 000 is being provided for installation of hand pump under the scheme of the government.

(iii) ***Fauna*** :— The wildlife of the district has greatly decreased in number and variety since the middle of the 19th century due to the clearance of jungles and the reclaimation of wild tracts and groves for cultivation. Though the wild animals has become quite unimportant, yet considerable species of birds, reptiles and fish are found in the District Sultanpur.

(iv) ***Animals*** :— The stray leopard which was occassionally seen in the Jungles of Kadu Nala has now become stinct. The wolf has become scarce. The Nilgai is seen in the jungles near Ram Nagar and few other places. Besides the monkey, jackel, fox and hare are common animals found througout the District Sultanpur.

(v) ***Birds*** :— The birds of the District Sultanpur are similar to those of the adjoining districts. The chief game birds found in the district are of several varieties of wild goose, duck, quail and partridge which are fairly plentiful during the winter. The large egret which is found throughout the district is shot for the sake of its plumage. Among other birds generally found in the District Sultanpur are parrot, peacock, red jungl, fowl, nightingale and sparrow. A large number of the migratory birds come to the swamps and jhiles in the southern part of the District Sultanpur.

(vi) ***Reptiles*** :— Various varieties of snakes and other reptiles are found everywhere in the District Sultanpur in the rural areas. Harmless snakes are found but some are deadly, *e.g.*, the Cobra. The Russel's Viper which is viviparous and hocturnal in its habits is commonly found in the district Sultanpur. Though the majority of snakes are non-poisonous, a few people die of snake bite almost every year. The other reptiles found in the District Sultanpur are chamaleon and monitor lizard, the later which was the fast becoming extinct due to netting, shooting, has been declared protected species in the Sultanpur District.

Thus the eco-system of the area has been degraded which has led to ecological, environmental crisis and socio-economic backwardness.

Conclusion

The land degradation and deforestation has caused severe ecological, environmental crisis and socio-economic backwardness. The symbiotic relationship between man and nature has been realized because the poor depends on the forest. The scheduled caste communities totally depends on the major forest produce, to grass and fallen drywood for fuelwood. The relationship between man and nature has been threatened. Agro-afforestation efforts, an endeavour, is rendered is more difficult since the needs of the community are at avariance with each other and it cannot be reconciled unless poverty amelioration programmes raise the level of living of those who are surviving below poverty line. The agro-afforestation programme must be initiated as a peoples movement.

Agro-afforestation is a system of land use along with the combined growing of agricultural crops with social forestry, horticulture, animal husbandry including vegetables, fuel-wood, fodder, fibre, fruits, fisheries, and foodgrains, etc. to fulfil the increasing demand of growing cattle and human population.

There is tremendous pressure of the human population which has led to deforestation and land degradation. The stabilization of population and participatory management for the reclamation of wastelands and agro-afforestation management for sustainable development.

The Forest Survey of India, Dehradun indicated in its report that there are 5.86 per cent forest land in Uttar Pradesh. Various programmes has been launched by the government to ensure successful afforestation programmes. There are 1297 sq. km. highly dense forest land out of which 210 sq. km., highly dense forest is found in Shrawasti District followed by 144 sq. km. in Balrampur District. There are 4699 sq. km. dense forest in Uttar Pradesh out of which 846 sq. km., dense forest is recorded in Sonbhadra District followed by 502 sq. km., in Kheri, 346 sq. km., in Chitrakoot and 316 sq. km. dense forest is found in Mirzapur District of Uttar Pradesh. There are 8122 sq. km., open forest in Uttar Pradesh out of which 1606 sq. km. open forest is found in Sonbhadra District followed by Kheri-446 sq. km., Shrawasti-347 sq. km., Chandauli-327 sq. km., open forest area. The forest land is found more along with the foodsteps of Himalayas and Vindhayan range and the Chambal and Gomati rivers.

Thus, in Uttar Pradesh, there are 14,118 sq. km., forest area which is 5.86 per cent to the total geographical area of the state which is very insignificant in comparision to the 33 per cent forest land earmarked by the Government. Very high afforested area is found in Sonbhadra District 2,469 sq. km., followed by Kheri - 1314 sq. km., forest land and Shrawasti District 811 sq. km., Mirzapur-782 sq. km., Pilibhit - 697 sq. km., Balrampur - 532 sq. km., Bijnore-423 sq. km., Chandauli - 519 sq. km., and Chitrakoot - 554 sq. km., forest area. It has been recorded that during 1977, there was 4.46 per cent forest land and during 2003 there has been 5.86 per cent forest area in Uttar Pradesh having 1.398 per cent growth in the forest land from 1977 to 2003, which is insignificant against 33 per cent forest land earmarked by the National Forest Policy and Uttar Pradesh State Forest Policy. The land degradation and deforestation is a great challenge to the planners and programme implementing institutions.

The agro-afforestation programmes in Sultanpur is not appropriately planned and properly implemented by the implementing agencies, because it requires joint endeavour and efforts of Agriculture- Horticulture - Social- Forestry and Fisheries departments of the District Sultanpur with the involvement of farmers.

The agriculture is the main occupation of the people of Amethi and Sultanpur. The area under cultivation is 73.86 per cent in Sultanpur followed by 0.44 per cent forest area.

The agriculture department has expended Rs. 6.68 lakh for high yielding variety seeds, fertilizer, agricultural implements, irrigation pipes, insecticides and pesticides and field demonstrations. Latest developed agricultural implements, agricultural cropping, etc. are practically demonstrated in the farmers field. Inspite of the above 4691.20 mt. tonnes seed and 5432.25 mt. tonnes fertilizers has been distributed among the farmers and a sum of Rs. 2873.35 lakhs cropping loan and 59340 farmers credit cards has been also provided to the farmers. It has been observed that about 25 to 30 per cent loss in the agricultural production is due to the insecticides starting from cultivation-cropping-crop harvesting and storage of the grain.

Appropriate application of insecticides and pesticides can reduce the loss in agricultural production.

Sultanpur District has 65.8 per cent net sown area. Proportionately, high percentage more than 70 per cent net sown area is found in Baldirai Block and Lambhua Block of the District Sultanpur while very low percentage 55.1 per cent net sown area to the total area is found in Bhadar Block of the District Sultanpur.

Horticultural cropping system has been strengthened in Sultanpur district covering 1000 hectares land under horticultural plantation. Intensive potato cultivation has been ensured in 5107 hectares land and 305 quintals potato seed has been distributed and hightech potato cultivation has been demonstrated in 520 hectares farmers land. Vegetables development programmes are being launched in 26,500 hectares farmers land providing 52.42 quintals seeds distributed and in the 1800 hectares land horticultural techniques has been demonstrated in the farmers field. Horticultural nurseries has been established through developing 6640 grafted nurseries plants at Kadipur and 34,640 grafted plants seedlings and about 10,000 grafted plants and 32,000 seedlings nurseries plants has been developed at Bhadar Nursery. There are 1.67 per cent horticultural land in Sultanpur District. Very high percentage 6.29 per cent horticultural land is found in Sangrampur Block and 3.41 per cent horticultural area is seen in Amethi Block of the District Sultanpur.

The afforested land in District Sultanpur is 3.17 per cent to the total area. Very high percentage 4.62 per cent forest land is found in Shukul Bazar Block followed by Musafirkhana having 2.43 per cent forest land and Pratappur Kamaicha 1.33 per cent forest land to the total area of the Block while Amethi Block is having only 0.05 per cent forest area to the total area of the Block which is very insignificant.

Social forestry division Sultanpur planted 2.53 lakhs plants covering 118.50 hectares land and 261.0 hectares land belonging to Gram Panchayat. There are 13 nurseries established in Sultanpur while one nursery at Amethi has also been established. In Amethi Block 8000 plants has been planted covering 5.0 hectares land and 9.03 lakhs plants has been planted covering 593.55 hectares land during 1996-98, in Sultanpur District.

Bhoomi Sanrakshan Adhikari (BSA) planted 70,875 plants covering 1055.50 hectares land.

District Horticulture Officer planted 9115 plants covering 100 hectares land in Sultanpur while 1200 plants has been planted in 12.0 hectares land. Indian Farm and Forestry Development Corporation (IFFDC) planted 19.13 lakh plants covering 1450.03 hectares land in Sultanpur District while Uttar Pradesh Land Development Corporation planted 59509 plants covering 95.22 hectares land. Thus, in Sultanpur District 29.56 lakh plants has been planted and 9200 plants has been planted covering 17.0 hectares land in Amethi Block.

The major part of the Sultanpur District was covered with the dhak, thorny bushes. A large dense forest tract extended in an unbroken stretch near Ram Nagar in Tehsil Amethi. The jungles area under Gram Sabha is about 3847 hectares and 1600 hectares forest land is controlled by the Forest Department, while 325 hectares forest land is found in the Tehsil Amethi.

The main species of trees found in the jungles are dhak, shisham, neem, babool, bel, pipal, bargad, goolar, rakar, and mahua. Among the species which has been introduced recently are mango, khair, safed siris, kala siris, kachnar, amaltas, jamun, sagaun, semal, arjun, bahera, zezyphus are commonly seen in the area under the forest departments along the roadsides in the Sultanpur District.

The fish are found in the rivers, lakes, ponds, canals, and artificial reservoirs of the District Sultanpur. The main species of the fish found in the district are bata, rehu, karuanch, singhi, hain, raia, bhakur and belgagra. The fish culture is scientifically and technically promoted and demonstrated in

Sultanpur District under various schemes launched by the Fisheries Development Agency, Sultanpur.

The flora and fauna and wildlife in Sultanpur district has greatly decreased in number, which are unimportant in the area.

The ecosystem of the area has been degraded which has led to ecological, environmental crisis and socio-economic backwardness of the area.

Thus agro-afforestation programmes in Sultanpur District and in Amethi Block has not been properly planned and appropriately implemented because it requires joint venture and efforts of the implementating agencies like Agriculture- Horticulture - Social - forestry and fisheries and with the participation, involvement of the local peoples. The agro-afforestation programmes should be implemented for the people, by the people and demonstrated in the farmers field in an integrated manner adopting latest developed and innovated scientific techniques.

5

Policy, Planning for Agro-Afforestation Management on Wastelands

Introduction

The increasing demand of the growing population as well as increased use of raw material for the industry has led towards the land degradation and rapid expansion of wastelands. Our country has 175 million hectares degraded land out of 328 million hectares land. The land degradation is mostly caused by both poverty and mismanagement of lands. The degradational cycle of common natural land resources proceeds from hacking, excessive grazing, over cropping, mismanagement, application of high doses of chemical festilizers, unscientific irrigational practices, cultivation on sub-marginal lands as well as natural calamities, all leading to land degradation. It has been indicated by the Satellite Imagery that we are loosing about 1.3 million hectares of forest per year. The national firewood requirement is about 130 million tonnes per year of which we are fetching about 50 million tonnes firewood from forest, which means 80 million tonnes of firewood has yet to be generated. Hence, the pressure shall mount heavily on the already disappearing forest cover. The excessive revenue generated through unplanned and unscientific cutting of forest, the greater distruction of the forest area. This must be stopped.

The problem of wastelands is mostly man-made and causes misery to the millions of the deprived rural poor. The reclamation of wastelands may be adopted as a strategy for the expansion of net sown area to increase the agricultural production and the plantation programme predominantly for the fuelwood, fooder to fetch the overall need of the rural poor. Therefore, it has been realized for an immense need for the formulation of Action Plan for the reclamation of wastelands for agro-afforestation, to meet the increasing demand of the fuelwood, fodder, fibre, fruits, fisheries and foodgrains, etc. Thus, a combined co-ordinated action plan must be drawn for the reclamation of wasteland and agro-afforestation management. The destruction of actual forest must be stopped and it is expected that social-forestry to compensate the forest degradation.

Keeping the above facts into consideration, it is necessary to describe the policies and planning initiated for the development and reclamation of wastelands to restore the ecological and environmental degradation on the one hand and the policies and planning formulation for agro-afforestation management and to ensure intensive agricultural multiple cropping system especially — agricultural cropping alongwith-horticultural, forestry, fisheries, animal husbandary and other activities for optimum utilization of available natural land resources and human/anthropogenic resources and to meet the increasing demand of growing cattle and human population for the fuel-wood, fibre, fruits, fisheries, fodder and foodgrain (F^6) restore and control the ecological and environmental degradation and maintain the ecological imbalances of the area and to improve the socio-economic crisis of the region.

Policies for Wastelands Development

Historical Perspectives

The problem of wastelands is not a new one, it has a long history. Initially *Apeman* survived on nature and lined as a barbarian. Later on he lost his ability to catch the animal, by throwing the stone at the animal and disabling the animal made it possible for him to catch the animal for his food. After few years, *apeman* formed the sharp stone for hunting purposes. In this way, the *apeman* disturbed the nature resulting in deforestation and ecological imbalances and growth of wastelands.

Histrocially, the *invaders* and *rulers* demarcated the wastelands during the 4th century B.C. during the Kallinga war — the good quality land was grabbed by upper class while hilly/degraded/wastelands was left for Sudras (low class people).

Emperor *Ashoka* used the wastelands for proper grading of the land. *Ambassador Megasthanese* had used the wastelands as neglected land. *Mughal Emperor Babar* used the term wastelands in different ways as the neglected land for grading the land for revenue collection. Later on, *Akbar The Great fixed* the value of land in *Annas* for the revenue collection from Taluqdars. Poor quality land/wastelands has been charged very nominal land revenue. While good quality land, 14 *Annas* to 16 *Annas* was levied while for the wastelands/neglected land no *land value/malgujari* was charged.

Britishers continued the same practice and no land revenue was charged for wasteland or the land which failed to yield a positive return to the cultivators.

It is observed that the development of wastelands started through the triangular force of man — nature — and technology, when man himself was interacting with nature for his survival, the concept of wastelands did not exist. But from the period of *apemen* including the sharpening of the stone and hunting of animals, the problem of wastelands started. It may be said that the development of technology has led to an increase in the wastelands. But one cannot say that one should stop the development of technology because it increase the wastelands. Thus efforts should be made to compensate the deforestation and land degradation through agro-afforestation management.

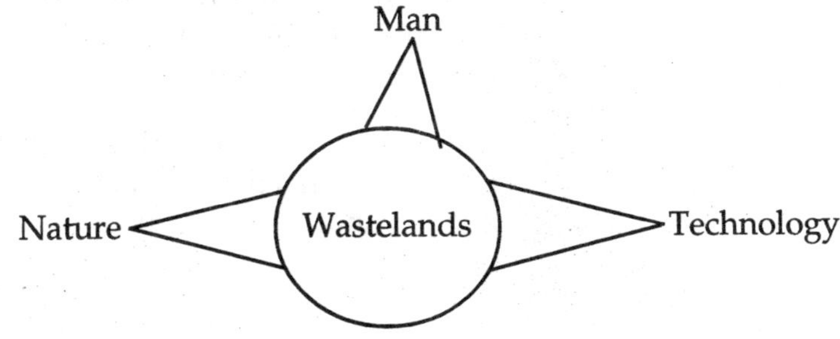

Post-Independence Policies

The magnitude of the problem of wastelands and environmental and land degradation has been given due priority and importance in the *Constitution of India.*

Article 48A, *of Constitution of India enunciates, "The state shall endeavour to protect* and *improve the environment* and *to safeguard the forest and wildlife of the Country."*

For the fulfilment of this objective the task of environmental protection has become of prime importance to the nation.

It was the vision and environmental zeal of Indiraji, that led to her pioneering statement on Environment at *Stockholm Conference* with the subsequent establishment of Department of Environment. We must prevent further degradation of natural resources and endowments, and life support system of land, water and vegetation.

National Bureau of Soil Survey and Land use Planning of the Indian Council of Agricultural Research has been established to restore the land degradation.

All India Soil and Land use Survey of the Department of Agriculture are engaged in performing the task of collecting and analysing the data on wastelands.

The preservation and protection of our environment and forests cannot be secured by statutory measures, government control and punitive mechanisms.

"Tree is India's life" and part of it would be an awareness that will reach out into generation in the future as well as in the historic words of late Smt. Indira Gandhi —

> "In his ignorance with his own increasing knowledge and ability man has ignored his dependence on the earth and has lost his communion with it. He no longer puts his ear to the ground so that the earth can whisper its secrets to him. The national song which inspired our freedom movement describes our land as one endowed with water and fruit, rich with greenness of growing plants. We must make this true not only of India but of all lands."

In her dream is to come true, one must no longer confine to the regulations and control to preserve and enrich our natural resources but one must put his ear to the ground and listen to what *Mother Earth* ask of him or her. And having listened, each one must do his or her bit for giving back to *Mother Earth* what centuries of despoliation has taken away so ruthlessly from her.

National Commission on Agriculture, in the Ministry of Agriculture, Government of India, indicated that 175 million hectares land out of 266 million hectares which are available for agricultural use are wastelands due to degradation of some form or the other.

Tremendous forest degradation and the associated ecological crisis and socio-economic crisis is related to it, that the then Prime Minister Late Shri Rajiv Gandhi in his address on January 5, 1985, mentioned the establishment of the "National Wastelands Development Board." Prime Minister called for ecological crisis and socio-economic crisis, which affects the poor much more significantly than any other part of the country. The major impact of the deforestation and ecological degradation that has taken place has been largely on the rural poor.

Half of our nation depends for its fuelwood and fodder on the common lands which has made not only their poverty much more acuse but the quality of life of the poor due to which the National Wasteland Development Board, has been more strengthen through developing a separate Department viz. Department of Wasteland Development under the Ministry of Rural Development for the restoration and reclamation of village community wastelands and individual wastelands. National Wastelands Development Mission was launched on 5th October 1989 by the Government of India to ensure wastelands development as peoples movement.

The basic objectives of the Wastelands Development Mission 1989 are as follows:

- To check and control the land degradation.
- To reclaim the wastelands for sustainable development.
- Greening the wastelands for availability of fuelwood, fodder, fruits, wood, etc.

The working policy for the Wastelands Development Mission was to develop peoples participation at Village Panchayat.

- To develop integrated land use system based on the integrated watershed developments.
- To implement working plant at village level.
- To regenerate the bio-mass, conservation and ecological balance.

- To emphasize on the production of wood, fuelwood and fodder.
- To solve the policy matters and extension of technology.

Target Areas

- The degradation forest land.
- The degradation grazing land and development of common land.
- To develop individual wastelands and dryland.

Mission Programme :— There are six mini-mission constituted to strengthen the wastelands development programme.

Mini-Mission - I – *Policy Planning* :– To develop policy planning and develop policy for land use system, grazing and animal husbandry management. Conservation of wood for fuelwood, establishment of wood, the distribution of benefits, accrued from common land, to strengthen the resources for mission programme to develop institutional finance and other support for farm forestry and to develop farmers industrial relation and it's promotion through financial support.

Mini Mission - II – *Peoples Participation* :— To develop capabilities and promote the programme at micro-level or village level.

Mini-Mission - III – *Technology Extension* :— Research extension with the objectives of reclaiming usar/banjar/ravine wastelands.

Mini - Mission - IV- *Restoration of Degradation Forest Land* :— Bio-mass pressure, fire, mismanaged grazing, and to remove the problems of wood and fuelwood.

Mini - Mission - V - *Greening the common land* :— To develop the bio-mass and reclaim the wastelands.

Mini - Mission - VI- *Farm Forestry* :— To develop the farm land to obtain fuelwood, fodder, wood and to develop land productivity.

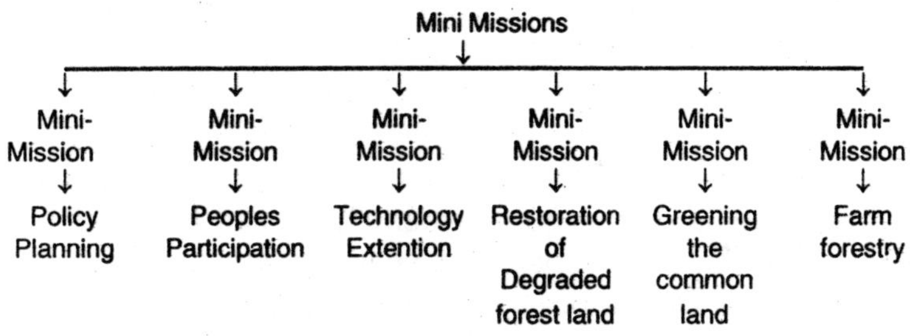

Fig. 5.1 : Wasteland Development Mission

The restoration and reclamation of forest degraded land has been controlled by the "*National Afforestation and Eco-Development Board*" (NAEB) in the Ministry of Environment and Forest, Government of India, with the view to restore and reclaim 40 million hectares degraded forest land out of 74 million hectares land. It is estimated that India is loosing 1.5 million hectares of foerst land per year.

Our former Prime Minister, Late Shri Rajiv Gandhi in his broadcast to the nation on January 5, 1985, said that-

> "continuing deforestation has brought us face to face with major ecological and socio-economic crisis. The trend must be halted, I propose immediately to set up a National Wastelands Development Board with the objective of bringing five million hectares of land every year under fuelwood and fodder plantations. We shall develop a peoples movement for afforestation."

The schemes of environmental protection, afforestation, prevention and reclamation of wastelands, better use of irrigation through scientific management and development of alternative sources of rural energy had been included in the 20-point Economic Programme.

However, at the State level in Uttar Pradesh data on land use is maintained by the Department of Agriculture on the old pattern of land use classification with no specific category of "*wastelands*". Thus, one can find a sound data base of wastelands at the national level, it is in a rudimentary form at the regional level. In the State of Uttar Pradesh, high power committee headed by the *Agriculture Production Commissioner* (APC.) comprising all the concerned secretaries and heads of departments of the government has been established during 1989. Later on seperate department viz. Department of Wasteland Development has been formed as per the pattern of Government of India.

Proper utilization of landuse and to maintain the diversification of agricultural land "National Soil Conservation and Land Use Board" has been established in the Ministry of Agriculture, Government. of India.

In Uttar Pradesh also "State Landuse Board" has been established under the Department of Planning, the Government of Uttar Pradesh with the view to maintain and manage and check and control the agricultural land for the other purposes.

Similarly, at the district level "District Landuse Board" in Sultanpur has been functioned under the Chairmanship of the District Magistrate, Sultanpur. The reclamation of wastelands and soil conservation programmes are being implemented by the Bhoomi Sanrakshan Adhikari (Gomati) under the Department of Agriculture, Government of Uttar Pradesh. World Bank supported scheme is also being implemented by the Uttar Pradesh Land Development Corporation (UPLDC) in Sultanpur and Department of Social Forestry and Department of Horticulture in the District Sultanpur has been engaged in the reclamation of wastelands for social forestry and horticultural purposes. The Fisheries Development Agency (FDA) and Fishermen Co-operative Societies corporation in Sultanpur has been engaged in the proper utilization of ponds and waterlogged land for fisheries programmes, providing scientific - technical back up and financial support system to the fishermen in the District Sultanpur.

Policies for Agro-Afforestation

The sustainable forest management and optimum conservation of natural resources and the orientation of technological and institutional changes in a manner to attainment and continued satisfaction of human needs for the present and future generations. The sustainable development of genetic resources viz. agriculture, horticulture, social-forestry and fisheries. The optimum utilization of the natural resources must be environmentally non-degrading, technologically - appropriate, socially suitable and economically viable.

The World Commission on Environment and Development 1997 defined the sustainable development as "Development that meets the needs of the present without comprising the ability of future generations to meet their own needs."

The sustainable development recognizes the utilization of natural resources which will change natural eco-systems. The sustainable agro-afforestation management is the Agriculture-Social forestry, Horticulture-fisheries component of the sustainable development, which aims at ensuring the values derived from the natural land resources to meet presently needs while at the same time ensuring their continued ability and contribution to long-term development needs of the common people.

The plants - animal - human life are closely interlocked with each other and disturbance in any one provides an imbalance in other elements. Our Constitution lays down provision for environment conservation. The part IV of the Constitution Policy which lays down the duties for the state to protect and improve the environment and safeguard the forests and wildlife of the country. Apart from this, the Constitution under Article 51 (g) states that, "it shall be the duty of every citizen of India" to protect and improve the natural environment including forests, lake, rivers, and wildlife and to have compassion for living creatures."

The ecological and forest management are normally determined on the basis of constitutional provisions, various legislations, current forest policy viz. 'National Forest Policy 1988' and National Conservation Strategy and Policy Statement on Environment and Development 1992, and Stockholm Conference 1974 on environment and Rio Summit 1991 on environment and development and latest environment conference at Kopenhagen 2009, and other international meetings, conventions and workshops help influenced agro-afforestation in management programmes immensely.

The first National Forest Policy was passed in the year 1894 while Second Forest Policy was announced in 1952 and Third Forest Policy i.e., New Forest Policy was announced in 1988. National Forest Policy 1988 :– New National Forest Policy was promulgated on 7th December 1988. Forest suffered serious depletion in India, there is a need to review the situation and to evolve a new strategy of forest conservation. Which includes preservation, maintenance, sustainable utilization, restoration and enhancement of natural environment. The objectives of the National Forest Policy are as follows :

(a) Maintenance of environment stability through preservation that has been adversely disturbed by serious depletion of the forests of the country.

(b) Conserving the natural heritage of the country by conserving the remaining natural forests with the vast variety of flora and fauna, which represent the remarkable biological diversity and genetic resources of the country :

- To check soil erosion and denudation in the catchment areas of rivers, lakes, reservoirs in the interest of soil and water conservation, for mitigating floods, droughts and for the retardation of siltation of reservoirs.
- To check the extension of sand dunes in the desert areas of Rajasthan and along the coastal tracts.
- Increasing sustainability of the forest, tree cover in the country through massive afforestation social forestry programmes.
- To meet the requirements of fuelwood, fodder, minor forest produce and small timber of the rural and tribal population.
- To increase the productivity of forests to meet the essential nation needs.
- To encourage efficient utilization of forest produce and maximizing substitution of wood.
- To develop massive people's movement with the involvement of women for achieving the objectives and to minimize pressures on existing forests.

The principal objective of the National Forest Policy is to ensure environmental stability and the maintenance of ecological balance including atmospheric equilibrium which are vital for sustenance of all life forms, human, animal and plants. Strategies of the National Forest Policy to achieve its objectives are as follows :

* The national goal is to have one third of the land area and the forest or tree cover. In hills and mountains areas two third of the area should be brought under forest as tree cover.
* Massive afforestation and tree plantation programme. A massive time bound programme of afforestation and tree planting with particular emphasis on fuel-wood and fodder development on all denued and degraded forest areas should be the national imperatives.
* Scientific management of State forests. Scientific and technical inputs should be applied to enhance the existing productivity of the forests.
* Linking rights with the carrying capacity of the forests, including grazing. The capacity of the forests should be optimized, through protection and development of forests.
* The diversion of forest land for non-forest use should be discouraged.
* Involvement of tribals in the development, protection and regeneration of forests.
* To discourage shifting cultivation.
* To control forests loss from encroachments, grazing and fires.
* To propogate and promote forest education research, data base management, extention and financial support for afforestation.
* The National Conservation Strategy and Policy Statement on Environment and Development, 1992.

The National Conservation Strategy and Policy Statement on Environment and Development, pertains the core issues of forest policy among other aspects having relevance to environment and afforestation. "The survival and well-being of a nation depend on sustainable development. Sustainable development is a process of socio-economic betterment that satisfies the needs and values of all interest groups without foreclosing future options. We must ensure that the demand on the environment from which we derive our sustenance does not exceed its carrying capacity for the present as well as future generations." (NCSPSED, 1992).

Ministry of Environment and Forest, Government of India, released a policy statement in 1992 outlining National Conservation Strategy on Environment and Development in which the Sustainable Development" the main objective. The basic objectives of the Policy was, "to ensure sustainable and equitable use of resources for meeting the needs of the present and future generation without causing damage to the environment." The various components of sustainable development and for the management of natural resources has been depicted in the Fig. 5.2.

The new policy may help to weave environmental fabric to our developmental process and national life and our commitment for reorienting policies and action in uniform with the environmental perspective.

The environmental problems, action taken in the environmental, field, constraints and agenda for action, priorities and strategies for action and development policies from environmental perspective, etc. has been the main sections of the National Conservation Strategy and the Policy Statement on Environment and Development.

The relevant aspects to *forest resources management* has been basically the agenda for the action, conservation of natural resources like land, water, bio-diversity and bio-mass and development policies for the forestry.

An integrated action plan on the part of the society, government institutions and individuals are the basic agenda for the action.

The conservation of natural resources includes land and water resources which includes classification, enactment of law, micro level planning extension and propogation compaign for restoration and reclamation of degraded land,

Fig. 5.2 : National Conservation Strategy and Policy Statement on Environment and Development (NCSPSED, 1992)

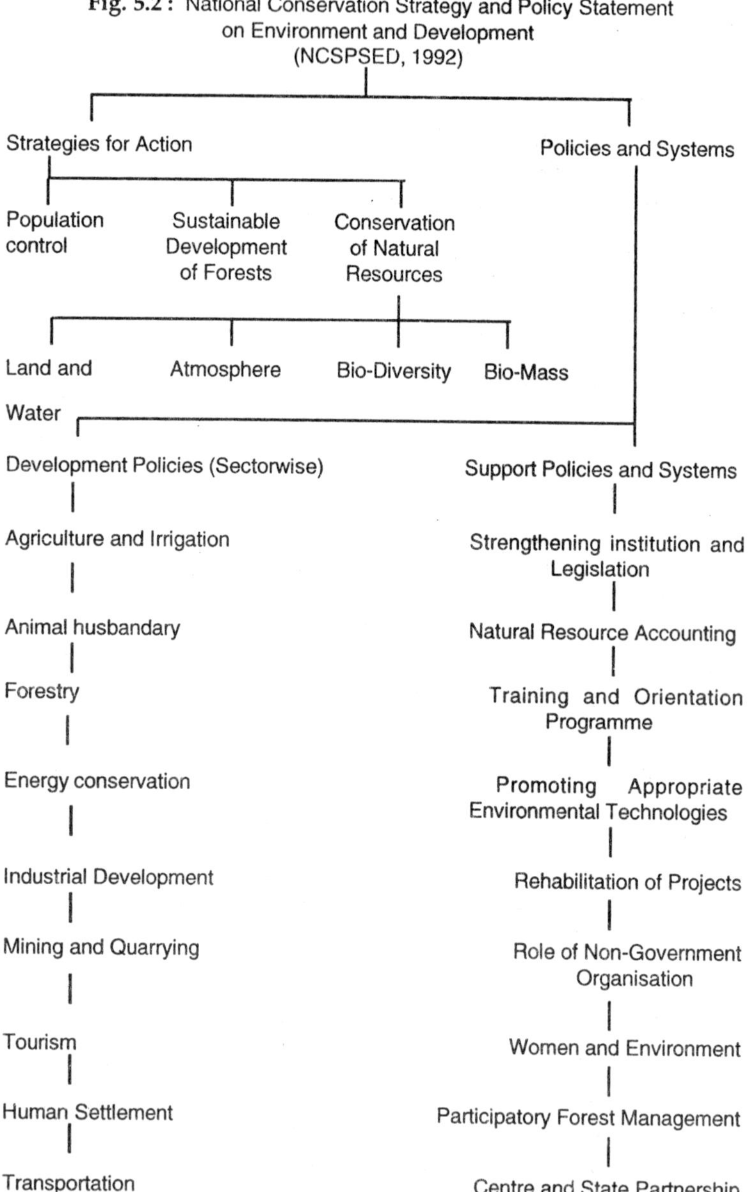

development of suitable agro-silvicultural techniques and conservation of the degraded lands for ensuring economic benefit for sustainable ecological development.

The biological diversity of India has been eroded due to various reasons which needs to preserved. The intensification of surveys of biological resources, conservation of bio-diversity, rehabilitation of rural poor, protection of sustainable plants, animals and genetic resources, developing methodologies through latest techniques of tissue culture and bio-technology has been the important action for conservation of biological diversity.

The explosive growth of population requires fuelwood, timber, fodder, fibre, fruits, fisheries and foodgrains, etc. The sustainable resource management and utilization of the biomass to meet the increasing requirements of the rural poor.

Conservation of common land and degraded forest resources, to reclaim and develop the wastelands, raising of fuelwood, fodder, fibre, fruits, foodgrains, fisheries and vegetables and not to promote the diversion of prime agricultural land and displacement of small and marginal farmers extensive research and development in agro-afforestation, development of scientific-technologies to enhance the efficiency of use of different bio-mass resources and to enable the rural artisans to sustain bio-mass based handicrafts.

Forestry Development Policies :— The main factors for ensuring conservation and sustainable development are use of environment friendly products and processes, low waste generating techniques and proper economic policies and fiscal incentives and disincentives. Raising of the forest cover and conservation of existing forest which are essential life support system and an important source of fuelwood, fodder, fruits, foodgrains, fibre, fisheries, etc. a concerted efforts must be initiated. To attain the target of having atleast one-third land area under forest and intensified measures must be adopted to commensurate mobilization of available natural resources to meet the growing demand of increasing human population.

Continued deforestation and land degradation and diversion of forest land for non-forest use and strengthening of the *Environment Protection Act 1986* and *Forest Protection Force* control of grazing, restriction removal of fuelwood as head loads and supply of alternate fuels has been an on-going programmes to check and control the indiscriminate deforestation. Intensification of Forest Management through *"Forest Conservation, Development and Regeneration"* has been the top priority of the government for which Rs. 111.50 crores in 2008-09 has been allocated by the Government of India.

A writ petition has been filed in the Hon'ble Supreme Court of India to check the indicriminate deforestation and diversion of forest-for non-forest use. In this regard Hon'ble Supreme Court was concerned and issued an order for appropriate action and to develop fund for the diversification and deforestation of the forest land for the non-forest used. The developed Compensatory Afforestation Fund will be utilized for re-afforestation of the alternate land. Before diversification of forest land usar agency will ensure availability of the land and compensate the fund resouce for the afforestation. The development of fund for re-afforestation on alternate land has been named as "*COMPA*" i.e., "Compensatory Fund for Afforestation Programme."

The Compensatory fund has been generated in the Southern State's like Karnataka, Tamil Nadu, Kerala and Andhra Pradesh while Northern States could not do the needful in comparasion to the diversification of forest land for non-forest use and deforestation and land degradation of the forest cover.

The Government of India also launched a programme, "Integrated Forest Protection Scheme (IFPS) later on this programme has been changed to "Intensification of Forest Management."

The National Afforestation and Eco-Development Programme has been initiated the Government of India through establishing "National Afforestation and Eco-Development Board" in 1992 with the principal objective of promoting afforestation tree planting, ecological restoration land eco-development in the country. Special attention is being given to the regeneration of degraded forest area and lands adjoining forest areas, national parks, sancturies, and other protected areas as well as the ecological fragile areas. The main scheme under this programme are *National Afforestation Scheme, Greening India* and *National Action Programme to Combat Desertification.* The increase in the forest cover to 33 per cent by 2012 is the thrust area for the Ministry of Environment and Forest which is very difficult task because without proper co-operation and co-ordination of the *State—District—Tehsil—Block—Village level* administrative authorities and sustained involvement of the *grassroot level workers* the earmarked target cannot be achieved. The implementation of the United Nation's Convention to Combat Deforestation and Social Forestry are also being covered under the ongoing schemes of the Intensification Forest Management.

Intensive Afforestation Management schemes, that should treats afforestation in a holistic manner and seeks to involve the communities and society in general in the preservation and conservation of forests has been deprived of funds. The afforestation scheme at village level "*Panchayat Van Yojana*" to be worked out with the Panchayats to ensure utilization of funds successful implementation of the afforestation programme.

Planning for Reclamation of Wastelands

Planning for the reclamation of wastelands is a process of observation, appraisal, analysis with regard to problems, constraints and compatible cause of action for reclamation of wastelands. The reclamation of wastelands for sustainable development needs a long-term planning for systematic, logical, scientific, technological and analytical action plan.

More than half of the population depends for it's subsistance for fuelwood, fodder, fibre, foodgrains, fruits and fisheries on the common land. The degradation of the common land has made not only their poverty much more acute but the quality of life of the rural poor has been going down. The reclamation of wastelands should be taken up as an important task for eradicating poverty, reducing unemployment and raising awareness among rural masses of the remote rural villages and to overcome the ecological, environmental and socio-economic crisis.

In continuation to the above, the following major points are suggested for successful planning of wastelands reclamation are as follows :

1. ***Identification of Wastelands*** :— Identification, definition of wastelands should be earmarked at grassroot level i.e., at village level, taking village Khasara Map as base map of the identification of wastelands.
2. ***Classification of Wastelands*** :— The classification of wastelands in terms of various factors, at village level, responsible for the growth of and formation of wastelands should be initiated at grassroot level in the intensified system.
3. ***Survey and Mapping*** :— Existing in adequacies in available wastelands information by various agencies, need to be verified through grassroot level field surveys.

   Mapping of various wastelands categories may be finalized with special attention to its suitabilities classification according to the factors responsible for the formation and growth of wastelands at village level based on the revenue village Khasara Map. Intensified and specified mapping and collection of wastelands formation should be carried out through Khasara Map.

   Land - Sat - Imagery and Survey of India –Toposheets, Maps from the Survey of India, Geological Survey of India should be assessed and super-imposed for proper understanding the problems of wastelands for integrated planning as per the needs of the local village people.

4. ***Capability Classification of Wastelands*** :— The capability classification of wastelands at field level/ plot level taking village Khasara Map as main unit of the study. The capability classification of wastelands should be worked out as per the soil fertility status and need of the local villages, the grass-root level user beneficiaries. The capability classification of wastelands should be worked out at field level taking Khasara Map as a base map. The viability of reclamation and classification of wastelands should be demonstrated to the actual needy beneficiaries/farmers.
5. ***Soil Testing*** :— Soil testing of the wastelands should be carried out to know the fertility status of the soil, to develop appropriate action plan for agro-afforestation.
6. ***Levelling and Bunding*** :— Levelling and bunding of the wastelands should be carried out with the involvement of the beneficiaries. Proper level of wastelands is important for appropriate water irrigation. Bunding of wastelands should be done for unwanted inlet of water and soil erosion.
7. ***Cleaning of the Wastelands*** :— Removal of the unwanted species and plants it should be implemented to bring the land for plantation and afforestation programme.
8. ***Leaching and Flushing*** :— Leaching of the land must be carried out for the percolation of the water and to break the Kankar Pan and the calcareousness of the soil. Proper flushing of the land to be carried out to flush the top saline or usar soil.
9. ***Tilling of the Wastelands*** :— Deep ploughing of the wastelands should be carried for proper mixing of the soil and mixing of the organic and inorganic

amendments and deep tilling of the wastelands will be helpful in the remaintenance of fertility status of the soil.

10. *Drainage System* :— Construction of the appropriate drainage system should be carried out for the flow of excess water and flushing of the water. Inside the field proper drainage system should be constructed for appropriate irrigation and proper drainage out of the excess water from the field.
11. *Irrigation System* :— Proper irrigation system and irrigation scheduling are needed for the reclamation misuse of the irrigation water.
    Mismanagement of canal irrigation should be checked which leads towards the waterlogging and deteriorates the fertility status of the soil. Tube-well irrigation will be appropriate source of irrigation.
12. *Green Mannuring* :— Sanai/Dhaincha growing in the land should be carried out for green mannuring of the land to maintain the fertility status of the soil and to develop appropriate condition for the growth of the bio-mass on the land.
13. *Application of organic and inorganic amendments* :— Proper application of organic and in-organic amendments should be managed. Compost fertilizer and green mannuring should be ensured including the proper doses of the NPK fertilizer as the requirements of the soil to maintain the fertility status of the soil.
14. *Cultivation of the land* :— Appropriate cultivation of the land should be carried out as per the requirement of cropping system and the crops or agro-afforestation programmes planned for the cultivation or plantation on the reclaimed wastelands.
15. *Greening of Wastelands* :— Greening of the reclaimed wastelands should be worked out to regenerate the bio-mass and to improve the ecological imbalances of the area. Scientific and technical back up support

system should be made available to the beneficiaries for greening of the wastelands.

16. ***Allotment of Wastelands*** :— The common degraded lands or the wastelands should be allotted to the needy and interested people on *patta* basis and such land can also be allotted on *tree patta* basis in which the land rights will remain with the Village Panchayat but the tree plantation benefits and its usufructs will be accrued by the *tree patta* allotted beneficiaries.
17. ***Co-operatives of Wastelands*** :— Wastelands reclamation co-operatives of land beneficiaries should be formed to avail various scientific and technical back up support system for the reclamation of wastelands, including soil testing and adoption of the various wasteland reclamation procedures.
18. ***Peoples Movement*** :— Reclamation of wastelands should be initiated as peoplement. The restoration and reclamation of wastelands or degraded land should be launched *by the people, for the people* and *with the people* because the deprived rural poors are the actual beneficiaries and the rural poors are the actual sufferers from the wastelands and degraded lands. The reclamation of wastelands should be planned and actually implemented by the rural poor itself.
19. ***Extension Programmes*** :— Appropriate propagation and extension programmes for the reclamation of wastelands for conservation of available natural land resources, restoration of degraded lands and wastelands reclamation adopting the C-2 scientific - technology i.e., the technology which is available within the villages itself should be applied for regeneration of the bio-mass.
20. ***Policies for Wastelands Development*** :— Various policies should be formulated for restoration and reclamation of wastelands and its accessibility to rural poor and for leasing the wastelands for the needy and interested people on *"Patta"* and *"Tree-Patta"*

basis. The *Wastelands Development Act* should be formulated in the pattern of *National Forest Policy* and *Environment Protection Act 1986.*

21. ***Agro-Afforestation Programmes*** :— Agro-afforestation programme should be implemented as per the suitability and capability of the soil or as per the fertility status of the soil.

There are six types of wastelands viz. usar, banjar, old fallow, fallow, waterlogged and other types of wastelands found in Amethi Block of the District Sultanpur. In view of the five main categories of wastelands predominant in five villages of Amethi Block viz. 1. *Parsanwa,* 2. *Benipur,* 3. *Loniapur,* 4. *Mahmodpur,* 5. *Bhaganpur* has been selected for the reclamation of the particular type of wastelands distributed in the selected respective village. The agro-afforestation programme planned for various types of wastelands as per the extent of wastelands has been depicted in the Fig. 5.3.

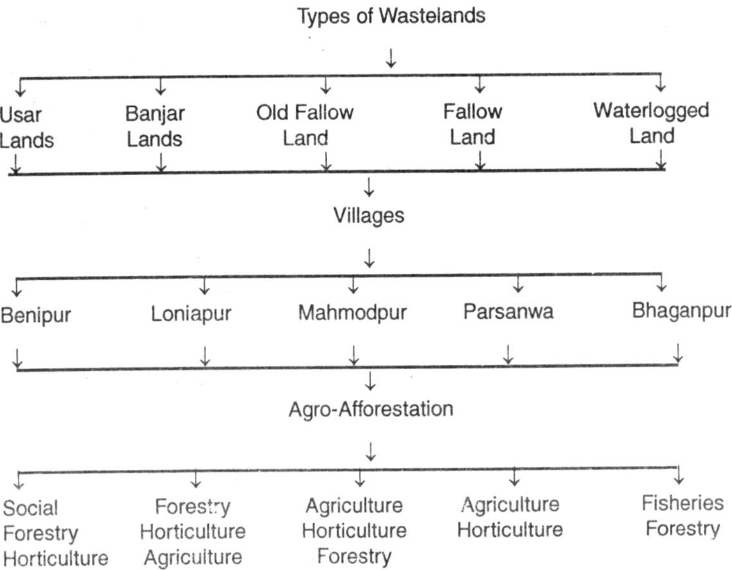

Fig. 5.3 : Wastelands Development

Thus in the *usar land* in village - *Parsanwa* social forestry - Horticulture, *Banjar Land* in village *Benipur* - Forestry - Horticulture - Agriculture, *Old fallow land* in village - *Loniapur* - Agriculture Horticulture - Forestry, *fallow land* - in village, *Mahmodpur* - Agriculture - Horticulture and in the *Waterlogged land* in village - *Bhaganpur* - Fisheries and forestry programmes are planned to meet the increasing demand of growing population for fuelwood, fodder, fibre, fruits, fisheries and foodgrains (F^6) in the selected five villages of Amethi Block, District Sultanpur.

Planning for Agro-Afforestation Management

The management of natural and human resource requires a proper planning. Agriculture - Forestry jointly called as Agro-Forestry being an important activity since time immemorial necessiated a management plan for generation of sustained fuelwood, fodder, fibre, fruits, fisheries, and foodgrains, production. The management plan in Agro-Afforestation parlance is termed as working plan. Agro-afforestation working management plan should be worked out so as to best to meet the interests and wishes of the owner of the reclaimed wastelands and indicate the means by which the agro-afforestation management purpose may be accomplished. The agro-afforestation management plan is a regulation prescribing the application of certain cultural rules and execution of certain agro-forestry programmes in order to produce a given result to obtain fuelwood, fodder, fibre, fruits, fisheries and foodgrains (F^6) to meet the increasing demand of growing population and to conserve the available natural and human resources and to check and control the environmental and land degradation and to restore the ecological crisis and improve the socio-economic conditions of the area.

The planning for agro-afforestation management for various types of wastelands viz. usar, banjar, old fallow, and waterlogged land for various *agri-horti-forestry* programmes in the selected five villages viz. *Benipur, Loniapur, Mahmodpur, Parsanwa* and *Bhaganpur* has been analysed respectively for the Amethi Block of District Sultanpur.

Planning for Social Forestry Horticulture on Usar land

The village Benipur of Amethi Block has been taken for the reclamation of usar land. The village Benipur is having 2.3 per cent usar land to the total area of the village which is proportionately high in comparison to the other villages of the Amethi Block.

An effort has been made to grow trees in highly sodic soils which had been largely unsuccessful in the various villages of Amethi from last two decades. Some scientists presented results of field experiments, the plantation of species such as Eucalyptus, Propopsis and Acacia Nilotica could be grown in highly alkali soils, provided of the soil in 90 × 90 meter pit was improved through application of gypsum and farmyard mannure.

Recent studies have shown that if tree seedlings are planted in auger holes filled with a mixture of original soil, 3-4 kg. gypsum and 7-8 kg. farmyard mannure, excellent growth of plants have been achieved.

In the present study, a favourable environment for root growth has been created in a limited area to a depth of 180 cm. in village Benipur of Amethi Block of the District Sultanpur. The basic aim of the present study has been to examine the feasibility of using afforestation techniques in usar land. The following planning for reclamation of usar land for afforestation with high pH value of the soil has been implemented :

1. Soil testing to know the pH value of the soil and to innovate the calcareousness of the soil and water percolability status.

2. Arrangement of appropriate irrigation system with good quality water preferable tube- well irrigation.
3. Breaking the hard Kankar Pan and removal of the Kankar pan from the digged pit.
4. Digging pits at 1 × 1 × 1 meter or 60 × 60 × 60 cm.
5. Taking out soil of the pit up to 0.5 meter dept, and replacing it with appropriate soil along with farm yard mannure and pyrite/gypsum proportionately as per the requirement of the soil.
6. Leaching and flushing of the salt affected soil.
7. Levelling and Bunding of the land.
8. Developing proper drainage system including water inlet and outlet.
9. Application of farmyard mannure, pyrite/gypsum, NPK fertilizer and organic and inorganic amendments to reduce the salinity status of the soil.
10. Plotting the land into small plots.
11. Developing trench fencing, live hudge and bio-fencing.
12. Establishing the nursery in the same area, for sustenance of the plants and tolerance of the plants with such usar land.
13. Plantation of *Prosopis cineraria, Prosopis Juliflora, Azadirachta Indica, Leucaena Leucocephala, Tamarix Indica, Albizia Procera, Pongamia Pinnata,* Amla, Ber, etc. in the reclaimed usar land.
14. Weeding and maintenace of the plants.
15. Top dressing of fertilizer.
16. Maintenance and management of the plants and replacements of the plants in case of low survival of plants.
17. Cutting the excess branches and leaves for appropriate growth of plants and to obtain fuelwood and fodder from the planted trees.
18. Appropriate distribution of the benefits accrued from the afforestation programme.

Planning for Forestry-Horticulture-Agriculture

The planning for forestry followed by horticulture and agriculture on the reclaimed Banjar land which has been left out of cultivation from more than five years has been implemented in the village - *Loniapur* of the Amethi Block of the District Sultanpur. The distribution of the banjar land in Loniapur village has been found proportionately high in comparision to the other villages of the Amethi Block.

The Forestry — Horticulture — Agriculture plantation on banjar land involves putting the degraded land into multiple use to meet the increasing demand of growing cattle and human population. The basic purposes of this study is to have trees and crops inter- and/or under planted to form an integrated system of biological production within the certain area. The planning for forestry - horticulture - agriculture in the banjar land has been implemented in the following system:

1. Levelling and bunding of the banjar land.
2. Diving the selected banjar field into different sub-plots.
3. Deep ploughing, leaching and flushing of the banjar land.
4. Preparation of drainage system for inlet and outlet of the excess water.
5. Construction of irrigation system through tube-well.
6. Soil testing.
7. Application of organic and inorganic amendments including farm yard mannure.
8. Cultivation of Sanai/Dhaincha for green mannuring.
9. Developing the nursery for the social forestry and horticultural plants in the same fields, for tolerance of the plants.
10. Digging of pits 1 × 1 × 1 meter or 60 × 60 × 60 cms.
11. Application of soil along with organic and in-organic amendments.

12. Inter planting the trees 4 × 1 meter spacing with cultivated fodder crop and other agricultural cropping.
13. Plantation of Prosopis Juliflora, Azadirachta Indica, Leucaena Leu cocephala, Amla, Ber, Guvava horticultural plants and inter cropping of Banjar and cropping of Sanai / Dhaincha and Patsan for fibre, etc.
14. The inter cropping of subaboor, a leguminous tree, with Leucena Rizka, a cultivated leguminious fodder crop which increases the overall nutrient content in the soil in terms of nitrogen level of the soil markedly.
15. Seeds from harvested crops being salt tolerant should be used subsequently in the reclaimed land.
16. Using the reclaimed banjar land for growing Bajara and other fodder crops.
17. Taking up the banjar land reclamation and cultivation for forestry-horticultural plants and agricultural crops depending upon the fertility status of the soil.
18. Top dressing of fertilizer including farm yard mannure.
19. Proper arrangement of irrigation as per the need of plants and crops.
20. Making the provisions of protective irrigation of trees and crops.
21. Maintenance and management of planted trees and cropping of the crops.
22. Cutting of excessing branches and leaves and crop harvesting.
23. Distribution of usufructs among the involved beneficiaries.

Planning for Horticulture - Agriculture - Forestry

The reclamation of *old fallow land* which has been left out of cultivation from 2-5 years has been implemented in the village - *Mahmodpur* of Amethi Block, for the *horticultural* plantation followed by the agricultural cropping and afforestation as per the fertility status of the soil and according to the need of the local village beneficiaries.

The horticultural—agricultural—afforestation programme on reclaimed old fallow land implies integration of trees and crops simultaneously or squentially. In a broad sense, horticulture - agriculture - forestry programmes with adequate attention to ecological and environmental aspects and dynamics of energy flow includes multi-cropping and optimum utilization of land resources. The planning for horticulture - agricultural afforestation activities being implemented in village Mahmodpur of Amethi Block are as follows :

1. Land levelling and bunding.
2. Plotting of land into sub-plants.
3. Deep ploughing and mixing of organic and inorganic amendments and farmyard mannure.
4. Developing irrigation channels.
5. Construction of drainage system for inlet and outlet of the water.
6. Installation of deep forebell/tube-well for appropriate irrigation.
7. Land preparation.
8. Green mannuring through sanai/dhainch cultivation.
9. Application of organic and inorganic amendments.
10. Digging of the pits and mixing of good quality soil along with organic and inorganic amendments.
11. Developing nursery for horticultural and forestry plants as per the needs of the local people.
12. Plantation of *Leucaena Leucocephala* on the border of the reclaimed old fallow land, along with *Prosopi Juliflora* and plantation of Amla, Guvava, Ber, Mango, Lemon, etc. plants and cultivation of barley, wheat, green fodder, sanwa and pulses.

13. Top dressing of fertilizer.
14. Maintenance and management of planted trees and crops.
15. Appropriate irrigation system as per requirements of the plants and crops.
16. Cutting of excessive grown branches and leaves and cropping and harvesting of the crops.
17. Distribution of usufructs obtained from the reclaimed old fallow land as per the participation of the local village beneficiaries.

Planning for Agri-Horti-Forestry Management

The planning for agriculture-horticulture and forestry programmes has been practically implemented in village — *Parsanwa* of Amethi Block through reclaiming follow land. The reclaimation of fallow land and planning for Agri-horti-afforestation management is as follows :—

1. Levelling, bunding of the fallow land.
2. Soil testing.
3. Sub-plotting of the fallow land.
4. Deep ploughing.
5. Mixing of farmyard mannure and organic and inorganic amendments.
6. Drainage construction for inlet and outlet of the water.
7. Provision of good quality irrigation water system.
8. Developing nurseries for horticultural and forestry plants.
9. Digging the pits and mixing of soil and organic and inorganic amendments.
10. Cultivation of foodgrain crops in the Kharif and Rabi cropping season followed by plantation of *Subabool* and *Prosopis juliflora* along the boundaries and plantation of Amla, Guvava, Papaya and vegetable cropping.

11. Top dressing of organic and inorganic amendments.
12. Provision of appropriate irrigation system including sprinkles irrigation system as per the requirements of plants and cultivated crops.
13. Maintenance and management of crops and plants.
14. Cutting of excess branches of plants and leaves and harvesting of crops.
15. Distribution of usufructs obtained from the reclaimed fallow land and afforested plants and cultivated crops among the involved beneficiaries.

Planning for Fisheries - Horti - Forestry Management

The reclamation of waterlogged land for fisheries programme followed by horticultural and forestry plantations on the funds has been implemented in village Bhaganpur of the Amethi Block because proportionately waterlogged land has been recorded comparatively high than the other villages of the Amethi Block. The planning for fisheries cultivation through developing pond and alongwith the fund horticultural and forestry plantations has been implemented :—

1. Testing of the soil to check the fertility status of the soil and to test the quality of water.
2. Provision of deep borewell and availability of tube-well for the availability of good quality sweet water for fisheries.
3. Construction of the pond for fisheries.
4. Preparation of bond/banks of the pond for horticultural/forestry plantation.
5. Digging of pits and mixing with good quality soil along with organic and inorganic amendments.
6. Preparation of inlet and outlet of excess water and appropriate construction of drainage system.

7. Preparation of pond for fish culture.
8. Development of nursery for forestry and horticultural plants for plantation on the funds/banks of the pond.
9. Development of hatchury/fish seed of high quality for successful fish culture.
10. Appropriate, scientific water of the pond.
11. Provision of the fish seed.
12. Plantation of Subabool, *Azadirachta Indica, Subabool, Tamarix Indica* and *Prospopis Juliflora* plantation along the Fund's outer side of the pond and plantation of Amla, Guvava, Ber, Mango hybrid/grafted plants and animal husbandry programmes.
13. Cropping of fish and cutting of the excess branches and leaves of the grown up plants.
14. Top dressing of farmyard mannure for the planted trees and proper watering of the pond.
15. Appropriate availability of good quality fish feed and fish seed.
16. Maintenance and management of fish culture and planted horticultural and forestry plants.
17. Appropriate distribution of benefits accrued among the involved beneficiaries as per their involvement.

The planning for the reclamation of various types of wastelands viz. usar land, banjar land, old fallow land, fallow land and waterlogged land, has been reclaimed in the various selected villages viz. Benipur, Loniapur, Mahmodpur, Parsanwa and Bhaganpur villages of Amethi Block respectively. As per need of the local people and beneficiaries—fuelwood, fodder, fibre, fruits, plantation has been organised and fisheries programme in the developed pond in waterlogged land and production of foodgrains has been planned with the involvement and participation of local village beneficiaries with the view to meet the increasing demand of growing cattle and human population on the one hand and restoration of degraded wastelands and to regenerated the degraded ecology and environment of the village and to improve socio-economic crisis of the selected villages of Amethi Block of District Sultanpur.

Conclusion

The land degradation and wastelands is caused both by poverty and mismanagement. The degradation cycle of common natural land resources proceeds from hacking, excessive grazing, over cropping, mismanagement, application of high doses of fertilizers, unscientific irrigational practices, cultivation, all leading to land degradation. The excessive revenue generated through unplanned unscientific cutting of forest, the greater destruction of the forest area, must be stopped and causes misery to the millions of the deprived rural poor.

The problem of wastelands is not a new one, it has a long history starting from Apeman to historical invadors, the wastelands has been formed. Emperor Ashoka used the term wastelands as neglected land, while Mughal emperor and Akbar The Great fixed the value of land in *Annas* for revenue collection from Taluqdars. Britishers continued the same practice and no land revenue was charged for the wastelands.

It is observed that wastelands development is the triangular interaction process between man–nature and technology.

After post independence, Article 48A of the Constitution of India enunciates, "The State shall endeavour to protect and improve the environment to safeguard the forest and wildlife of the country."

National Bureau of Soil Survey and Land Use Planning and All India Soil and Land Use Survey has been engaged in the collection and analysis of the data on wastelands.

National Commission on Agriculture also surveys the land degradation information. On January 5, 1985 National Wastelands Development Board was established for the reclamation of wastelands. National Level Wastelands Development Mission was launched on 5th October 1989 having 6 Mini-Missions viz. Policy Planning, Peoples Participation, Technology Extension, Restoration of the degraded forests, Greening of the common land, and Farm forestry, wasteland development has been also included in the 20-point economic programme. Department of Wastelands Development was established in the Government. of India.

In the State of Uttar Pradesh, high level power committee was headed by the Agriculture Production Commissioner of Uttar Pradesh. Later on Department of Wastelands Development was established in the Government. of Uttar Pradesh. In the pattern of National Soil Conservation and Land Use Board, Government of India, in the Uttar Pradesh 'State Land Use Board' is also functional in the Department of Planning, Government of Uttar Pradesh.

The District Land Use Board is also functional at District level, Bhomi Sanrakshan Adhikari, and Uttar Pradesh Land Development Corporation and Social Forestry Departments are engaged in the restoration of degraded land and reclamation of wastelands.

The Constitution of India lays down provision for environment conservation. The Constitution under article 51 (g) states that "it shall be the duty of every citizen of India to protect and improve the natural environment including forests, lakes, rivers and wildlife to have a compassion for living creatures."

National Forest Policy 1988 and National Conservation Strategy and Policy Statement on Environment 1992 has been formed to protect National Forest Policy was formed in 1988, while National Environment Protection Act 1986 was also formed, to protect the environment. The National Conservation Strategy and Policy statement on Environment and Development comprises with strategies for action and policies and systems for conservation and development of environment.

Forest Resource Management and Forestry Development Policies includes the main factors for ensuring conservation and sustainable development processes, low waste generating techniques and proper economic policy and fiscal incentives and disincentives. Raising of the forest cover and conservation of existing forests which are essential life support system and an important source of fuelwood, fodder fruits, foodgrains, fibre, fisheries, etc., a concerted efforts must be initiated.

Compensatory Fund for Afforestation Programme (COMPA) has been developed for deforestation and diversion of forest land for non-forest use.

Integrated Forest Protection Scheme and Intensification of Forest Management has been also launched. National Afforestation and Eco-Development Board has been established in the Ministry of Environment and Forest, Government of India with the objective of National Afforestation Scheme Greening India and National Action Programme to combat desertification to increase 33 per cent forest cover by 2012, which can be achieved with proper co-ordination and co-operation of the State — District — Tehsil — Block — village level administrative authorities and sustained involvement of the grassroot level workers, the proposed earmarked target may be achieved and *Panchayat Van Yojana* must be strengthened at grassroot level.

Planning for the reclamation of wastelands is a process of observation, appraisal, analysis with regard to problems, constraints and compatible cause, for reclamation of wastelands. The reclamation of wastelands for sustainable development needs a long-term planning for systematic, logical, scientific-technological and analytical action plan including identification of wastelands, classification of wastelands and survey and mapping of wastelands, capability classification of wastelands, soil testing, levelling and bunding, cleaning, leaching and flushing, tilling and deep ploughing, drainage system irrigation system, green mannuring, application of organic and inorganic amendments, cultivation, greening of wastelands, allotment of wastelands, co-operatives of wasteland developing beneficiaries, peoples movement, extension programmes, policies for reclamation of wastelands and agro-afforestation has been implemented in Parsanwa, Benipur, Loniapur, Mahmodpur, and Bhaganpur villages for Social Forestry, Forestry, Horti-Agriculture, Agri-Horti-Forestry, Agri-Horticulture and Fisheries-Forestry managements respectively.

Planning for agro-afforestation management has been formulated taking one unit of wastelands in selected five villages of Amethi Block.

Planning of *Social Forestry-Horticulture* has been formulated and the reclamation of usar land has been implemented in village- Benipur of Amethi Block. The reclamation of usar land and land preparation, developing nursery and plantation of suitable social-forestry and horticultural plants has been planted on the reclaimed usar land with the involvement of local village level beneficiaries to meet the increasing demand of growing population for fuelwood, fodder, fruits, etc.

Forestry- Horticulture- Agriculture management planning and reclamation of banjar land has been done in the village Loniapur of Amethi Block of District Sultanpur. The Forestry-Horticulture-Agricultural plantation and cropping has been carried out on the reclaimed banjar land with the involvement of village level beneficiaries to grow fuelwood, fodder, fibre, fruits and foodgrains to meet the increasing demand of growing cattle and human population.

Planning for *Horticulture-Agriculture-Forestry* management has been implemented in the reclaimed old fallow land in village Mahmodpur of Amethi Block with adequate attention to ecological, and environmental aspects and dynamics of energy flow includes multi cropping and optimum utilization available natural land resources.

The appropriate planning for *Agriculture- Horticulture - Forestry* managment programme has been implemented on the reclaimed fallow land in village– Parsanwa of Amethi Block, for optimum utilization of available natural and human resources with the view to restore ecological and land degradation and improve socio-economic crisis and to meet the increasing demand of growing cattle and human population.

Planning for the reclamation of waterlogged land has been implemented in village– Bhaganpur of Amethi Block. The waterlogged land has been reclaimed through construction of pond for fisheries cultivation along with horticultural and afforestation programme on the bund and banks of the pond for optimum utilization of waterlogged land to regenerate the bio-mass and improve ecological imbalances of the area.

Thus the planning for reclamation of usar land in Benipur village, Banjar land in Loniapur, old fallow land in Mahmodpur village, fallow land in Parsanwa village has been implemented with the involvement of rural poor beneficiaries. The reclamation of various wastelands for Agro- Horti- Forestry - fisheries has been implemented with the view to obtain - fuelwood, fodder, fibre, fruits, foodgrain, fisheries (F^6) to restore the degradation of land and wastelands development to meet the increasing demand of growing cattle and human population to check and control the ecological environmental degradation and improve ecological imbalances, regenerate the bio-mass and improve socio-economic conditions of the deprived rural multitudes of the Amethi Block of the District Sultanpur.

6

Reclamation of Wastelands

Introduction

Tremendous forest degradation and associated ecological crisis and the associated socio-economic crisis affects the rural poor much more significantly than any other. The major impact of deforestation and land degradation and ecological degradation that has taken place has been largely on the rural poor, because half of our nation depends for its fuelwood and fodder on the common lands and it is the degradation of these common lands which has made not only their poverty much more acute but the quality of life of the poor, infact, has been going down because of these shortages and degradation. We have lost 50 per cent of our forest cover out of 75 million hectares which are considered to be forest area, about 40 million hectares are considered without sufficient tree cover. In terms of grazing lands we have lost anywhere from 26 to 52 per cent of our grazing lands, so again, the impact has been largely on the rural poor. The reduction in the land resources and land resources productivity and land degradation and it is not producing the fuelwood, fodder which people require. The increasing cattle and human population has led to the crisis which is very significant.

Our nation is loosing 1.5 million hectares of forests and 12000 million tonnes of top soil every year due to deforestation and runoff. The nations fuelwood requirement is about 130 million tonnes every year of which we are fetching about 50 million tonnes of firewood from forest. It means the balance of 80 million tonnes has yet to be generated. The purpose shall mount heavily on the already disappearing forest cover.

The problem of wastelands is mostly man-made and causes misery to millions of the rural poor. The reclamation of wastelands must be adopted as a strategy for the extention of net sown area according to it's suitability to increase the overall agricultural production through agricultural cropping or for the afforestation programme predominently for the fuelwood, fodder, fibre, fisheries, fruits and foodgrains for the integrated development of the rural poor. Thus a co-ordinated action plan with the involvement of local rural poor beneficiaries must be formulated for agro-afforestation management on wastelands at village level or grassroot level.

Keeping the above facts into consideration various types of wastelands viz. usar land, banjar land, old fallow land, fallow land and waterlogged land of village, Benipur, Loniapur, Mahmodpur, Parsanwa and Bhaganpur has been selected as per the extent of the particular wastelands, for its reclamation. In the selected patch of wastelands complete reclamation process including development of nursery and plantation of social-forestry and horticultural plants and agricultural cropping for both Rabi and Kharif cropping season has been practically demonstrated to the cultivators with their continued involvement and participation to obtain the fuelwood, fodder, fibre, fruits, fisheries, and foodgrains to meet their increasing demand and restore the ecological imbalances of the area and check the environmental and land degradation and also to improve the socio-economic crisis of the deprived rural poors of the Amethi, District Sultanpur.

Reclamation Capability of Wastelands

Land degradation and deterioration of the fertility status of the soil leads towards formation of wastelands. The capability classification of wastelands may help to plan the reclamation process of the various wastelands types in Amethi. Capability classification of wastelands is an imperative grouping and grading of soils, according to the fertility status of the soil, potentialities and limitations, their capability of producing agricultural crops and horticultural and afforestation of various plants, and its responsiveness for the management of agricultural cropping practices. Reclamation capability classification is a system to make a sound and complex process for conservation plant to find out the suitability of wastelands for specific agricultural, horticultural and afforestation programmes. The method of reclamation capability classification of wastelands is a systematic segregation of different kinds of wastelands which are distinguished from one to another by variation in the kind and degree of the various use imposed by soil characteristics, morphometric, hydrologic, climatic and other environmental factors.

Thus the fundamental purpose of wastelands capability classification is to utilize the available natural wasteland resources according to their reclamation capabilities through rational planning.

The wastelands capability classification in Amethi, District Sultanpur is basically based on the environmental parameters of morphometric (slope, ruggedness number) climatic (rainfall) hydrological (drainage density, quality of water in pH and behaviour of water table), inherent soil characteristics and personal field observation. In view of the above the following reclamation capability classification has been ascribed for the vairous types of wastelands observed in Amethi Block at village level or at field level.

Capability class I — Very Easily Reclaimable.
Capability class II — Easily Reclaimable.

Capability class III — Reclaimable with certain difficulty
Capability class IV — Reclaimable with moderate difficulty.
Capability class V — Reclaimable with difficulty.

The reclamation capability classification of various wastelands viz. usar land, Banjar land, old fallow land, fallow land, waterlogged land and other types of wastelands, at village level in Amethi Block has been depicted in the figure illustrated below —

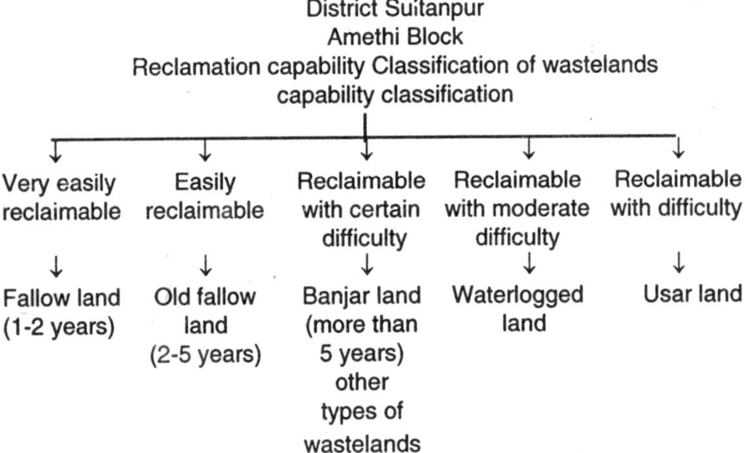

Fig. 6.1 : Capability classification of wastelands

Thus the wasteland's reclamation capability classification is the best illustration of the useful work. It may be remarked that the reclamation capability classification is of immense importance and of the practical utility for the reclamation of wasteland for agro-afforestation management. Although it needs enormous labour and technical knowledge and scientific backup support system together with huge funds, it would help greatly in predicting the suitability and adoptability of wastelands for various social forestry and horticultural plantations and agricultural cropping system. On the basis of reclamation capability classification of wastelands. It has been recorded that fallow land can be very easily reclaimed, old fallow land can be easily reclaimed, Banjar land and other types of wastelands can be reclaimed with certain difficulty, waterlogged land can be reclaimed for fisheries programme with moderate difficulty and usar land can be reclaimed with difficulty due to high pH value of soil and calcareousness of the soil which requires more financial and human labour inputs and scientific and technical back up support system.

Reclamation of Wastelands

The explosive population growth and excessive exploitation of natural resources deforestation and land degradation has brought us face to face for ecological and environmental crisis and also leading towards socio-economic crisis among the deprived rural multitude for fetching fuelwood, fodder, fibre, fisheries, fruits and foodgrains (F^6) to fulfil the increasing demand of growing cattle and human population. Hence, the conservation attempt i.e., protecting the exisiting cultivable land and reclaiming the already depleted wastelands figures predominently among the priority tasks of the planning process. Various reclamation measures have been adopted for different types of wastelands in the selected villages of Amethi Block, District Sultanpur. Some of the wastelands reclamation measures has been observed unsuccessful after some time because the lands reverted to its original condition due to mismanagement and the unscientific way in which the reclamation measures has been adopted. The planning for wastelands reclamation methods, due attention must be paid to input cost factor. The inputs and outputs must be balanced with benefits accruing from the land over the years. Time involved in the reclamation of wastelands is an additional factor to be considered. It has been observed that cheaper amendments are slower in reaction and provide uneconomic returns at the initial stage of reclamation. Certain ameliorative factors, such as surplus farm commodities or industrial wastes may be available in an area but their costs may prove prohibitive or they may be available with difficulty at an other place. Such factors have to be taken into consideration before deciding upon a particular method for reclamation of wastelands for social-forestry, horticultural and agricultural cropping. An appropriate analysis has also to be made for the environmental and anthropogenic factors responsible for the growth of the various types of wastelands at village level in Amethi Block of the District Sultanpur.

The reclamation of various types of wastelands cannot be considered in totality because for various types of wastelands, different reclamation measures are required for agricultural, horticultural and afforestation programmes. Respective measures to be adopted for the reclamation of different types of wastelands has been analysed practically as implemented in the selected villages of Amethi Block. Various wasteland reclamation procedures and time requirement starting from land development, nursery raising, agri-horti-forestry plantation is depicted in the Fig. 6.2.

In this study, the reclamation capability classification of wastelands has been analysed to assess the fertility status of the soil for cropping and afforestation programmes and the input requirements for its reclamation. It has been observed that the waterlogged lands are reclaimable with difficulty while usar lands are reclaimable with moderate difficulty

The banjar lands are reclaimable with certain difficulty. The old fallow lands can be easily reclaimed while fallow lands can be very easily reclaimed which is depicted in Fig. 6.3.

In view of the reclamation capability classification the usar land in village Benipur has been selected for social forestry and afforestation programme. The banjar land in village Loniapur has been selected for the forestry -

Sl. No.	*Item of work*	*Time required*
1.	Mobilization, motivation and education of beneficiaries	1
2.	Identification, demarcation of wastelands	½
3.	Demarcation of wasteland for nursery raising and land preparation	½
4.	Bio-scientific training and soil analysis for banjar land reclamation	½
5.	Preparation of Nursery raising land	½
6.	Reclamation, irrigation, Bio-fertilizer application for land preparation for nursery	½
7.	Filling of polythene bags and seedlings	½
8.	Maintenance and management of nursery plants, adoption of tissue culture techniques	4
9.	Reclamation, cleaning, levelling of banjar patta land	½
10.	Med Bunding for bio-fencing and preparation of drainage system	½
11.	Land Preparation/cultivation	½
12.	Irrigation management/sprinkler system	½
13.	Leaching	½
14.	Flushing	½
15.	Mechanical Processing	½
16.	Green Manauring	½
17.	Application of Gypsum and Pyrite	½
18.	Bio-Fertilizer and Composting of Waste	½
19.	Shifting of nursery plants to the reclaimed land site and demonstration of agricultural equipments/accessories	½
20.	Plantation of Biofencing, fuelwood, wood, fruits plants	2
21.	Multi-inter-cropping of vegetable, fodder and foodgrain crops (Kharif and Rabi)	8
22.	Irrigation Management/sprinkler system	2
23.	Application of Bio-fertilizer and compost fertilizer	1
24.	Application of Insecticides and pesticides	1
25.	Bio-scientific management of plantation and multi-inter-cropping system	2
26.	Scientific demonstration of Harvesting techniques	1
27.	Recycling of crop waste for bio-fertilizer	1
28.	Training and demonstration of Post-Harvest Technology	1
29.	Training for Agro-processing	1
30.	Agri-Horti-Afforestation Management Bio-remediation and Eco-Management and follow-up action	2

Fig. 6.2 : Processes of wastelands Reclamation

horticulture - agriculture activities. The old fallow lands in village Mahmodpur has been taken up for Agriculture - Horticulture and forestry programmes and fallow lands in village Parsanwa has been taken for agricultural and horticultural programmes while waterlogged land in village Bhaganpur has been selected for fisheries and forestry

Wastelands		*Class*		*Reclamation capability Type*
Waterlogged land	—	V	—	Reclamation with difficulty.
Usar land	—	IV	—	Reclaimable with moderate difficulty.
Banjar land	—	III	—	Reclaimable with certain difficulty.
Old fallow land	—	II	—	Easily Reclaimable.
Fallow land	—	I	—	Very Easily Reclaimable.

Fig. 6.3 Reclamation Capability of Wastelands

programmes to produce fuelwood, fodder, fibre, food grain, fruits and fisheries to meet the increasing demand of the growing cattle and human population. The adoption of Agri-Horti-afforestation programmes in the various villages of Amethi Block has been depicted in the Fig. 6.4.

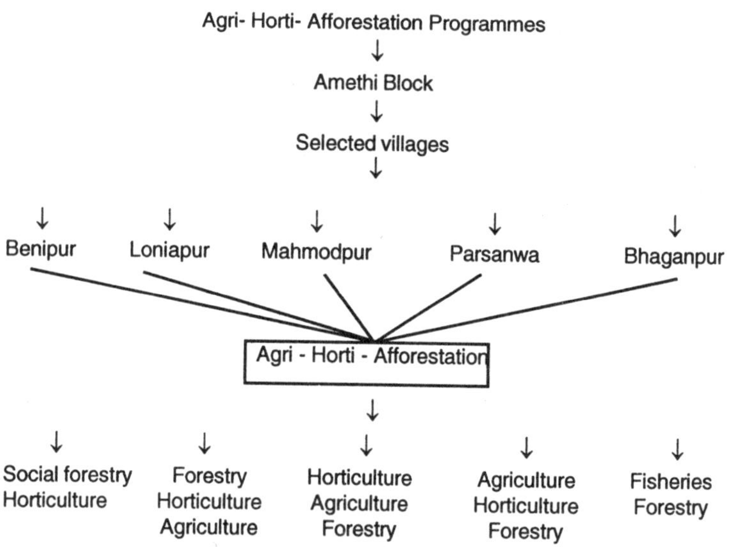

Fig. 6.4 Agri- Horti- Afforestation Programmes

Thus the reclaiming exercise is mostly dependent on the reclamation capability classification of wastelands in the selected five villages of Amethi Block in the District Sultanpur.

Techno-economic viability of the Reclamation of Wastelands

Bio-scientific reclamation techniques for the reclamation of usar land, banjar land, old fallow land, fallow land and waterlogged land owned by the deprived rural multitude beneficiaries belonging to Benipur, Loniapur, Mahmodpur, Parsanwa and Bhaganpur respectively, through Agri-Horti-Afforestation programmes to meet the increasing demand of vegetables, wood, fuelwood, fibre, fruits, fisheries, fodder and foodgrains (VWF^6) of growing cattle and human population, to restore the degraded wasteland natural resources to control the ecological and environmental crisis, and improve the socio-economic crisis and to generate sustained employment and increase their income. No doubt the reclamation of wasteland for agro-afforestation management will be helpful in improving the ecological imbalances of the area and it will be helpful for the integrated development of the deprive village beneficiaries.

The eco-sustainability through bio-scientific reclamation of various types of wastelands for Agri-Horti-Afforestation programme for income and employment generation. The Agri-Horti-Afforestation programme is technically, economically viable and self-sustaining with the environment of local village people. The viability of the reclamation of wastelands for agro-afforestation management is depicted in the Fig. 6.5.

Socially	—	Acceptable
Scientifically	—	Suitable
Environmentally	—	Viable
Ecologically	—	Sustainable
Technologically	—	Feasible
Economically	—	Beneficial
Individually	—	Manageable
Practically	—	Adoptable

Fig. 6.5 : Techno-Economic viability of the Reclamation of wastelands

The technological and economic viability of the reclamation of various types of wastelands in the different villages of Amethi Block has been feasible and suitable to the deprived rural multitude because restoration of degraded land for Agri-Horti-Afforestation programmes to produce fuelwood, fodder, fibre, fruits, foodgrain and fisheries to meet the increasing demand of growing cattle and human population and it will be an asset in improving the ecological imbalances of the area and socio-economic crisis of the rural poors. The reclamation of wastelands for Agri-Horti- Afforestation programmes in the initial years, it will be less profit making excercise but in the subsequent years, the cost of cropping and maintenance of afforested and horticultural plants because the input cost will be lower that the output accrued from the reclaimed wastelands. Technically, the reclamation of the wastelands is viable and feasible and economically benefical to the deprived rural multitudes of the people's of Amethi.

Reclamation of Usar Land for Afforestation

Various reclamation measures for usar land for social-forestry programme in one bigha usar land has been practically demonstrated to the rural poor beneficiaries in village - Benipur of Amethi Block, District Sultanpur.

The village - Khasara Map has been traced and cartographic techniques has been adopted to draw the Gata land and show the necessary boundaries based on the village Khasara Map of Benipur village. The settlement area, Ponds, Garden, Doyam, Goyad, Domat, Matiyar, Doyam Matiyar Soyam and Awwal land based on Anna value system of the land at field level has been earmarked for the village Benipur. The land use system has been depicted in the Map-44. The Goyad land having 14-16 Anna value land which is very fertile and Rabi, Kharif and Jaid cropping season's crops are cultivated and multiple cropping is also adopted in the village while Doyam land having low fertility status of the soil is found in most of the areas of the village Benipur. The usar land in village Benipur is found 2.32 per cent to the total area of the village. The pH value of the soil in village Benipur is found more than 8 %, which indicates that salanity and calcareousness in the soil is found very high which creates hinderance in the agricultural cropping and afforesation is also not successful due to which the usar land has been left out of cultivation. Various scientific and technological packages for the reclamation of usar lands has been adopted. Important usar land reclamation measures has been mechanical, leaching, flushing, application of organic and inorganic amendments and growing of salt tolerant

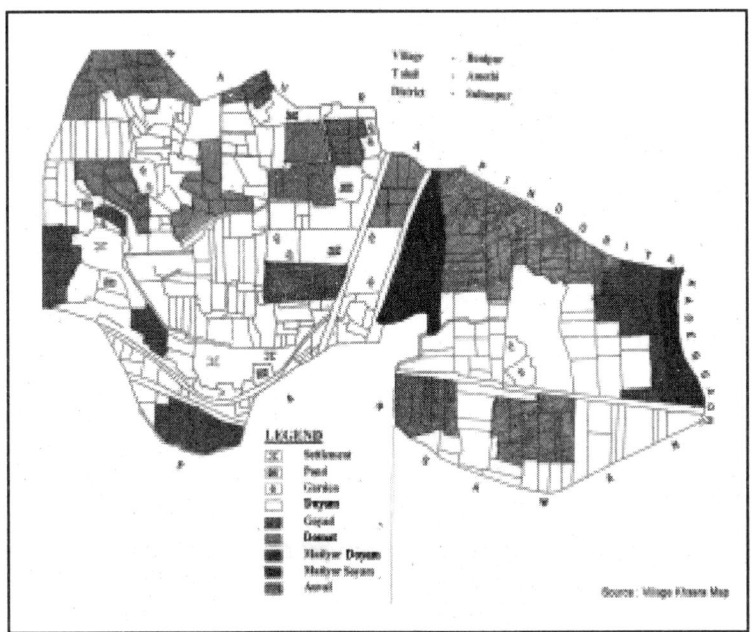

Map-44 : Cropping Quality of Land-Benipur

crops. The adoption of suitable methods, have to be encouraged such as total input cost, availability of good quality water, type of soil, nature of terrain, local agro-climatic conditions and agricultural cropping practices. However, reclamation measures adopting organic and inorganic amendments etc. are considered feasible when the deterioration of the soil has been found and beneficial effects appear to be of short duration.

Reclamation of usar land adopting all the agricultural/horticultural/afforestation practices of scientific — technologies rather than to use the pick and choose approach. Provision of good quality of water for irrigation is an essential prerequisite. The essential components of usar land reclamation which has been adopted are as follows :

- *Levelling and Bunding* :— Proper levelling of the land has been done. *Med bundi* has been constructed, in the field. The land has been divided into convenient size plots with small earthen embankments in accordance with slope. Small suitable drains has been constructed for the removal of rainwater and excess irrigation water. Leaching with rainy water and irrigated water has been carried out to fluch the salt affected soils. Water percolation has been assured through deep digging of pits and to break the Kankar pan augerhole system has been applied.
- *Soils Testing* :— Soil testing has been ensured to know the nature of the soil and requirement of the fertilizer to produce the crop. In the first season 20 quintals of gypsum has been applied alongwith 50 kg. area, 25 kg. Shakti khad and 25 kg.m. Potash and compost khad has been applied. Easily decomposable organic mannure (Dhaincha) has been applied before rain. Gypsum in the powdered form has been mixed with

copper 10 cms. of soil. After application of gypsum water is needed for 10-15 days before afforestation. Pyrite can also be applied as per requirement of the soil.

- *Irrigation* :— Light but frequent irrigations has been managed as per requirement of the land. It is much useful to grow Dhaincha as a green mannure crop when sufficient irrigation water is available.

The land preparation, soil testing and irrigation techniques can be adopted in a suitable modified system to meet the requirements of the soil. But before any reclamation programme is taken into hand, there should be adequate levelling of the land, improvement of the existing drainage system and supply of the ample good quality irrigation water. A scheme for the reclamation of such usar land/cultivated land, big or small, can be an economic proposition if planned on scientific lines. In most of the cases the deterioration caused to the soil by salt is more easily reclaimable and maintenable than caused due to soil erosion. Infact it is due to the land prices have gone up and there is scarcity of land, so that the reclamation schemes must be carried out to meet the increasing requirements of the local village people.

An attempt to grow trees in highly sodic soils has been largely unsuccessful. Some scientists have presented results of field experiements to show that some species such as Eucalyptus, Prosopis Juliflora, and Acacia Nilotica could be grown in highly alkali soils. Recent studies have shown that if tree plantations has been done through augerholes filled with a mixture of original soils, 3-4 kg. gypsum and 7-8 kg. farmyard mannure, excellent growth of plants can be achieved. An attempt has been made in this study to provide a favourable environment for root growth has been created in a limited area to a depth of 180 cm. in village Benipur of Amethi Tehsil/Block respectively. The main objective of this exercise was to examine the feasibility of using afforestation technology in usar land. The following are among the measures required for the reclamation of usar land for afforestation programme along with Amla and Ber, etc. horticultural plantations :

* Testing of the soil has been done to find out the fertility status of the soil and to know the nature of the soil and strata of the Kankar pan and calcareousness of the soil.
* Arrangement of appropriate irrigation facility before taking of afforestation programme in the usar land.
* Breaking of the Kankar pan and removal of the Kankar pan through digging one meter deep pit.
* Digging of pits at 1 × 1 × 1 meter or 60 × 60 × 60 cms. spacing.
* Taking out the soil of the pit upto 0.5 meter depth and replacing it with soil of appropriate pH value of the soil adding to a farmyard mannure and pyrite in appropriate proportions.
* Leaching out, the soil along with rain water, salt soil responsible for the salinity of the soil.
* Application of farmyard mannure, pyrite/gypsum nitrogen and zinc sulphate to reduce the salinity of the soil.
* Plantation of prosopis and other plants, which has salt tolerance capacity, in the reclaimed usar land.
* Sub-plotting of the land and construction of small bunds.
* Provision of live hedge and bio-fencing on the bunds of the reclaimed usar land.
* Provision of adequate irrigation facility through tube-well irrigation to ensure availability of good quality water.
* Weeding of the planted land.
* Application of organic and inorganic amendments in the afforested reclaimed usar land in appropriate times as per requirements of the soil and plants.

* Provision of appropriate drainage system for the removal of excess rainy water and irrigation water and flushing out the saline soils.

The one Bigha usar land in village Benipur of Amethi Block has been selected for practical reclamation and for afforestation programmes with the involvement of the local village beneficiaries in the following phases of usar land reclamation processes :

A. Phase-I—Usar land Reclamation/Land Development :

- Cleaning and levelling of the usar land.
- Bunding and *Med-bundi* of the land.
- Land preparation for afforestation.
- Irrigation arrangements (tube-well and sprinkler system).
- Leaching.
- Flushing of the usar soil.
- Mechanical processing of the usar land reclamation.
- Green Mannuring.
- Application of gypsum/pyrite.
- Application of Bio-fertilizer and agro-waste composting.

B. Phase - II — Nursery Raising :

- Nursery land preparation.
- Bio-fertilizer/sand/soil etc.
- Poly bags filling.
- Seedlings of the *Prosopis cineraria, Karonda, Prosopis Juliflora, Azadirachta Indica, Leucaena Leucocephala* (Subabool), *Eucalyptus tereticormis, Tamarix Indica, Albizia procera, Pongamia pinnata,* and other plants seedlings.

- Provision of appropriate irrigation system for the nursery plants.
- Maintenance and Management of nursery plants and adoption of tissue culture techniques.
- Hybrid seeds of the plants for fuelwood, fodder, etc.

C. Phase-III — Afforestation

- Diging of Pits.
- Mixing of the fresh soil along with organic and inorganic amendments.
- Bio-fencing on the bunds and plantation.
- One meter inside after hedge plantation on Med-bund wood plantation.
- Shifting of plants from Nursery land to the plantation site.
- Plantation of *Prosopis Cineraria, Karonda, Prosopis, Juliflora, Azadirachta Indica,* Leucaena, *Leucaena leucocephala, Eucalyptus tereticornix, Tamrix Indica, Albizia procera, Pongamia pinnata, Jeropha* and other plants in the reclaimed land.
- Proper bio-scientific application of bio-fertilizer appropriate irrigation system including sprinkler system.
- Use of insecticides and pesticides.
- Appropriate management of plants and afforested land.
- Integrated techniques of afforestation management.
- Application of organic and inorganic amendments.
- Application of Bio-fertilizer and compost.
- Recycling of afforested plants waste for the bio-fertilizer.

D. Phase - IV – Post-Afforestation

- Demonstration of post-afforestation techniques including cutting of excessive leaves and branches of plants for fuelwood and fodder use of the beneficiaries.

- Demonstration of bio-remediation of afforestation management on usar land.
- Recycling of afforested plants leaves, etc. for the bio-fertilizer.
- Follow up of the afforested plants including appropriate irrigation system.
- Appropriate application of organic and inorganic amendments in the afforested land.

Reclamation of Banjar Land for — Forestry - Horticulture-Agriculture

The banjar land which is left out of cultivation from more than 5 years has been reclaimed in one Bigha plot of banjar land in village — Loniapur of Amethi Block. The cropping quality of the land as per the fertility status of the soil has been depicted in the Map-45, which indicates that the Goyad land is found only in the limited area while Domat land which is less fertile is found in two-third area of the village. The banjar land in village Loniapur is found 3.27 per cent to the total of the village.

The successful reclamation of banjar land through organic and inorganic amendments alongwith scientific and technological inputs and understanding of the behaviour of water table and knowledge of the pH value of the soil and fertility status of the soil are necessary. Various reclamation measures which has been applied for the reclamation of one Bigha banjar land in village Loniapur of Amethi Block has been explained. The reclaimed banjar land has been afforested, horticultural plantations and partially agricultural cropping.

- The banjar land has been properly levelled for ensuring uniform distribution of irrigation water,

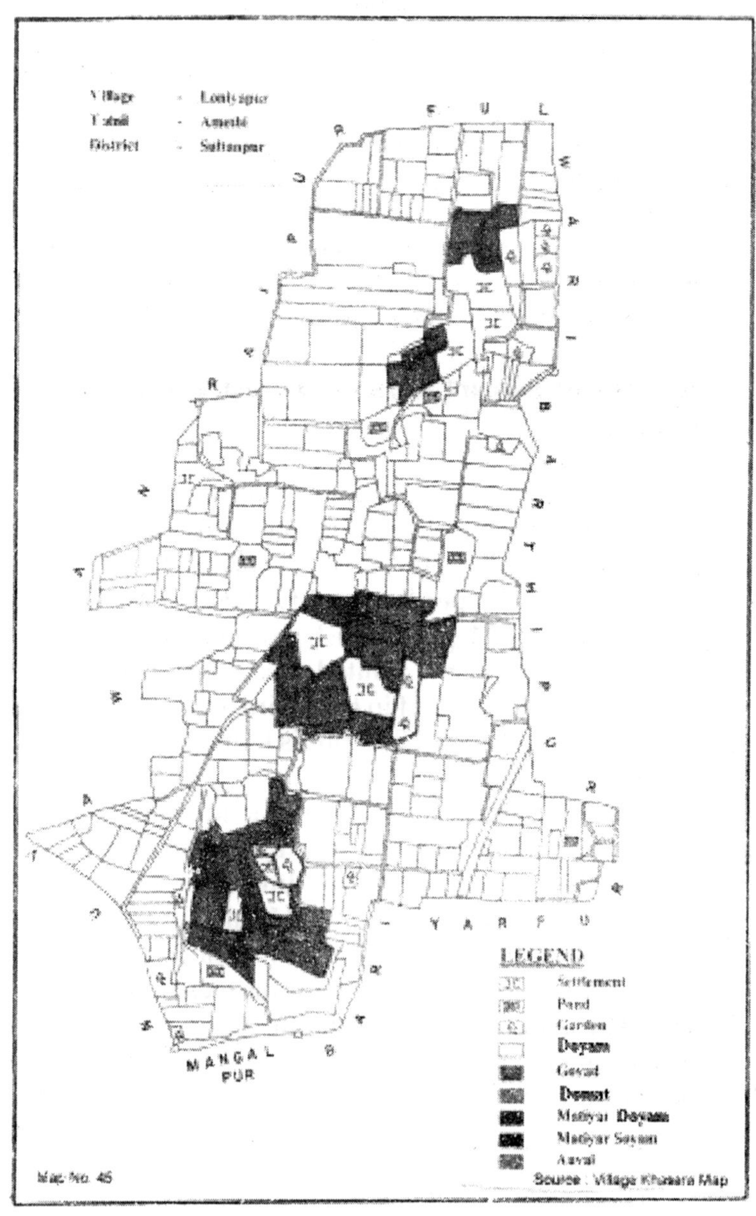

Map-45 : Cropping Quality of Land : Loniapur

fertilizer, and uniform growth of crops and appropriate organic and inorganic amendments.

- The land has been divided into different size plots for judging proper levelling of the land along with bunds. The bunds are made because it is required essentially to prevent the entry of run-off water from outside area.
- The surface drainage is necessary and it is made along the out side of the bunds for providing proper out flow for the water. Good quality water is necessary for irrigation and it is being tested before its use for irrigation purpose.
- Testing of the soil has been done and according to the nature and requirement of the soil to produce a good crop, urea, Shakti khad, Potash has been applied. The gypsum/pyrite has been used and it is mixed in the upper 10 cm. with light ploughing 15-20 days before afforestation. After application of organic and inorganic amendments, appropriate irrigation has been ensured till 5-7 cms. Water level is obtained. Green mannuring has been done before the afforestation on the reclaimed banjar land. The one bigha banjar land in village Loniapur of Amethi Block in Sultanpur District has been reclaimed for the Forestry - Horticulture - Agriculture programmes adopting the following measures :—

Phase - I,-- Land Preparation

- Bunding/Med-bundi.
- Land levelling.
- Sub-plotting of the land.
- Top dressing of fertilizer.
- Deep ploughing.
- Leaching and flushing of the soil.
- Irrigation management/sprinkler system of irrigation.

- Mechanical processing of banjar land reclamation.
- Green mannuring.
- Application of gypsum and pyrite.
- Application of bio-fertilizer, NPK.
- Micro-organism based bio-fertilizers and bio-pesticides.

Phase II – Nursery Raising

- Land preparation for the nursery.
- Irrigation arrangement/sprinkler system.
- Mixing of soil, sand, bio-fertilizer and it filling in the polythene bags.
- Seedling of horticulture and forestry plants.
- Maintenance and management including application of irrigation and bio-fertilizer, etc.
- Procurement of hybrid seeds viz. *Prosopis Cineraria, Prosopis Juliflora, Azadirachta Indica, Shisham, Leucaena Leucocephala, Tamrix Indica, Albizia Procera, Pongamia Pinnata, Jetrokha, Karonda* and *Eucalyptus tereticornis* plants.
- Arrangements of tissue culture raised plants.
- Shifting of nursery raised plants to the plantation site.

Phase III – Plantation/agricultural cropping

- Digging of pits.
- Mixing of the soil alongwith organic and inorganic amendments and filling in the pits..
- Plantation of fuelwood, fodder, fibre, fruits and food-grains viz. *Prosopis Cineraria, Prosopis Juliflora, Azadirachta Indica, Shisham, Leucaena Leucocephala, Tamrix Indica, Albizia Procera, Pongamia Pinnata, Jetropha, Karonda, Amla, Eucalyptus tereticornis* plants.
- Agricultural cropping of Barley in Rabi season and Sanai/Dhaincha in Kharif season and Urad/mung in the Jaid season of agricultural cropping.

- Appropriate arrangements of irrigation system including sprinkler system.
- Application of bio-fertilizer/compost khad.
- Use of insecticides and pesticides.
- Bio-scientific management of multi-inter-cropping on the reclaimed banjar land.
- Appropriate management and maintenance of the planted trees and crops in the Rabi, Kharif and Jaid agricultural cropping season.

Phase-IV – Post Harvest System

- Scientific demonstration of harvesting techniques.
- Recycling of the crop waste for bio-fertilizers.
- Cutting of grown up branches of trees and leaves for fuelwood and fodder.
- Training and demonstration of Post Harvest Technology.
- Training for Agri-Horti processing to obtain appropriate price for the produced materials.
- Appropriate distribution of benefits accrued from the reclaimed banjar land among the involved beneficiaries.

Reclamation of Old Fallow Land for Agri - Horti - Forestry

The reclamation of old fallow land in one bigha has been implemented in village - Mahmodpur of the Amethi Block. The Goyad (good quality) land has been found along with the settlement and Domat, Matiyar Doyam, Matiyar Soyam and Avval quality land as per the fertility status of the soil has been significantly found in the village - Mahmodpur which is depicted in the Map-46. The agricultural cropping quality of the land has been based on the fertility status of the soil to produce different crops.

The old fallow land has been left out of cultivation from two to five years, with the view to maintain the fertility status of the soil. The old fallow land can be easily reclaimed through adopting various reclamation measures —

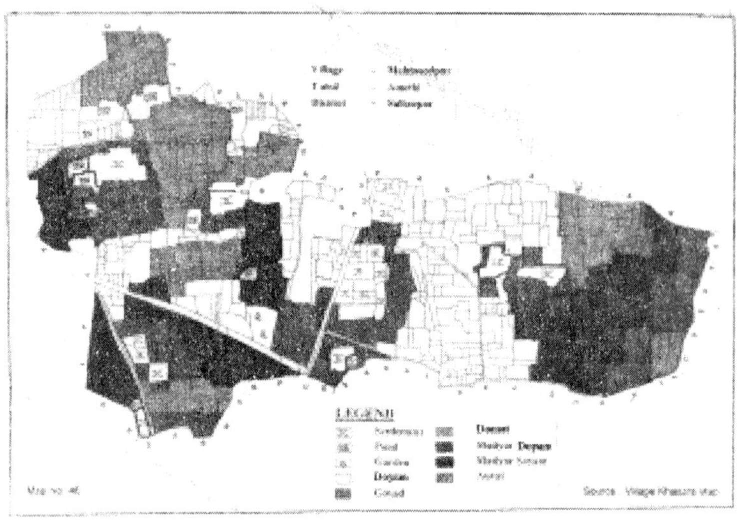

Map-46 : Cropping Quality of Land

A. Land Preparation

The old fallow land which is left out of cultivation from 2 to 5 years to maintain the fertility status of the soil.

- Bunding and Med-bundi of the land.
- Sub-plotting of the land.
- Levelling of the land.
- Top dressing of the land.
- Deep ploughing and cultivation.
- Irrigation management including adoption of sprinkler system of irrigation.
- Leaching and flushing of the land.
- Mechanical processing of the land.
- Green mannuring of the land.
- Application of organic and inorganic amendments.
- Application of bio-fertilizers/NPK.

- Micro-organism based bio-fertilizers and bio-pesticides.

B. *Nursery Development :*

- Land preparation for the nursery.
- Irrigation management.
- Mixing of the soil, sand, bio-fertilizer and filling in the polythene bags and seedlings.
- Maintenance and management of nursery plants and adoption of tissue culture techniques.
- Procurement of high yielding variety of seeds for Agri - Horti - Afforestation.

C. *Plantation :*

- Digging of the pits.
- Mixing of the soil along with organic and inorganic amendments and filling in the pits.
- Bio-fencing along the bunds.
- One meter inside after hedge plantation on med-bund wood and fodder plantation has been planted.
- *Fuelwood Plantation* :– Prosopis cineraria, Prosopis Juliflora, Azadirachta Indica, Tamarix Indica, Albizia Procera, Pongamina Pinnata.
- *Fodder Plantation* :– Leucaena Leucocephala, Nopier grass, M.P. Chari, Mustard, Barseem.
- *Fruits Plantations* :– Ber, Amla, and Karonda Plantation.
- *Wood Plantations* :– Shisham and Sagaun Plantation.
- *Fibre Plantations* :– Mulbury plants and Arjun Plantation, Sanai, Dhaincha, etc.
- *Foodgrains* :– Paddy, Wheat, Barley, Mung, etc.

Inside the land multi-inter cropping techniques has been adopted for production of Agri-Horti-Afforestation i.e., fuelwood, fodder, foodgrain, fruits, fibre, wood plantation and agricultural cropping has been ensured. Proper bio-scientific application of bio-fertilizer appropriate irrigation including sprinkler irrigation system.

- Use of insecticides and pesticides.
- Appropriate agricultural cropping techniques has been demonstrated on the reclaimed old fallow land.
- Integrated multi-inter- cropping techniques has been practically demonstrated to increase— Agri - Horti - Afforestation productivity.

D. *Post-Harvest Technology :*

- Cutting of growing additional branches of trees and leaves.
- Harvesting of foodgrain crops for the rabi-kharif and jaid cropping season.
- Waste management from the straws and other afforested plants and agricultural cropping for bio-fertilizer.
- Scientific demonstration of post-harvest techniques.
- Recycling of crop waste for bio-fertilizers.
- Training and demonstration of post harvest technology.
- Demonstration of agro-horti-processing techniques to obtain appropriate price of the Agriculture - Horticulture and Afforestation produce items.
- Appropriate distribution of benefits accrued from Agri - Horti - Afforestation in programmes among the involved village beneficiaries.

Reclamation of Fallow Land for Agri - Horti - Afforestation

Reclamation of fallow land for Agriculture, Horticulture and afforestation programmes has been practically implemented and demonstrated in village - Parsanwa of Amethi Block, District Sultanpur.

The cropping quality of the land based on soil fertility status of the soil has been demarcated as per the Khasara map of village Parsanwa. The Goyad land neighbouring settlement areas has been found significantly in the village followed by Gomat, Matiyar Doyam, Matiyar Soyam and Avval quality of land. The Doyam quality land is found in significantly in the Parsanwa village. Quality of land based on fertility status of the soil has been depicted at plot or gata field level in the Map-47.

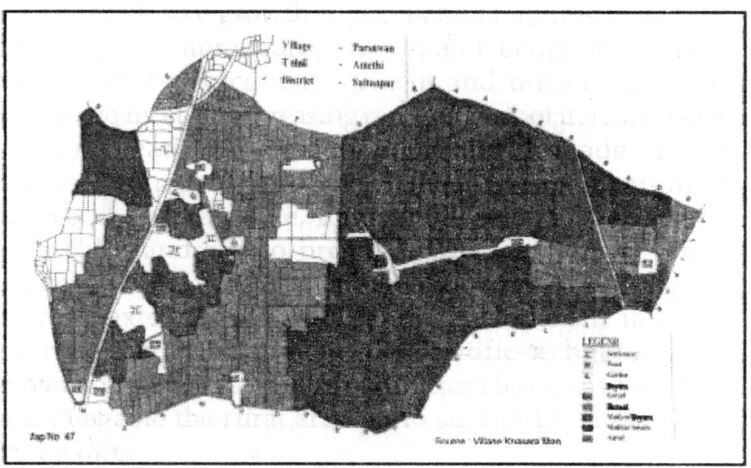

Map-47 : Cropping Quality of Land : Parsanwa

The proper identification and demarcation of fallow land has been insured and one bigha fallow land has been taken for reclamation with the involvement of local village beneficiaries. The reclamation of fallow land with the involvement of local beneficiaries has been implemented adopting various scientific and technological measures.

I. *Land Development*

- Bunding/Med-bundi of the land.

- Sub-plotting of the land for proper equal distribution of irrigation water.
- Deep ploughing of the land.
- Leaching and flushing of the land.
- Irrigation management.
- Mechanical management.
- Mechanical processing for reclamation of land.
- Green mannuring.
- Application of organic and inorganic amendments.
- Use of bio-fertilizer/NPK fertilizer.
- Micro-organism based bio-fertilizers
- Use of insecticides and pesticides.

II. Nursery Development

- Land preparation for the nursery raising.
- Irrigation management including sprinkler irrigation system.
- Mixing of soil, sand, bio-fertilizer and its filling in the polythene bags.
- Seedling of hybrid quality Agro-Horti-Afforestation for fuelwood, fodder, fibre, fruits.
- Maintenance and management including application of irrigation and bio-fertilizer etc.
- Procurement of hybrid seeds for agricultural cropping.
- Arrangement of tissue culture raised, horticulture and afforestation plants.
- Appropriate maintenance and management of nursery plants including replacement of non-surviving plants.

III. Plantation of Horticulture - Afforestation Plants

- Bunding/Med-bundi.
- Land preparation.

- Irrigation management.
- Mechanical processing for land reclamation.
- Green mannuring.
- Application of Bio-fertilizer/composting of waste.
- Digging of pits.
- Mixing of good quality soil, sand alongwith organic and inorganic amendments and filling in the digged pits.
- Agricultural cropping –Paddy crop in Kharif season; Wheat and Barley crop in Rabi season; Mung and Urad crops in Jaid season
- Plantation of Horticultural and Afforestation Plants.
- Shifting of nursery plants to the reclaimed fallow land site.
- Demonstration of agricultural equipments and accessories.
- Plantation of multi-inter-cropping alongwith fuelwood, fodder, fibre, fruits and foodgrain crops.
- Application of Bio-fertilizer, NPK and compost fertilizer.
- Appropriate application of irrigation through sprinkler irrigation system.
- Proper application of insecticides and pesticides.
- Bio-scientific demonstration of plantation on multi-inter-cropping techniques.
- Appropriate management and maintenance of the planted trees and agricultural crops for good quality production to meet the increasing demand of growing cattle and human population for fuel-wood, fodder, fibre, fruits and foodgrain and to restore the ecological imbalances of the village and improve the socio-economic conditions of the deprived rural multitudes.

Fuelwood	Fodder	Fibre	Fruits	Fisheries	Foodgrains	Wood	Vegetables
Prosopis-	Leucaena-	Mulbury	Karonda	Rohu	Wheat	Shisham	Brinjal
Cineraria	Leucocephala	Arjun	Amla	Bhakar	Barley	Sagaun	Tomato
Prosopis-	(Subebool)	Sanai	Guvava	Nain	Paddy		Lady finger
Juliflora	Napier Grass		Papaya	Silver corp	Peas		Chilli
Azadirachta-	M.P. Chari		Ber		Lobia		Potato
Indica	Mustard		Banana	Grass corp etc.	Mung		Cauliflower
Tamrix	Barseem				Urad etc.		Cabbage
Indica							Onion, etc.
Albizia							
Procera,							
Pongamia-							
Pinnata,							
Ecualyptus-							
tereticornis							
Jetropha, etc.							

Fig. 6.6. : Agri-Horti-Afforestation

IV Post-Harvest Technology :

- Scientific demonstration of harvesting techniques.
- Cutting of branches of trees and leaves for the fuelwood and fodder.
- Recycling of crop waste for bio-fertilizers.
- Training and demonstration of Post-Harvest Technology.
- Training for agro-processing to obtain appropriate price for the Agri - Horti - Afforestation produce for the involved beneficiaries.
- To ensure proper follow up action.
- Demonstration of Agri-Horti-Afforestation - Multi-inter-cropping management and post harvest technology programmes.
- Agri-Horti-Afforestation management, Bio-remediation and Eco-management.

Reclamation of Waterlogged Land for Fisheries — Afforestation

The reclamation of waterlogged land has been implemented in village - Bhaganpur of the Amethi Block, because there is 9.85 per cent waterlogged land to the total area of the village which is comparatively high than the other villages of Amethi Block. It has been observed that cropping good quality of land which is Goyad is found around the settlement area. Domat land, Matiyar Doyam, Matiyar Soyam and Avval land is very insignificantly distributed in the village. The Doyam land has been significantly found in the village which is found in the two-third area of the village various cropping quality of the land and land use system has been depicted in the Map-48.

The reclamation of waterlogged has been done for fisheries programme alongwith the bunds forestry and

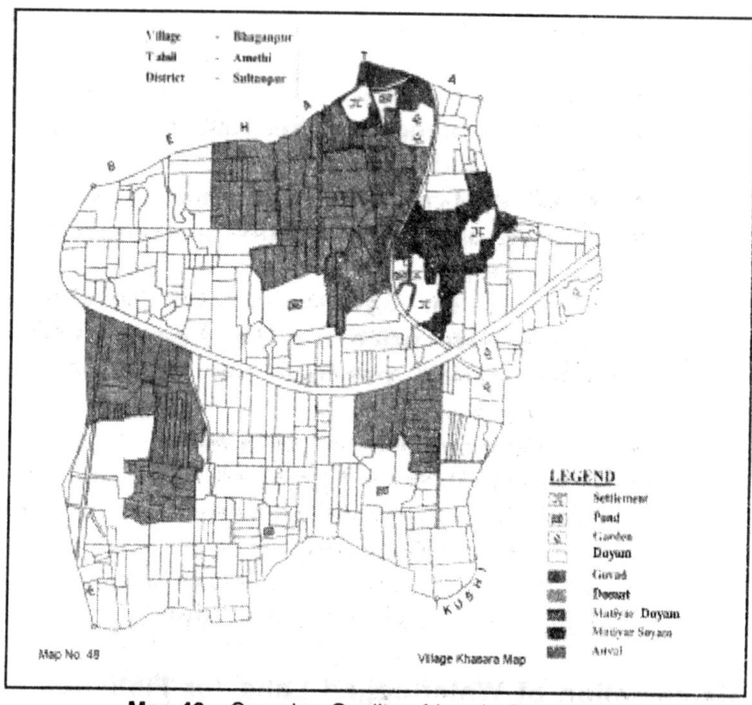

Map-48 : Cropping Quality of Land : Bhaganpur

horticultural plants has been planted, because the waterlogged land can reclaimed for the fisheries programme while waterlogged land reclamation can be implemented with difficulty for Agricultural-Horticultural and afforestation programmes.

The reclamation of waterlogged land for fisheries followed by foresry and horticultural plantation has been implemented in the village Bhaganpur of the Amethi Block.

I Land Development

- Land development for fisheries.
- Construction of pond.
- Testing of the soil.
- Testing of the underground water.

- Proper construction of drainage system for inlet and outlet of the water.
- Proper construction/development of the bunds of the pond.
- Proper development of the pond.

II Nursery Development

- Preparation of land for nursery raising.
- Land levelling and bunding for the nursery.
- Arrangement of the irrigation system.
- Provision of the organic and inorganic amendments.
- Soil preparation for the nursery raising.
- Good quality soil, sand and fertilizer mixing and filling in the polythene bags.
- Seedling of the hybrid quality forestry and horticultural plants seeds in the polythene bags.
- Maintenance and management of nursery plants.
- Adoption of tissue culture techniques for good qualitiy growth of plants.

III Fisheries Programme

- The development of pond for fisheries culture.
- Fill in the pond appropriately with the water.
- Training to the beneficiaries for fisheries culture.
- Development of Mini-Hatchury.
- Development of high yielding variety fisheries sheed viz. Rohu, Bhakur, Nain, Carmal, Corp, Silver corp, Grass corp, etc. with the support of Uttar Pradesh Fisheries Development Corporation at the Government concessional rate.
- Testing of the soil and water.
- Inspection of the growth of fishes and provision of scientific and technical assistance.

IV Plantation of Horticulture and Forestry Plants

- Digging of the pits alongwith the banks and bunds of the pond.
- Mixing of the soil with organic and inorganic amendements and filling in the digged pits.
- Shifting of horticultural and forestry plants from the nursery land to the pond's site.
- Plantation of *Prosopis Cineraria, Prosopis Juliflora, Azadirachta Indica, Tamrix Indica, Albizia Procera, Eucalyptus Tereticornis,* and *Leucaena Leucocephala* plants under the social forestry programmes.
- Plantation of Amla, Papaya and Guvava plants alongwith the banks of the ponds.
- Maintenance and Management of the planted horticultural/forestry plants.

V. Post-Harvest Technology

- Demonstration of fish cropping and marketing.
- Recyling of fisheries culture and seedling of the fishes.
- Cutting of the additionally grown up branches and leaves of the trees for fuelwood and fodder use of the beneficiaries.
- Maintenance and management of the fish pond and forestry and horticultural plants.
- Proper distribution of the benefits accrued out of the fisheries programmes and the horticultural and forestry plantations.
- Ensuring the follow up action of the fisheries and horticultural and forestry plantation.

Conclusion

Explosive population growth has caused tremendous forest

degradation, leading towards ecological crisis and associated socio-economic crisis, affects the rural poor much more significantly than any other. We are loosing 1.5 million hectares of forest and 12000 million tonnes of top soil every year due to deforestation and run-off. The nation's fuelwood requirement is about 150 million tonnes every year of which we are fetching about 50 million tonnes of firewood from the forest. The balance of 80 million tonnes has yet to be generated.

The problem of wastelands is mostly man-made and causes misery to millions of the rural poor. The reclamation of wastelands must be adopted as a strategy for the extension of net sown area according to its suitability to increase the overall agricultural production through agricultural cropping and horticultural and afforestation programmes, predominantly to fetch the fuelwood, fodder, fibre, fruits, fisheries and foodgrains for the integrated development of the deprived rural poor.

The reclamation capability classification of wastelands has been made, based on the fertility status of the soil, potentialities and limitations, their capability of producing agricultural crops and horticultural and afforestation plantations. It has been observed that the fallow land (1-2 years) are very easily reclaimable for agricultural - horticultural and afforestation programmes. The old fallow land (2-5 years) are easily reclaimable for agricultural - horticultural and forestry plantations. The banjar land which has been left out of cultivation from more than five years are reclaimable with certain difficulty for forestry-horticultural and agricultural cropping system. The usar land is reclaimable with difficulty for forestry and horticultural plantations, while the waterlogged land is reclaimable with moderate difficulty for fisheries, forestry and horticultural plantations.

The eco-sustainability through bio-scientific reclamation of various types of wastelands for Agri-Horti-Afforestation programme for income and employment generation. The Agri-Horti-Afforestation programme is technically and economically viable, scientifically, suitable and socially acceptable, because it will fulfil the increasing demand of the growing cattle and human population.

The reclamation of usar land for social-forestry-horticultural programmes has been demonstrated in the one Bigha of usar land in village - Benipur of the Amethi Block. Various reclamation measures such as levelling, bunding, soil testing, application of organic and inorganic, appropriate arrangement of irrigation system leaching and flushing of the top soil and deep ploughing and breaking of the Kankar pan, etc. has been the important task which has been adopted for the reclamation of usar land. Nursery for various social-forestry and horticultural plants and adoption of the tissue culture based techniques has been ensured. Various social forestry plants viz. *Prosopis cineraria, Prosopis Juliflora, Azadirachta Indica, Leucaena Leucocphala* (Subabool), *Jetropha, Eucalyptus Tereticornis, Tamrix Indica, Albizia Procera, Pongamia pinnata* and Amla, Ber, Karonda, Guvava etc. horticultural plants has been planted. Post-harvest technology and follow up action of the reclaimed land has also been practically demonstrated to deprived rural poor beneficiaries.

The reclamation of banjar land has been demonstrated in the village - Loniapur, where 3.27 per cent banjar land has been observed. The reclamation of banjar land in the village-Loniapur has been initiated through levelling, bunding, deep ploughing, top dressing of fertilizer, irrigation management, mechanical processing, organic and inorganic amendments and micro-organism based bio-fertilizers and bio-pesticides. Nursery raising various horticultural and social-forestry plants has been implemented. The plantation of various social-forestry and horticultural plants has been planted and agricultural cropping of Sanai/Dhainch for fibre and green mannuring and Barley, Urad, Mung, etc. has been cultivated in the reclaimed banjar land. The bio-scientific management of multi-inter-cropping on the reclaimed land has also been demonstrated. Proper scientific demonstration of harvesting techniques and recycling of the crop waste for bio-fertilizers has been implemented with the involvement of deprived rural poor beneficiaries. Proper distribution of benefits accrued has been ensured among the involved village beneficiaries. Demonstration of post-harvest technology and proper follow up action has been ensured.

The reclamation of old fallow land which is left out of cultivation from 2 to 5 years due to some reason or the other has been taken up in the village - Mahmodpur of the Amethi Block. The agricultural cropping quality of the land-based on the fertility status of the soil has been analysed.

The land development of the old fallow land has been ensured through levelling, bunding, deep ploughing, top dressing of fertilizers, irrigation system, leaching and flushing of the top soil, mechanical processing, green mannuring, organic and inorganic amendments and bio-fertilizers/NPK and micro-organism based bio-fertlizers and bio-pesticides. Land preparation for the nursery raising, irrigation management, mixing of the soil, sand, bio-fertilizers and filling in the polythene bags and seedling of hybrid quality seeds.

Digging of pits, mixing of the soil with organic and inorganic amendments and filling in the digged pits. Trench making and bio-fencing, hedge plantation on med bund has been implemented. Various fuelwood, fodder, fibre, fruits plantations has been done and agri-cultural cropping for paddy, wheat, barley, mung, Sanai/Dhaincha has been ensured. Inside the land multi-inter cropping techniques has been adopted. Post-harvest technology and follow up action has been practically demonstrated to the involved beneficiaries.

The reclamation of fallow land, which is left out of cultivation from 1-2 years, for Agri-Horti-Afforestation programmes has been implemented in the village- Parsanwa of the Amethi Block in Sultanpur District. Levelling, bunding, deep ploughing, irrigation management, green mannuring, organic and inorganic amendments, application of micro-organism based bio-fertilizer and use of insecticides and pesticides has been done for the reclamation of fallow land. Nursery has been developed, irrigation management of nursery plants, mixing of soil, sand, bio-fertilizers and filling in the polythene bags, seedling of the hybrid variety of horticultural and social forestry plants. Arrangement of tissue culture raised horticultural and social-forestry plants and maintenance and management of nursery plants.

The plantation of various horticultural and social forestry plants in the digged pits alongwith organic and inorganic amendments. Demonstration of agricultural cropping for wheat, paddy, barley, mung, urad and Sanai/Dhaincha for green mannuring and fibre requirements. Demonstration of bio-scientific plantation techniques on multi-inter-cropping system. Practical demonstration of post-harvest technology and follow up action of agricultural cropping system and horticultural and social-forestry plantation and distribution of the benefits accrued from it among the involved village beneficiaries.

The reclamation of waterlogged land for fisheries and afforestation has been implemented in village - Bhaganpur of Amethi Block. The land development and construction of pond has been implemented testing of soil and under groundwater has been done. Nursery raising for horticultural and social forestry plants has been ensured adopting various techniques for nursery raising. The constructed pond has been developed for fisheries and banks of the pond has been utilized for horticultural and social-forestry plantations. Fisheries hatchury has been developed and various types of fish like Rohu, Bhakur, Nain, Karmal corp, Silver corp, Grass corp, etc. has been developed. Requisite scientific and technological inputs has been applied for the successful development of fisheries programme alongwith horticultural and afforestation on the banks of the pond. Proper follow up action has also been demonstrated to the involved rural poor village beneficiaries.

Thus the reclamation of various types of wastelands viz. usar land, banjar land, old fallow land, fallow land and waterlogged land has been practically implemented in the Benipur, Loniapur, Mahmodpur, Parsanwa, and Bhaganpur villages of Amethi Block respectively. The Agri- Horti-Afforestation and Fisheries cultivation/plantation has been done in the selected villages. It has been observed that the various types of wastelands distributed in the various villages of Amethi Block can be reclaimed with proper scientific and technological inputs. The reclamation of wastelands has been an asset in restoring the degraded land to produce fuelwood, fodder, fibre, wood, fruits, fisheries and foodgrains to meet the increasing demand of growing cattle and human population. The reclamation of wastelands is also an asset in checking and controlling the environmental and ecological crisis and improving the socio-economic crisis of the deprived rural poor villagers of the Amethi.

7

Economics of Wastelands Reclamation for Agro-Afforestation Management

Introduction

The reclamation of wastelands for Agri-Horti-Afforestation programme is essential, with the view to obtain the increasing demand of growing cattle and human population for vegetable, wood, fuelwood, fodder, fibre, fruits, fisheries, and foodgrains (VWF^6), which is worthwhile from the point of view of economic development through increasing agricultural production by increasing additional area under cultivation. The pressure of cattle and human population on land is growing rapidly, the extension of cultivated land has been stagnant from the several years but the cultivated land has been getting deteriorated due to some reason or the other. The over exploitation and excessive cultivation, high doses of fertilizer and canal irrigation are one of the basic reasons for growth in the wastelands area. The such wastelands and degraded cultivated lands has been within the reach of the common farmers of Amethi. Most of these lands are not suitable for agricultural use. The reclamation of various types of wastelands is a time taking and costly affair and requires scientific and technological back up support. The adoption of various reclamation measures for wastelands as accentuate soil erosion is not desirable from the long-term point of view. In view of the above constraints, it is essential that pros and cons of wastelands reclamation are made amply clear to the farmers, so that they can adopt most appropriate remedial measures. No doubt high expenditure is involved in practising most of the wastelands reclamation remedial measures in the initial stages of the reclamation process, subsequently, the farmers begin to derive considerable benefit from the reclaimed lands. The farmers can be trained, motivated to adopt various measures for the reclamation of wastelands only by disseminating to them the information regarding the economic benefits in the form of additional agricultural production, which ultimately paves the way for socio-economic development and restoration of the ecological and environmental crisis of the Amethi.

The economics of the reclamation of various types of wastelands has been closely linked to the management aspects. The cost of reclamation of wastelands depends upon the nature and extent of degradation of the wastelands has undergone. In this study, an attempt has been made to work out the average expenditure involved in the reclamation of one Bigha wastelands of the different types. Mainly the usar land, banjar land, old fallow land, fallow land and waterlogged land has been selected for the reclamation of wastelands according to their suitability for - Agriculture-Horticulture - Social Forestry and fisheries programmes. The broad criteria in this aspect has been to reclaim usar land, banjar land, old fallow land, fallow land and the waterlogged land for Agri - Horti - Afforestation - Fisheries programmes. The input- out analysis for the reclamation of various types of wastelands has been done after reclamation of each types of wastelands in the various villages of Amethi Block.

The important factors that needs to be taken under consideration in attempting to reclaim various types of wastelands are the cost of reclamation and the anticipated benefits in terms of additional-fuelwood, fodder, fibre, foodgrains, fruits, fisheries, wood and vegetables produced from the reclaimed wastelands. The economics of the reclamation of different types of wastelands has been worked out with the involvement and continued participation of farmers and concerned scientific and technical personnel belonging to different impementing agencies engaged at Amethi, District Sultanpur.

Economics of Reclamation of Usar Land

The most important measures for the reclamation of usar land with high pH value of the soil is land levelling, bunding, deep ploughing, appropriate irrigation management, construction of proper drainage system for inlet and outlet of the water, leaching and flushing of the top sodic soils, breaking of the Kankar pan and the application of organic and inorganic amendments. The quantity of fertilizer and application of the organic and inorganic amendments to be used depends on the requirements of the soil. Hence, the cost of usar land reclamation also varies with the extent of usarization and the prevailing cost of commodities and labour.

Usar land with reh encrustation has a high content of soluble salts, while encrustations and reh powder appearance in the soil on earth surface in the summer season. Such usar land be reclaimed by leaching and flushing with good quality of water and ensuring proper drainage system for outlet of the water. The expected benefits and the encouragements, propagation, motivation induced among the farmers/ cultivators to reclaim the usar land and its maintenance and management for agricultural cropping, horticultural and afforesation programmes, has inspired the beneficiaries for the reclamation of usar land. Therefore, it is important to make concurrent assessment of reclamation of usar land especially interms of investment requirements, posible output and benefits. It would help in formulating suitable reclamation policies in relation to credit requirements, returns and repayment capacity. Based on the past experiences at cultivators field, the cost-benefit analysis has been done during the both Rabi and Kharif cropping season. The reclamation of usar land has been implemented in the village — Benipur of Amethi Block. The important reclamation work involved has been basically levelling, bunding, deep ploughing, leaching and flushing, drainage system, application of organic and inorganic amendments, provision of good quality irrigation water, etc. An adequate attention has been given for the improvement of drainage system and breaking of the Kankar pan, to allow the water percolation. Green mannuring and application of compost khad has been used. The organic and inorganic amendments has been applied as per the requirement of the soil. Various salt tolerant horticultural and forestry plants has been planted on the usar land.

The economics of usar wastelands reclamation has been practically implemented in one Bigha usar land in village Benipur of the Amethi Block, District Sultanpur. The input cost for reclamation of usar land specially land development, nursery raising, plantation/afforestation and post- plantation management has been depicted in the Table 7.1.

The usar land development has been implemented through cleaning, levelling, sub-plotting, med-bunding, bio-fencing, deep ploughing, leaching and flushing, mechanical processing, green mannuring, land preparation/cultivation, application of gypsum/pyrite, management of irrigation, organic and inorganic amendments Bio-fertilizer and agro-waste management, in which a sum of Rs. 35,100 has been invested during the first year of usar land reclamation process and a sum of Rs. 16, 600 has been incurred during the second year of the usar land reclamation.

Nursery land preparation, soil, sand, bio-fertilizer mixing and filling in the polythene bags, seedling for hybrid quality fuelwood, fodder, fruits seeds, irrigation system, mainenance and management of nursery plants adopting tissue culture techniques, availability of hybrid seeds and shifting of nursery from the established nursery to the land reclamation site expending a sum of Rs. 20,100 during the first year of nursery raising and a sum of Rs. 10,200 only has been expended during the second year of nursery raising to ensure the mortality of plants in the nursery as well as plantation site.

The digging of pits, the mixing of soil, fertilizer and filling in the digged pits, plantation of fuelwood, fodder, fruits plant, arrangement of irrigation bio-fertilizer/compost khad, application of insecticides and pesticides. Bio-scientific management, organic and inorganic amendments and plantation equipments/accessories activities Rs. 57,300 has been incurred in the first year and a sum of Rs. 18, 500 only has been spent for the replacement of the plants and unsurvived plants and other important activities for the successful growth of plants during the second year of usar land reclaimation activities.

Table 7.1 : Economics of Usar land Reclamation in Villages-

Sl. No.	*Item of work*	*Input cost in Rs. (One Bigha land)*		
		Ist year	*second year*	*Total*
A.	***Usar land Development***			
1.	Cleaning and levelling.	3,500	500	4,000
2.	Sub-plotting and Med-bunding.	3,000	1, 000	4,000
3.	Bio-fencing.	2, 000	1, 500	3,500
4.	Deep ploughing.	1, 500	1, 000	2, 500
5.	Leaching and Flushing.	2, 000	500	3,400
6.	Mechanical Processing.	2, 400	1, 000	3,400
7.	Green Mannuring.	1, 800	800	2, 600
8.	Land Preparation/cultivation.	2, 100	500	2, 600
9.	Application of gypsum/pyrite.	2, 900	1, 600	4,500
10.	Irrigation System.	5,600	3,000	8,600
11.	Organic and inorganic amendments.	5,100	3,800	8,900
12.	Bio-fertilizer and Agro-waste composting.	3,200	1, 500	4,700
	Total	35,100	16,600	51,700

B.	***Nursery Raising***			
1.	Nursery Land Preparation	3,000	500	3,500
2.	Soil, Sand, Bio-fertilizer mixing	2, 000	500	2, 500
3.	Poly bags and filling	2, 500	1, 000	3,500
4.	Seedling	3,000	1, 000	4,000
5.	Irrigation System	3,500	1, 500	5,000
6.	Maintenance and management of Nursery plants/tissue culture system	3,000	1, 200	4,200
7.	Hybrid seeds of fodder/fuelwood, etc.	2, 300	1, 000	3,300
8.	Shifting of Nursery Plants	800	500	1, 300
	Total	20,100	10,200	30,300
C.	***Horti-Afforestation,***			
1.	Diggin of pits	12, 800	3,500	16,300
2.	Mixing of soil/fertilizer and filling in pits	8,000	3,200	11, 200
3.	Plantation – fuelwood	5,000	2, 800	7,800
	– fodder	5,000	2, 000	7,000
	– fruits	3,500	1, 500	5,000
4.	Irrigation Management	6,,500	3,500	10,000
5.	Bio-fertilizer/compost	3,500	1, 500	5,000
6.	Insecticides/Pesticides	1, 200	800	2, 000
7.	Bio-Scientific Management	1, 500	1, 000	2, 500
8.	Organic and inorganic amendments	4,500	2, 600	7,100
9.	Plantation Equipments/accessories	5,800	1, 800	7,600
	Total	57,300	18,500	75,800
D.	***Post-Harvest Technology***			
1.	Recycling of crop waste for Bio-fertilizer	4,800	2, 800	7,600
2.	Cutting/pruning of branches/leaves	3,500	3,000	6,500
3.	Plantation Management	6,500	4,500	11, 000
4.	Follow up	3,000	2, 800	5,800
	Total	17,800	13,100	3,09,000
	Output Cost			
1.	Fodder	20,000	31, 000	51, 000
2.	Fuelwood	10,500	12, 500	23,000
3.	Fruits	12, 000	15,500	27,500
4.	Waste management/compost	2, 000	2, 500	4,500
	Total	44,500	61, 000	105,500
E.	***Cost-Benefit Analysis***			
	Input Cost (A + B + C + D)	1, 30,300	58,400	188,700
	Output Cost - Fodder	20,000	31, 000	51, 000
	Fruits	12, 000	15,500	27,500
	Fuelwood	10,500	12, 500	23,000
	Waste management/compost	2, 000	2, 500	4,500
	Total output	44,500	61, 000	105,500

Note :– Benefit received from reclaimed one Bigha usar land is not beneficial during the Ist and second year of reclamation process but in the subsequent years the input cost will be very low and output will be increased which will subside the input cost and profit will be increased later on hence it will be economically beneficial.

Recycling of crop waste for bio-fertilizer, cutting/pruning of branches and leaves of trees post-plantation management and follow up action activities a sum of Rs. 17,800 has been spent during the first year while a sum of Rs. 13,100 has been spent during the second year of usar land reclamation in village - Benipur of Amethi Block.

Thus a sum of Rs. 130,300 has been spent during the first of usar land reclamation of land preparation, nursery raising, horti-afforestation and post-plantation management while a sum of Rs. 58,400 has been incurred during the second year of usar land reclamation. Thus total Rs. 1,88,700 has been incurred during the land reclamation in the selected one Bigha usar land in village Benipur of the Amethi Block, District Sultanpur. It is to be noted here that in the afforestation, horticulture plantation in the reclaimed usar land in the initial year, the reclamation cost is very high which decreases in the subsequent years and output-cost will increase in the next years. It has been observed that in the first year of reclamation a sum of Rs. 20,000 obtained from fodder, Rs. 12,000 from planted fruits, and fuelwood, provided Rs. 10,500 output and Rs. 2,000 obtained through waste management and compost khad. The total output cost received in the first year has been only Rs. 44,500 and Rs. 61,000 only during the second year of usar land reclamation process. It has been recorded that in the first year the input expenditure has been very high while out cost in comparison to the input cost has been low but in second year of the reclamation process the input cost was lowered but the output cost was increased. Thus it is clear that in the Ist year the investment of the usar land is permanent expenditure which may be considered as an asset and accordingly the output cost may be considered while analysing the economics of usar land reclamation.

Thus it is clear from the process of usar land reclamation that the input cost during the first year is higher than the output cost which is Rs. 44,500 while during the second year input cost was Rs. 58,400 and output cost achieved was Rs. 61,000 which is beneficial very nominally. No doubt in the third year the input cost will be lowered and output cost will be increased hence it is economically viable and benefical to reclaim the usar land and it will restore the ecological and environmental crisis on the one hand and it will improve the socio-economic conditions of the deprived rural multitudes of Amethi.

Economics of Banjar Land Reclamation

The banjar land is reclaimable with certain difficulties. The banjar land reclamation has been implemented in village-Loniapur of Amethi Block. The reclamation process of banjar land has been practically demonstrated in the village — Loniapur in one bigha land. Initially, the land preparation and banjar land development has been reclaimed through adopting the various process of cleaning, levelling, plotting and bunding. Bio-fencing, hedge making, deep ploughing and cultivation, irrigation system, organic and inorganic amendments, bio-fertilizer and agro-waste composting process in which a sum of Rs. 21,500 has been incurred while a sum of Rs. 11,900 has been expended during the second year of the banjar land reclamation. The economics of banjar land reclamation has been depicted in the Table 7.2.

In the second phase nursery raising has been implemented in which land preparation for nursery, soil, sand, bio-fertilizer, mixing, polybags and filling the poly-bags, hybrid variety seeds availability and seedlings in the polybags, irrigation system, maintenance and management of nursery plants and shifting of nursery plants has been done and a sum of Rs. 15,300 has been incurred and in the second year Rs. 6,800 has been spent as precautionary measures for the replacement of unsurvived plants.

Afforestation and horticultural plantations along with multi-inter-cropping techniques has been applied. Various high yielding variety of fuelwood, fodder, fibre, fruits, plantation has been done in the reclaimed land and agricultural cropping of maize, barley and mung, urad crops has been sown in the Kharif and Rabi and Jaid cropping seasons respectively. The irrigation management, bio-fertilizer and compost, insecticides and pesticides, Bio-scientific management, organic and inorganic amendements and plantation equipment/accessories etc. procedures has been adopted and implemented in which a sum of Rs. 40,000 has been spent during the first year and a sum of Rs. 26,800 has been incurred during the second year of the reclamation process of banjar land.

Table 7.2 : Economics of Banjar land Reclamation Villages

Sl. No.	*Item of work*	*Input cost in Rs. (One Bigha land)*		
		Ist year Rs.	*IInd year* Rs.	*Total* Rs.
A.	***Banjar land Development***			
1.	Cleaning, levelling	3,000	—	3,000
2.	Plotting and Bunding	2,000	500	2,500
3.	Bio-fencing/Hedge making	1,000	500	1,500
4.	Deep ploughing/cultivating	1,500	500	2,000
5.	Mechanical Processing	1,200	600	1,800
6.	Green Mannuring	1,500	1,500	3,000
7.	Land Preparation and Cultivation	4,500	2,500	4,000
8.	Irrigation system	1,200	800	2, 000
9.	Organic and inorganic amendments	3,500	1,500	5,000
10.	Bio-fertilizer and Agro-waste composting	2,100	1,500	3,600
	Total	21,500	11,900	33,400
B.	***Nursery Raising***			
1.	Land Preparation for Nursery	2,500	2,000	4,500
2.	Soil, sand, Bio-fertilizer mixing	1,500	500	2,000
3.	Poly bags and filling	2,500	1,000	3,500
4.	Seedlings - Fodder, fuelwood, fibre, fruits	2,500	800	3,300
5.	Irrigation System	3,000	1,000	4,000
6.	Maintenance and Management of Nursery Plants/tissue culture system	2,500	1,000	3,500
7.	Nursery Plants shifting	800	500	1,300
Total		15,300	6,800	22,100

Table 7.2 : *(Contd...)*

C. Afforestation - Horticulture - Agriculture			
1. Digging of Pits	8,000	4,500	12,500
2. Mixing of soil/fertilizer filling in pits	7,000	3,000	10,000
3. Plantation – Fuelwood	3,000	2,000	5,000
– Fodder	1,500	500	2,000
– Fibre	2,000	1,000	3,000
– Fruits	3,500	2,500	6,000
Agricultural cropping – Maize	2,000	2,000	4,000
– Barley	1,500	1,500	3,000
– Mung/urad	1,000	1,000	2,000
4. Irrigation system	5,000	4,000	9,000
5. Bio-fertilizer/compost	2,000	1,000	3,000
6. Insecticides/pesticides	1,000	1,000	2,000
7. Bio-scientific management	1,500	1,000	2,500
8. Organic and inorganic amendments	1,000	1,000	2,000
9. Plantation Equipment/accessories	1,000	1,000	2,000
Total	40,000	26,800	66,800
D. Post-Harvest Techniques			
1. Recycling of crop waste for Bio-fertilizer	2,500	2,500	5,000
2. Cutting/Pruning of branches and leaves of trees	2,500	2,500	5,000
3. Cropping/plantation management	5,500	3,500	9,000
4. Follow up action	3,000	2,500	5,500
Total	15,500	12,000	27,500
E. Output - Cost :			
1. Fuelwood	12,500	10,000	18,500
2. Fodder	25,000	25,000	50,000
3. Fibre	10,000	12,000	22,000
4. Fruits	13,000	25,000	38,000
5. Foodgrains (Kharif, Rai, Jaid, cropping seasons)	8,000	10,000	18,000
Total	68,500	82,000	150,500
F. Cost Benefit Analysis :			
Input cost	92,300	57,500	149,800
Output cost	68,500	82,000	120,500
Benefit	23,800	24,500	700

The post-harvest technology has been adopted and demonstrated. The recycling of crop waste for bio-fertilizer, cutting/prunning of branches and leaves of trees, cropping and plantation management and follow up action has been implemented in which a sum of Rs. 15,500 has been incurred in the Ist year and a sum of Rs. 12, 000 has been incurred in the second subsequent year of banjar land reclamation.

The output cost has been estimated based on the produce obtained from the fuelwood, fodder, fibre, fruits, plantations and agricultural crops produced. It has been approximately estimated that a sum of Rs. 68,500 has been obtained during the first year of reclamation of banjar land and a sum of Rs. 82,000 has been obtained during the second year from the reclaimed banjar land. It has been observed that during the first year of reclamation of banjar land the input cost in the Afforestation - Horticultural - Agricultural cropping is higher than the output cost achieved from the reclaimed land but during the subsequent second year input cost has been lower and output cost has been found higher than the input cost. Thus during the second year a sum of Rs. 24,500 profit has been obtained but subsequently for the both years the profit was very nominal because of higher input cost and low output in the Ist year of the reclamation of banjar land. It is observed that the reclamation of banjar land for social forestry- Horticultural - Agricultural not beneficial during the Ist year but during the second year the profit has been increased and in the subsequent years the output cost will increase and input cost will be reduced. Thus, the reclamation proposition because it provides fuelwood, fodder, fibre, frutis and foodgrains to meet the increasing demand of growing cattle and human population and it is economically viable and beneficial in the subsequent years. It has been helpful in restoring the ecological, environmental and degradation of land and it has also improved the socio-economic crisis of the deprived rural multitudes and also helpful in improving the ecological crisis of the area.

Economics of Old Fallow Land Reclamation

The economics of old fallow land reclamation has been assessed in one Bigha old fallow land in village Mahmodpur of Amethi Block. The old fallow land is easily reclaimable. The old fallow land has been reclaimed for Agricultural-Horticultural and afforestation programme with the involvement of the local village beneficiary and owner of the land. The old fallow land has been reclaimed through adopting various processes of reclamation. The economics of old fallow land reclamation has been depicted in the Table 7.3. The reclamation of old fallow land has been initiated through adopting cleaning and levelling, plotting and bunding, bio-fencing and hedging, deep ploughing and cultivation, mechanical processing, green mannuring, land preparation and cultivation, irrigation management, organic and inorganic amendements, bio-fencing and agro-waste composting, etc. practices has been implemented in which a sum of Rs. 18,900 has been incurred in the Ist year reclamation of old fallow land while a sum of Rs. 8,900 has been expended during the second year of old fallow land reclamation.

A nursery has been established to faciliate horticultural and forestry plants. The land preparation for nursery, soil, sand, bio-fertilizer, mixing, polybag filling, high yield variety seeds procurement and seedling in polybags, irrigation management maintenance and management of nursery, nursery plants shifting, etc. activities has been implemented in which a sum of Rs. 12,800 has been expended and a sum of Rs. 8,500 has been incurred during the second year of old fallow land reclamation.

The wheat, mung, urad and paddy agricultural crops have been shown in the Rabi, Jaid and Kharif agricultural cropping season followed by Sanai and Dhainch cultivation for fibre and green mannuring to increase the fertility status of the soil. Digging of pits and mixure of the soil, sand and bio-fertilizer, etc. have been filled in the digged pits for plantation of Amla, Papaya, Amrapali Mango, Karonda, Eucalyptus Tereticornis, Leucaena Leucocephala, Arjun, Prosopis cineraria, etc. plantation has been planted, bio-fertilizer/compost, irrigation management, insecticides and pesticides, bio-scientific management, organic and inorganic amendments and procurement of plantation equipments, etc.

Table 7.3 : Economics of Old Fallow Land Reclamation in village — Amethi, District-Sultanpur

Sl. No.	Item of work	*Input cost in Rs. (One Bigha land)*		
		Ist year Rs.	*2nd year* Rs.	*Total* Rs.
A.	***Old Fallow land Preparation***			
1.	Cleaning and Levelling	3,000	200	3,000
2.	Plotting and Bunding (Mend)	1,500	500	2,000
3.	Bio-fencing and Hedge making	1,000	500	1,500
4.	Deep ploughing/cultivation	1,500	500	2,000
5.	Mechanical Processing	1,200	600	1,800
6.	Green mannuring (Sanai/Dhaincha)	1,000	1,000	2,000
7.	Construction of drainage system	1,200	800	2,000
8.	Irrigation management	3,500	2,300	5,800
9.	Organic and inorganic amendments	3,000	1,500	4,500
10.	Bio-fencing and agro-waste management	2,000	1,000	3,000
	Total	18,900	8,900	27,800
B.	***Nursery Establishment :***			
1.	Nursery land Preparation	2,500	2,000	4,500
2.	Soil, sand, Bio-fertilizer mixing	1,500	1,000	2,500
3.	Polythene bags and filling	1,500	1,000	2,500
4.	Seedling (Agri-Horti-Plants)	2,000	1,500	3,500
5.	Irrigation management	2,000	1,500	3,500
6.	Maintenance and management of Nursery	2,500	1,000	3,500
7.	Shifting of Nursery plants	800	500	1,300
	Total	12,800	8,500	21,300
C.	***Agri - Horti - Afforestation :***			
1.	Agricultural cropping –			
	Wheat	4,000	3,000	7,000
	Urad/Mung	1,000	800	1,800
	Paddy	3,000	2,500	5,500
2.	Horticultural Plantation – Digging of pits	5,000	4,000	9,000
	Amla	2,000	1,000	3,000
	Papaya	1,000	1,000	2,000
	Mango-Amrapali	2,500	2,000	4,500
	Karonda	1,500	500	12,000
3.	Afforestation – Eucalyptus tereticornis			
	Leucaena	1,000	1,000	2,000
	Leucaephala	1,500	500	2,000
	Arjun	1,500	1,000	2,500
	Prosper cinesis	1,000	1,000	1,000
4.	Bio-fertilizer/compost	2,000	1,000	3,000

Table 7.3 : *(Contd...)*

5.	Irrigation Management	4,500	3,500	8,000
6.	Application of Insecticides and Pesticides	1,000	800	1,800
7.	Bio-Scientific management	1,000	1,000	2,000
8.	Organic and inorganic amendments	1,000	500	15,000
9.	Equipments and accessories	1,200	500	1,500
	Total	35,700	25,600	61,300
D.	***Post-Harvest Technology***			
1.	Recycling of crop-waste management for the Bio-fertilizers	2,000	1,500	3,500
2.	Cutting and prunning of branches and leaves	2,000	1,000	3,000
3.	Cropping and plantation management	4,000	3,000	7,000
4.	Follow up action	2,000	1,500	3,500
	Total	8,200	7,000	15,200
E.	***Output cost***			
	Fuelwood	18,000	21,800	39,000
	Fodder	18,000	21,500	39,500
	Fibre	8,000	11,000	19,000
	Fruits	12,000	19,000	31,000
	Foodgrains	18,000	24,000	42,000
	Total	74,000	96,500	17,500
F.	***Cost Benefit analysis***			
	Input cost (A + B + C + D)	75,600	50,000	125,600
	Input cost - output cost = Benefit	1,600	16,500	44,900
	Total Benefit during 2nd year		Rs. 44,900	

has been done in which a sum of Rs. 35,700 has been incurred and a sum of Rs. 25,600 has been expended during the second year of the reclamation of old fallow land.

The post-harvest techniques have been applied for recycling of crop waste for bio-fertilizer, cutting and prunning of leaves and branches of trees, agricultrual cropping and plantation management and follow up action have been ensured in which a sum of Rs. 8,200 has been expended during the first year of the reclamation of old fallow land and a sum of Rs. 7,000 has been incurred during the second year of reclamation process of the old fallow land.

It has been observed that during the first year a sum of

Rs. 75,600 has been incurred while Rs. 50,000 has been expended, against which a sum of Rs. 74,000 has been obtained from fuelwood, fodder, fibre, fruits, foodgrain cropping during the Ist year. It indicates that there is negative profit of Rs. 1,600 has been obtained during the Ist year of the reclamation of old fallow land while a sum of Rs. 4,6500 has been achieved from fuelwood, fodder, fibre, fruits and foodgrains during the second year of the reclamation of old fallow land against the total expenditure of Rs. 50,000. Thus there has been net profit of Rs. 46,500 during the second year of the reclamation of old fallow land. In general there has been net profit of Rs. 44,000 only during the first and second year of the reclamation process of old fallow land.

Thus, it has been recorded that the old fallow land reclamation for Agriculture-Horticulture and afforestation programme is economically beneficial to the rural poor because it has fulfilled their increasing demand of fuelwood, fodder, foodgrains, fibre, fruits, etc. and it has also been helpful in restoring the ecological crisis and socio-economic crisis of the rural poor.

Economics of Fallow Land Reclamation

The economics of fallow land has been implemented in the village - Parsanwa of the Amethi Block. The agricultural - horticultural activities followed by the afforestation programme has been implemented in the reclaimed fallow land. The various reclamation measures of the fallow land has been adopted and practically implemented. The economics of fallow land reclamation has been depicted in the Table 7.4. Initially the land preparation, sub-plotting, bunding, hedging and bio-fencing, deep ploughing, and cultivation, mechanical processing, green mannuring (Dhaincha and Sanai) drainage system, irrigation management, organic and inorganic amendments, agro-waste management and bio-fencing activities has been implemented in which a sum of Rs. 17,900 has been incurred during the first year of fallow land reclamation and a sum of Rs. 9,300 has been expended during the second year of the fallow land reclamation.

Nursery has been established for raising afforestation and horticultural plants. Land preparation for nursery raising, soil, sand, bio-fertilizer mixing, polythene bag procurement and filling in the poly bag, hybrid, variety horticultural and afforestation plantation, irrigation management, maintenance and management of nursery and shifting of nursery plants to the plantation field activities has been implemented for which a sum of Rs. 9,500 has been expended during the first year and for the replacement of unsurvived plants nursery raising has been ensured during the second year of reclamation process of which as sum of Rs. 6,800 has been expended for the successful implementation of horticultural and plantation programme.

Table 7.4 : Economics of Fallow land Reclamation village —

Sl. No.	*Item of work*	*Input cost in Rs. (One Bigha land)*		
A.	***Fallow land Reclamation***			
1.	Land Preparation	4,000	1,500	5,500
2.	Sub-plotting and Bunding	1,200	1,000	2,200
3.	Hedging and Bio-fencing	1,000	500	1,500
4.	Deep Ploughing and cultivation	1,500	500	1,500
5.	Mechanical Processing	1,200	800	20,000
6.	Green Mannuring (Dhaincha and Sanai)	1,500	1,000	2,500
7.	Drainage system	1,000	500	1,500
8.	Irrigation Management	2,500	2,500	5,000
9.	Organic and Inorganic amendments	3,000	500	3,500
10.	Agro-waste management and Bio-fencing	1,000	500	1,500
	Total	17,900	9,300	27,200
B.	***Nursery Development :***			
1.	Land Preparation for Nursery raising	1,500	1,000	2,500
2.	Soil, sand, bio-fertilizer mixing	1,000	500	1,500
3.	Polythene Bag procurement and filling	1,000	1,000	2,000

Table 7.4 : *(Contd...)*

4.	Seedling	1,500	1,000	2,500
5.	Irrigation management	1,500	1,000	2,500
6.	Maintenance and management of nursery	2,000	1,500	2,500
7.	Shifting of Nursery plants	1,000	800	1,800
	Total	9,500	6,800	16,300
C.	***Agri-Horti-Afforestation Programme***			
1.	Agricultural cropping			
	Wheat	4, 000	3,000	7,000
	Mung/urad	1, 000	800	700
	Paddy	2,500	2,000	4,500
2.	Horticultural Plantation			
	Amla	2,000	1,000	3,000
	Mango	2,000	1,500	3,500
	Papaya	1,000	500	1,500
	Guvava	1,000	500	1,500
3.	Digging of pits	4,000	3,000	7,000
4.	Afforestation –			
	Prosopis cineraria	1,000	1,000	2,000
	Leucaena Leucaephala	1,500	500	2,000
	Eucalyptus tereticornis	1,600	400	2,000
5.	Bio-fertilizer/compost	1,500	1,000	2,500
6.	Irrigation management	3,000	2,000	5,000
7.	Insecticides and pesticides	1,000	800	1,800
8.	Bio-scientific management	1,000	500	1,500
9.	Equipments/accessories	1,800	800	1,800
10.	Organic and inorganic amendments	1,200	600	1,800
	Total	28,200	21,000	50,200
D.	***Post-Harvest Technology***			
1.	Recycling of crop waste land arrangement for Bio-fertilizer	1,500	1,000	2,000
2.	Cutting and Prunning of branches and leaves of trees	2,000	1,000	3,000
3.	Agricultural cropping/Plantation management	3,000	2,500	5,500
4.	Follow up action	1,500	1,000	2,500
	Total	8,000	5,500	14,500
E.	***Output cost***			
	Foodgrains	25,000	27,000	52,000
	Fruits	12,000	16,000	28,000
	Fibre	6,000	8,000	14,000
	Fuelwood	13,000	16,000	29,000
	Fodder	19,000	21,500	40,500
	Total	*69,000*	*88,500*	*1,57,500*
F.	***Benefit***	4,400	46,500	50,900

Agricultural cropping and horticultural–afforestation plantation programme has been implemented in the reclaimed fallow land in which a sum of Rs. 4000 for wheat crop, Rs. 1,000 for mung and urad crop and for paddy cropping Rs. 2,500 has been incurred for the Rabi, Jaid and Kharif cropping seasons respectively. Similarily, Amla, Mango, Papaya, Guvava horticultural plantation and Prosopis, Cineraria, Leucaena Leucaephala and Eucalyptus treticornis social - forestry plantations has been ensured along with bio-fertilizer, irrigation management, insecticides and pesticides, bio-scientific management, equipment and accessories, for agricultural cropping and horticultural and afforestation plantation, organic and inorganic amendments etc. practices has been implemented in which a sum of Rs. 29,200 has been incurred during the first year and Rs. 21,000 has been expended during the second year of the fallow land reclamation.

Post-harvest technology has been implemented in which recycling of crop waste management and follow up action practices has been implemented in which a sum of Rs. 8,000 has been expended during the first year of the reclamation process and a sum of Rs. 5,500 has been incurred during the second year of the reclamation programmes.

Output achieved from the horticultural and afforestation plantation and agricultural cropping has been recorded satisfactory in which a sum of Rs. 25,000 has been obtained from foodgrains productions during the Kharif, Rabi and Jaid cropping seasons, while Rs.12,000 achieved from the produced fruits, Rs. 6,000 from fibre especially from Sanai/ Patson fibre, Rs. 13,000 from fuelwood and Rs. 19,000 from fodder. The total output achieved during the first year has been Rs. 69,000 and a sum of Rs. 88,500 has been obtained during the second year of the fallow land reclamation process. Thus a sum of Rs. 4400 has been achieved as net profit during the Ist year while the profit has been increased during the second year of the reclamation process because in this year the input cost has been reduced and output estimated cost was increased upto Rs. 46,500 during the second year of the reclamation process of the fallow land and a sum of Rs. 50,900 has been achieved as a net profit during the two years of fallow land reclamation process.

It has been observed that the reclamation of fallow land is economically beneficial to the local village people because this process has been an asset in restoring the ecological and environmental degradation and controlling the ecological crisis and improving the socio-economic crisis of the area. It has been an asset in fulfilling the increasing demand of fuel-wood, fodder, fibre, fruits and foodgrains of the growing cattle and human population of the selected villages of Amethi Block in the District Sultanpur.

Economics of the Waterlogged Land Reclamation

The economics of waterlogged land reclamation has been impelemented in the village - Bhaganpur of the Amethi Block of the District Sultanpur. The input cost and output cost for the reclamation of waterlogged land for fisheries programme along with horticultural and afforestation programme on the banks of the pond has been implemented. The detailed reclamation process of waterlogged land for the fisheries programme along with the afforestation and horticultural plantation, etc. has been depicted in the Table 7.5. The selected waterlogged land in village Bhaganpur of Amethi Block has been initially developed and pond has been constructed for the purpose of fisheries cultivation.

Waterlogged land reclamation programme has been initiated through demarcation and plotting of waterlogged land, digging and construction of pond, construction of the banks of the pond. Development of drainage system for inlet and outlet of water, soil testing and under groundwater testing, installation of tubewell and procurement of diesel engine etc., Hedge making on out side the banks of the pond,

Table 7.5 : Economics of Waterlogged land Reclamationin villages -

Sl. No.	Item of work	Cost in Rs.
A.	***Input Cost***	
1.	Demarcation and Plotting of waterlogged land	1,500
2.	Digging/construction of pond	35,000
3.	Construction of the banks of the pond	4,500
4.	Development of drainage system for inlet and outlet of water	3,500
5.	Soil testing and underground water testing	1,500
6.	Installation of Tubewell and Diesel Pump etc.	48,000
7.	Hedge making on out side the banks of the pond	2,200
8.	Digging of pits for plantation	3,100
9.	Water filling in the pond approximately three times	9,200
10.	Developing fisheries Hatchury and Procurement of fish seeds	16,500
11.	Procurement of social forestry and Horticultural Plants	3,500
12.	Fisheries cultivation	8,900
13.	Management of fish feed	12,000
14.	Soil, fertilizer mixing and filling in the pits	3,600
15.	Horticulture - Forestry Plantations/Bio-fencing	1,800
16.	Maintenance/management of fisheries culture and plants	15,000
17.	Bio-scientific management of fishing and plants	5,800
18.	Follow up programmes	2,500
	Total Input cost	1,78,100
B.	***Output cost - Horticulture***	8,000
	Social forestry	7,500
	Fisheries	48,000
	Total	63,500

digging of pits for plantation, water filling in the pond approximately three times, developing fisheries hatchury and procurement of fish seeds, procurement of social forestry and horticultural plants, fisheries cultivation, management of fish feed, soil, fertilizer mixing and filling in the pits, horticulture-social forestry plantations and bio-fencing plantations maintenance and management of fisheries culture and plants, bio-scientific management of fishing and plants, ensuring follow up programmes of fisheries programmes etc. has been properly implemented for successful fisheries cultivation and horticultural and social forestry plantation in which a sum of Rs. 1,78,000 has been incurred out of which a sum of Rs. 35,000 has been incurred for the construction of pond and installation of tubewell and availability of diesel engine for irrigation/watering in the pond for which Rs. 48,000 has been expended and these expenditures has been the permanent asset for the beneficiary. Thus a sum of Rs. 83,000 has been incurred as permanent expenditure and availed as a permanent asset for which no investment shall be required for the second year. Similarly, most of the expenses are not required for the second year except the fisheries culture management, fish feed, fish seed for hatchury, watering, etc. In the first year a sum of Rs. 63,500 has been achieved from the horticulture and forestry plants and fisheries culture while in the second year the input cost will be minimized and output cost will be increased input cost including permanent cost and in the subsequent years the farmers will be able to manage their cost of pond construction and installed tubewell and diesel engine and will be able to increase there income from the fisheries cultivation and from the horticulture and social forestry plants.

Thus, the fisheries and horticultural and social forestry plantation on waterlogged land is an economic proposition and beneficial from the second year because during the first year the permanent input cost could not provide significant benefit. The reclamation of waterlogged land for fisheries - horticulture - forestry programme is economically viable and beneficial in the long run and in improving the socio-economic and ecological crisis of the area. The reclamation of waterlogged land is environmentally and economically viable and feasible to the beneficiaries.

Conclusion

The restoration of ecological and land degradation is the need of the hour for deprived rural poors because the explosive population growth tremendous deforestation, ecological and environmental degradation has brought us face to face for the scarcity of fuelwood, fodder, fibre, fruits, foodgrains, fisheries, vegetable and wood for the day-to-day requirements of the common people. The over-exploitation and excessive cultivation, high doses of fertilizer, canal irrigation are one of the basic reasons for the growth of wastelands. Such wastelands and degraded cultivated lands has not been within the reach of the common farmers.

The adoption of various reclamation measures for wastelands, as accentuate soil erosion is not desirable for the long-term point of view. In view of the above constraints, it is essential that pros and cons of wastelands reclamation are made amply clear to the farmers, so that they can adopt most appropriate remedial measures in the initial stages of reclamation tenure, subsequently, the cultivators will be able to derive considerable benefit from the reclaimed land. The cultivators must be trained, motivated, to adopt various measures for the reclamation of wastelands only by disseminating to them the information regarding the economic benefits in the form of additional agricultural production, which ultimately paves the way for socio-economic development and restoration of the ecological and environmental crisis of the villagers.

The economics of the reclamation of the different types of wastelands is closely linked to the management aspects. The cost of reclamation of wastelands depends upon the nature and extent of degradation of the wastelands has undergone. The broad criteria has been to reclaim usar land, banjar land, old fallow land, fallow land and the waterlogged land for Agri - Horti - Afforestation - Fisheries cultivation and plantation respectively. The input-output cost analysis for the reclamation of various types of wastelands has been done, after the reclamation of each types of wastelands in the selected villages of Amethi Block. The economics of the reclamation of various types of wastelands has been estimated with the involvement and continued participation of farmers and involved scientific and technical personnel belonging to different impelementing agencies engaged in Amethi Block, District Sultanpur.

The most important reclamation measures for the reclamation of usar land with high pH value of the soil has been the land levelling, bunding, deep ploughing, appropriate irrigation management, construction of proper drainage system for inlet and outlet of the water, leaching and flushing of the top sodic soils, breaking of the Kankar pan, and application of organic and inorganic amendments. The quality of the fertilizer, and application of organic and inorganic amendments depends on the requirement of the soil. The cost of the usar land reclamation also varies with the extent of usarization and prevailing cost of commodities and labour.

It has been observed that a sum of Rs. 130,300 has been incurred for the usar land reclamation including land preparation, nursery raising horticultural - afforestation and post-plantation managament activities and a sum of Rs. 58,400 has been incurred during the second year of the usar land reclamation process. Thus a total sum of Rs. 1,88,700 has been incurred during the subsequent two years of the usar land reclamation in the one Bigha land in village Benipur of the Amethi Block. It has been noticed that in the initial year of usar land reclamation the input cost was very high which has decreased in the second year but out cost has increased in the next year. It has been recorded that a sum of Rs. 44,500 achieved in the first year while Rs. 61,000 obtained during the second year of plantation while the input cost during the first year was very high but during the second year the input cost has decreased. In the subsequent years also the input cost will decrease and output cost will increase, which indicates that the reclamation of usar land is costly affair in the initial year but the input cost has decreased and output cost has increased significantly hence it is economically viable and beneficial to reclaim the usar land, to restore the ecological and environmental crisis and improving the socio-economic crisis of the villagers.

The banjar land reclaimable with certain difficulty has been implemented in the village Loniapur of the Amethi Block. It has been recorded that a sum of Rs. 92,300 has been incurred for the banjar land development, nursery raising, Afforestation - Horticultural plantation and agricultural cropping and implementation of post-harvest techniques during the first year while a sum of Rs. 57,500 has been expended during the first year of the reclamation of banjar land, while Rs. 68,500 has been achieved as output cost from fuelwood, fodder, fibre and fruits during the first year and Rs. 82,000 has been achieved in the second year of the banjar land reclamation process. It has been noticed that in the first year the benefit was in minus but in the second year it increased and the farmer was benefited with Rs. 24,500. Thus during the two subsequent year very nominal benefit has been accrued from the banjar land reclamation.

It has been observed that the reclamation of banjar land for afforestation - horticulture - Agricultural cropping was not beneficial during the initial year but in the second year the benefit was increased because in the subsequent year the banjar land reclamation input cost decreases and the output cost has increased simultaneously overall the reclamation of banjar land is an economic position because it provides fuelwood, fodder, fibre, fruits and foodgrains to meet the increasing demand of growing cattle and human population and also in improving the ecological and socio-economic crisis of the villages of Amethi.

The old fallow land has been reclaimed in one Bigha land of village - Mahmodpur of Amethi Block. The old fallow land has been reclaimed for Agricultural cropping – horticulture and afforestation programmes. It has been recorded that sum of Rs. 75,600 has been expended for land preparation nursery raising, Agri - Horti - Afforestation, plantation and agricultural cropping followed by post harvest technology during the first year of the reclamation of old fallow land and a sum of Rs. 50,000 has been incurred in the second year of the old fallow land reclamation process, while a sum of Rs. 74,000 has been obtained from fuelwood, fodder, fibre, fruits, foodgrains with a negative profit of Rs. 1,600 while a sum of Rs. 96,500 achieved as output cost during the second year and there has been net profit of Rs. 46,500 in the second year from the reclaimed old fallow land. It has been recorded that during the subsequent first and second year of old fallow land reclamation a net profit of Rs. 44,900 has been achieved.

The reclamation of old fallow land for Agri-Horti - Afforestation programme in village Mahmodpur of Amethi Block has been economically benefiable to the village beneficiaries and also an asset in improving socio-economic crisis and ecological imbalances of the village.

The reclamation process of fallow land has been implemented in village-Parsanwa of Amethi Block. Agricultural cropping - Horticultural Afforestation activities has been carried out in the reclaimed fallow land. It has been recorded that a sum of Rs. 64,600 has been expended during first year of the reclamation of fallow land during first year of the reclamation of fallow land for fallow land reclamation, nursery raising, Agricultural - Horticultural - Afforestation programme and demonstration of post-harvest techniques to the beneficiaries while during the second year a sum of Rs. 42,000 has been incurred out of which a sum of Rs. 69,000 has been achieved as output cost in the first year and Rs. 88,500 output cost during the second year from the reclaimed fallow land and a total output cost of Rs. 1,57,500 for subsequent two years has been obtained.

It has been observed that a sum of Rs. 4,400 has been achieved as net profit during the first year of fallow land reclamation and Rs. 46,500 has been obtained as a net profit during the second year and a sum of Rs. 50,900 has been achieved as a net profit during the subsequent two years of the reclamation of fallow land in village - Parsanwa of Amethi Block. It has been recorded that the reclamation of fallow land is economically viable in improving the socio-economic crisis of the rural poors and also restoring the ecological crisis of the area.

Reclamation of waterlogged land has been implemented in the village - Bhaganpur of Amethi Block. The waterlogged land reclamation has been initiated mainly through the construction of pond, drainage system, development of the banks of the pond, installation of tubewell and procurement of diesel engine, developing fish hatchury, procurement of fish seeds, arrangement of forestry and horticultural plants and bio-scientific management of fisheries culture and plants etc. for which a sum of Rs. 1,78,000 has been incurred in the first initial year of waterlogged land reclamation, out of which a sum of Rs. 35, 000 has been incurred for the construction of pond and installation of tube well and availability of diesel engine Rs. 48, 000 has been incurred which are the permanent assets of the beneficiary. Thus a sum of Rs. 83,000 has been incurred as permanent asset's expenditure for which no investment is required in the second year and most of the incurred expenses are not required for the subsequent years. It has been observed that a sum of Rs. 63, 500 has been obtained as a output cost from the reclaimed waterlogged land for fisheries and horticultural and social forestry plantation and the output cost will be increased in the subsequent years, the farmers will be able to manage their cost of pond's construction and installed tube-well and diesel engine and the beneficiaries will be able to increase their income from the fisheries cultivation along with afforestation and horticultural plantation. It is observed that the waterlogged land reclamation for fisheries - horticulture - afforestation programme is economically viable and beneficial in long run in improving the ecological crisis and socio-economic crisis of the rural poor beneficiaries.

Thus the reclamation of usar land, banjar land, old fallow

land, fallow land and waterlogged land for Agri - Horti - Affrestation - Fisheries programme has been economically viable and beneficial proposition to village beneficiaries because it has provided fuelwood, fodder, fibre, fruits, food-grain, fish to the village beneficiaries to meet the increasing demand of growing cattle and human population on the one hand and it has been helpful in restoring the ecological, environmental land degradation and improving the socio-economic crisis of the deprived rural multitudes of the Amethi, District Sultanpur. The scientific and technical support system and infrastructural availability to the villagers for the reclamation of usar land, banjar land, old fallow land, fallow land, and waterlogged land in the various villages in Amethi Block must be linked with various other programmes being implemented by the line departments will be a milestone in the reclamation of wastelands and restoration of socio-economic and ecological crisis of the villages of Amethi.

8

Strategies for Agro-Afforestation Management on Wastelands

Introduction

The distribution of various types of wastelands at village level in Amethi Block and at Block level in District Sultanpur and the major natural and human factors and various indicators has been discussed in the previous chapters. The policies and planning for agro-afforestation management on wastelands, status of agro-afforestation programmes in Amethi and Sultanpur has been described while practical reclamation process of usar land, banjar land, old fallow land, fallow land, waterlogged land and economics of the reclamation of such wastelands for Agri - Horti - Forestry - Fisheries programmes in the various selected villages of Amethi Block has been analysed in detail in the previous chapters of this study.

An attempt has been made in this part of the study to analyse and suggest the strategies to be adopted for obtaining the best suitable results from the reclamation of the various types of wastelands for Agro-Afforestation management. In such circumstances it is necessary to devote adequate attention to policy formulation with the involvement of the village beneficiaries and then the reclamation of wastelands for agro-afforestation and fisheries management to restore the ecological and socio-economic crisis of the villages of Amethi.

The management implies the way responsibility is delegated and decisions made, the way of the functions are differentiated and co-ordinated, the way managing personnel are selected, promoted and rewarded, and the information is dissiminated to the right interested beneficiaries at the right time. Thus, the strategies related to the management and structure building for wastelands reclamation for agro-afforestation management plays an important role in the overall integrated development of the villages. The importance of management is not only in knowing the various scientific-technical inputs but in doing or implementing its test is not logic but in the actual results of the reclamation of wastelands for the agro-afforestation management.

In real sense strategies to be adopted include the provision of several packages of the most suitable technological and scientific inputs, credit support, building up of a strong social infrastructure and arranging marketing support system. In the planning for the reclamation of various types of wastelands, due attention is also required for the different supporting activities viz. motivation of the deprived poor farmers and the people belonging to the weaker sections of the society, including landless farmers/ agricultural labourers to adopt appropriate scientific and technological inputs and arrangement of the distribution systems for such wastelands for meeting the minimum needs of the weaker sections in respect of such inputs as they cannot manage the reclamation of wastelands at their own limited available resources.

It has been observed and noted that so far no organised/ systemetic efforts has been made by the Central-State - District-Tehsil-Block level Government agencies to formulate action oriented planning strategies for the effective utilization of wastelands resources. As a result of this, such lands continue to be put to sub-optimal use and in many cases to even destructive use. Thus, the deprived rural multitudes are to be motivated to be participated in these programmes and an active role of the Concerned Government/Non-Government implementing agencies has to be ensured, through restoring the degraded lands, improving the ecological crisis of the poor villagers. The reclamation of wastelands for Agri- Horti - Forestry - Fisheries and to fulfil the increasing need of fuelwood, fodder, fibre, fruits, foodgrain, fisheries for the growing cattle and human population. Therefore, the strategies for the reclamation of wastelands with the involvement of rural poor beneficiaries for agro-afforestation management has been described and people's participation to ensure man-nature-technology relationship in an appropriate system, so that the natural resources are properly exploited to meet the day-to-day requirements of the common below poverty line people living in the remote rural villages.

Strategies for the Reclamation of Wastelands

Appropriate strategies, structures, policies and planning should be derived and adopted so that the various types of wastelands are reclaimed fodder, fruits, fisheries, fibre, foodgrains, etc. to meet increasing demand of growing cattle and human population.

Coordinating agencies for the reclamation of wastelands at village level should be established to support the resourceless farmers, are having access to scientific-technological inputs and preventing the formation of wastelands. Another function of the co-ordinating agencies should be to create awareness among farmers for the reclamation of various measures. District and Block level officials should support the farmers in aquiring the wastelands on the lease or *Patta* basis or for the *tree patta* system and post-harvest technological information and the marketing of agro-base produce.

Imaginative strategies for communication with the village beneficiaries should be systematized and extended at grassroot level. Appropriate use of different mass media, such as television, radio, local newspapers, films, and various audio-visual techniques should be made available to motivate the farmers to participate enthusiastically in the programmes related to the reclamation of wastelands and greening of degraded lands. Just like *Green Revolution* there should be integrated programme of *Greening of Wastelands* with the active involvement of Research and Development Organizations, extension agencies, voluntary organisations and the farmers. Peoples involvement and participation is necessary in all operations of the reclamation of wastelands, nursery raising, agro-forestry, *Patta* land and *tree patta* land allotment to the needy interested beneficiaries including appropriate incentives to the beneficiaries for the reclamation of wastelands.

Identification of the Wastelands

The first essential task is to identify the wastelands, the problems and prospects at micro level or grassroot level i.e., village levels. It is imperative to undertake village level or evel at plot level wastelands and soil survey and to draw maps indicating their detailed distribution. It is equally important to accumulate information on the proportionate distribution of wastelands and percentage growth of various types of wastelands at village level with the continued involvement of village account and (Lekhal/Patwari), village heads, interested farmers, personnel of the soil conservation, Revenue Officials, Agriculture Officer, Horticulture Officer, Forest Officer and Block Development Officers for the identification of the problems of wastelands and factors responsible for the formation and the instant growth of the area under wastelands must be analysed at field/plot level for the formulation of planning for the reclamation of the wastelands.

Factors in Wastelands

The various factors responsible for the formation and increase in the area under wastelands should be identified. The important natural and human factors at micro-level should be identified and analysed as a precautionary measures to check and restore the growth of wastelands. The man-made problems viz. high doses of irrigation and high doses of fertilizer application, excessive cultivation, over cultivation must be controlled, limited as per the fertility status of the soil. The soil and irrigation water testing must be carried out at least alternate cropping system. Therefore, natural and anthropogenic factors should be analysed before initiation of the reclamation of various types of wastelands.

Genesis of the Wastelands

On the basis of the various factors responsible for the formation and growth of wastelands, the genesis of the wastelands must be analysed in the context of the status of the wastelands in question i.e., the extent of the degradation of land, which has undergone. This means the classification of land into three categories : marginally degraded land, partially degraded lands and severely deteriorated lands. The suitable strategies to be worked out which will depend on the category to particular type of wastelands based on the genesis and formation of wastelands.

Capability Classification of Wastelands

The categorisation of wastelands on the basis of it's capability for the reclamation. Thus, it will then form the basis for evolving models for the action plan. The capability classification should be based on the factors like determinants of wastelands, genesis of the wastelands, limitations of the natural resources and locations of the affected degraded lands. The reclamation capability classification of wastelands viz. very easily reclaimable, easily reclaimable, reclaimable with certain difficulty, reclaimable with moderate difficulty and wastelands reclaimable with difficulty, etc. should be analysed based on the fertility status of the soil to produce agricultural crops and afforestation and horticultural plantation.

Structure of the Wastelands

The selected patch of the wastelands should be properly levelled, to ensure uniform application of irrigation water, fertilizers, organic and inorganic amendments. Further, the land must be divided into sub-plots of appropriate sizes to ensure adequate levelling and proper bunding of the land.

The constructed bunds must be strong enough to check the entry of run-off water from outside as well as to prevent outflow of the water from the field. Surface drainage should be provided outside the bund to ensure proper outflow of the water during the reclaiming operation. Proper use should be made of rainwater during rainy season to leach and flushout undesirable compounds from the soil. The good quality water should be used for irrigational purpose of the agro-afforestation programmes.

Testing of the soil should be carried out for its proper characterization and the determinants of the wastelands growth including the soils requirement of organic and inorganic amendments for increasing the productivity of the land. Gypsum and Pyrite application are ideal amendments are to added in the upper 10 cm. layer with light ploughing, 15 to 20 days before the paddy cropping.

After organic and inorganic amendments of the soil,

irrigation should be carried out freely upto 5-7 cm. water level is obtained. Green mannuring before and after cultivation helps to maintain the fertility status of the soil.

Based on the type of soil, environmental conditions, various types of wastelands can be developed for Agriculture-Horticulture - Social forestry - Fisheries programmes as per suitability of the soil. In most of the cases of wastelands reclamation, no extensive physical and chemical scientific reclamation techniques except bunding the land and rain water irrigation are required.

Irrigation facilities are required for the agricultural crops. There is no need for seperate irrigation facilities for tree plantations, protective irrigation is sufficient for plantation programmes. Irrigation sources like tubewells are to be created in selected patches of wastelands for the reclamation purposes. Trees for fuelwood, fodder, fibre, fruits may be planted as per the fertility status of the soil and also as per need of the local people.

Action Oriented Planning

Within a specified timeframe, the concerned implementing agencies should prepare and make available a reliable data base for various types of wastelands after their identification and suitability for different purposes–agricultural-horticulture-forestry-fisheries.

The concerned implementing agencies are required to assist the beneficiaries, particularly in the demonstration of improved methods of cultivation and arranging the supply of the requisite inputs for the reclamation of wastelands for various purposes. It includes the arrangement of financial supports for the small, marginal and *patta* land allottee landless farmers and people from the weaker sections of the society to enable components of the programme is an organised publicity campaign, integrated programmes for training the farmers at various levels on the different aspects of the utilization of wastelands. The scientists can apply an effective role by suggesting necessary changes in the cropping patterns particularly for the drought prone and desert areas, where there are serious moisture stress-related bottlenecks in the work of programmes concerned with the wastelands reclamation. The other tasks of the scientists include selection of appropriate hybrid variety species, for fodder, fuelwood, fodder trees and agricultural crops according to the nature of wastelands in question, making provision for supply of seeds of high yielding variety, requisite extension support pertaining to choice of cropping pattern, methods of cropping and post-harvesting techniques.

Implementing agencies concerned with the integrated rural development programmes should ensure availability of raw material inputs on the subsidized basis, whereever justified. This is particularly necessary in respect of gypsum and pyrite and other organic and inorganic amendments needed for the reclamation of the different types of wastelands.

The soil testing laboratories including the mobile one, should ensure prompt and accurate testing of soils. In addition they should provide guidence to the farmers for the use of organic and inorganic amendments according to the nature and requirement of the soil.

The pedogenic and hydrologic scientists from various implementing agencies should visit the villagers to advice the farmers in respect of simple but better water management steps for controlling the soil erosion and overflow of water which damage the fertility status of soil.

Appropriate facilities required for augmenting irrigation facilities should be arranged to the farmers in respect of the programmes related to the reclamation of wastelands. The proper guidance should be made available regarding control and restoration of waterlogging and the consequential usarization of the land.

The beneficiaries farmers co-operative societies should be formed, enlightening individual farmers should be made available to the interested needy farmers for their encouragement and incentives in respect of the reclamation of various types of wastelands. Appropriate scientific technologies for the wastelands reclamation should be made available to the beneficiaries belonging to the landless and weaker sections of the society.

The mining activity should be curved in such areas where it is leading towards the growth of wastelands. The steps should be taken to find alternative sources of such essential raw materials, whose supply gets interrupted due to this. A collective efforts need to be made to check and control the soil losses through water and wind erosion and to prevent the collapse of irrigation system through siltation of the soil.

The planning for the reclamation of various types of wastelands including — land preparation, levelling, bunding, sub-plotting, leaching and flushing, good quality, irrigation system, application of gypsum/pyrite, organic and inorganic amendments, green mannuring, bio-scientific management of wastelands development should be devised and adopted at various levels especially at field level and village levels should be properly integrated, Action in respect of various operations related to reclamation should be co-ordinated, keeping in view the capability and suitability of the different types of wastelands various purposes including Agriculture-Horticulture - Forestry - Fisheries with the view to fulfil the increasing need of fuelwood, fodder, fibre, fruits, foodgrains, fisheries, (F^6), growing cattle and human population and to restore the ecological imbalances of the villages.

Extension Programmes

Appropriate attention should be given to the organisation of training, demonstration, and extension programmes for creating awareness among weaker sections in the remote interior villages on various aspects of the wastelands reclamation programmes. Motivation, propogation of the problems and prospects of wastelands and allotment of *patta* and tree *patta* lands to the landless and agricultural labourers and pros and cons of the wastelands development should be extended upto village level and also for the wider publicity to control the formation of wastelands and also the reclamation of wastelands for various Agricultural - Horticultural - Forestry - Fisheries programmes as per needs of the local people.

Strategies for the Nursery Raising

Nursery should be established at village level for which land preparation for the nursery, procurement of the polythene bags, mixing of sand, fertilizer, compost khad, soil and filling in the polybags, seedlings, proper arrangement of irrigation system, maintenance and management of nursery must be demonstrated at village level. High level yield variety species like. *Prosopis Cineraria, Prosopis Juliflora, Azadirachta Indica, Tamrix Indica, Albizia Procera, Pongamia Pinnata, Eucalyptus Tereticornic, Leucaena Leucocephala, Shisham* and *Sagaun* plants nurseries should be established to fulfil the increasing demand of fuelwood, fodder, fibre, fruits, etc.

Strategies for the Agriculural Cropping

Agricutural cropping i.e., Kharif-Rabi, Jaid, cropping seasons as per the suitability of the soil and capability of the land must be demonstrated to the farmers. The green mannuring i.e., Sanai and Dhaincha especially for fibre, paddy, wheat, barley, mung, urad, etc. cropping should be adopted in the reclaimed land. In the usar land barley and Sanai/Dhaincha may be cultivated while in the banjar land, old fallow land, fallow land paddy, wheat, barley, mung/urad, etc. may be cultivated in Kharif, Rabi and Jaid cropping seasons to meet the increasing demand of foodgrains, fodder and fibre of the growing for human population.

Strategies for the Horticultural Plantations

Nursery raising for horticultural plants should be established as per needs of the local villagers. The Amla, Papaya, Ber, Mango, Guvava, Karonda, Lemon, Banana, horticultural plants are may be planted as per suitability and fertility status of the soil along with Subabool, a leguminous tree, besides being salt tolerant, it helps in fixation of nitrogen of the soil. The multi-inter-cropping along with horticultural plantations must be propagated at village level along with vegetable cropping as per the need of the local village beneficiaries.

Strategies for the Afforestaton

Afforestation strategies should be promoted and the plantation of *Prosopis Cineraria, Prosopis Juliflora, Azadirachta Indica, Tamrix Indica, Albizia Procera, Pongamia Pinnata, Eucalyptus tereticornis, shisham, Sagaun, Leucaena Leucacephala* social forestry plantations should be promoted and demonstrated. If the land is not suitable for growing agricultural crops, the growing the leguminous tree species is recommended for improving the fertility status of the soil. Subabool a leguminous tree besides being salt tolerant, helps in fixation of nitrogen. One the forestry is developed, the land can be taken up for cultivation of foodgrain crops after a period of 3-7 years depending upon the extent of usarization of the land in the beginning. Protective irrigation is sufficient for afforestation, irrigation sources like tubewells may be managed in the selected patches of the wastelands for reclamation. Plants for fuelwood should be planted at 1.5 × 1.5 meter spacing. In the case of mixed plantations, trees should be planted at 4 × 1 meter spacing along with cultivated fodder crops. Seeds of the harvested crops should be collected and used for growing subsequent crops in the same land, because plants growing from such seeds are more salt-tolerant and productivity of the crop obtained by sowing seeds secured from outside. The reclaimed land can be used for afforestation programmes for fuelwood, fodder, fibre, etc. In terms of financial returns multi-intercropping of afforestation is more profitable in the agricultural cropping.

Strategies for Fisheries

The waterlogged land may be reclaimed for the construction of ponds for fisheries cultivation and the banks of the pond may be utilized for afforestation and horticultural plantations. The hybrid quality fish seed like, Rohu, Bhakur, Nain, Karmal corp, Silver corp, Grass corp, fish seeds hatchury should be developed and fish cultivation should be promoted in the constructed pond through reclaiming the waterlogged with the view to restore the ecological and environmental imbalances and in improving the socio-economic crisis of the villagers.

Gram Banjar Bhoomi Vikas Yojana

Gram Banjar Bhoomi Vikas Yojana at village level should be launched under the chairmanship of village Pradhan. The village level and development programmes should be linked together with the wastelands development programme. *National Rural Employment Gurantee Act* (NAREGA) should be linked with the wastelands development programme, involving the NAREG A beneficiaries for reclaiming the *Patta* or *Tree Patta* allotted wastelands for restoring the ecological land degradation.

Greening Gram Yojana

Greening the Gram Yojana should be launched through involving the village Panchayat people and plantation on the common land of village and individual lands plantation should be promoted, with the view to restore the environmental and land degradation of the village and also to improve the socio-economic crisis of the villagers.

Compensatory Fund for Afforestation (COMPA)

As per the directives of the Hon'ble Supreme Court of India, States District - Block, village level compensatory fund for Afforestation Programme should be initiated for re-afforestation against the deforestation and land degradation.

Panchayat Van Yojana

Every village Panchayat should intend to achieve the target of 33 per cent forest cover by 2012, the only scheme that treats afforestation in a holistic manner and seeks to involve the communities and the society in general in the preservation and conservation of forests has been deprived of funds. The *Panchayat Van Yojana* scheme should be launched to ensure the utilization of funds and successful implementation of the reclamation of wastelands for afforestation programmes. The village Panchayat should formulate effective strategies to create mass awareness about afforestation among the poor people who depends on the forest resources in different forest cover but would also provide better opportunity empowerment, livelihood, and security to the villagers.

Intensification of Agro-Afforestation Management

The intensification of agro-afforestation management at village level should be extented and the promotion of afforestation, tree planting, ecological restoration and eco-development at village level and also regeneration of degraded forest land. The agro-afforestation management on wastelands should be intensified at village level with the involvement of the villagers and local level concerned implementing agencies — strategies should be formulated to check indiscriminate deforestation and diversion of forest land for non-forest use, strengthening of forest protection force, control of grazing and restriction on removal of fuel-wood, as head loads and availability of alternate fuels.

Education/Training for Agro-Afforestation Management on Wastelands

The village level training, education for agro-afforestation management on wastelands including exhibitions and training programmes should be organised by the concerned line departments. The main activities under this scheme are:

- Agro-afforestation management on wastelands awareness campaign.
- Agro - afforestation clubs.
- Greening the land.
- Mass awareness.

Agro-afforestation management on wastelands in a broad perspectives, the younger generation should be made fully aware of the environmental concerns that are attracting the attention at the village level. The agro-afforestation management education and trainning by imparting non-formal education at the school level also should be promoted for wider publicity. Mass awareness programme should be launched at village level to propogate the reclamation of wastelands for agriculture-horticulture-forestry-fisheries programmes to fulfil the increasing demand of growing cattle and human population for fuelwood, fodder, fibre, fruits, foodgrains, and fisheries, and also to restore the ecological crisis and improve the socio-economic crisis of the villagers.

Appropriate strategies should be adopted for education/ training/propagation of the reclamation of wastelands for agro-afforestation management to meet the increasing demand of growing cattle and human population and also to restore the ecological and socio-economic crisis of the villagers.

Conclusion

The strategies formulation and adoption of various measures

for the reclamation of wastelands include the provision of several packages of the most suitable technological and scientific inputs, credit support, building up of a strong social infrastructure and arranging marketing support system. The strategies for the reclamation of wastelands with the involvement of rural poor villagers for agro-afforestation management for appropriate exploitation of natural resources to meet the day-to-day requirements of the common people living in the remote rural villages.

Imaginative strategies for communication with the village beneficiaries should be systematized and extended to grassroot level beneficiaries. Appropriate use of mass media and audio-visual techniques should be made available to motivate the farmers for their enthusiastically in reclamation of wastelands and *'Greening of the Wastelands'* with the active involvement of the deprived rural poor people. Peoples participation and involvement is necessary in all operations of the reclamation of wastelands for agro-afforestation management incentives to the beneficiaries.

Identification of wastelands, classification of wastelands and it's distribution at village level should be analysed i.e., usar land, banjar land, old fallow land, fallow land, waterlogged land and other types of wastelands in the various villages of Amethi has been identified and its distribution has been also analysed.

Various natural and human factors responsible for the growth of wastelands has been explained at village level in Amethi Block of the District Sultanpur.

The genesis of the wastelands and the various determinant responsible for the growth and formation of wastelands has been explained. The genesis of wastelands has been classified into three categories viz. marginally degraded land, partially degraded land and severely degraded lands. The suitable strategies should be worked out for various types of wastelands based on genesis and formation of wastelands.

The capability classification of wastelands as per suitability of the soil to produce the crops has been analysed and strategies must be adopted to analyse the capability classification of wastelands based on the reclamation capability of the wastelands.

Testing of the soil, land preparation levelling and bunding, leaching and flushing, green mannuring, organic and inorganic amendments, appropriate irrigation management, bio-scientific management etc. should be adopted for the reclamation of wastelands.

Action oriented planning within a specified timeframe should be adopted for reclamation of wastelands. Stepwise proper planning for the reclamation of wastelands starting from land preparation, soil testing, irrigation management organic and inorganic amendments as per requirement of the soil for agricultural cropping and horticultural - afforestation programmes should be formulated and demonstrated to the needy poor beneficiaries of the villages.

Extension programmes for the reclamation of wastelands for agriculture - horticulture - forestry- fisheries programmes should be practically demonstrated to the deprived resourceless poor beneficiaries.

Strategies for nursery raising including land preparation, polythene bag filling with mixed sand, soil, fertilizer, and seedlings, and irrigation management and maintenance and management of nursery should be appropriately demonstrated to the village beneficiaries.

Agricultural cropping for the Kharif, Rabi, Jaid cropping seasons especially paddy, wheat, barley, mung and urad and Sanai/Dhainch, etc. should be properly demonstrated on the reclaimed wastelands and agricultural cropping should be planned as capability classification of wastelands and fertility status of the soil.

Strategies for horticultural plantations including — Amla, Papaya, Ber, Mango, Guvava, Karonda, Lemon, Banana, etc. should be demonstrated on the reclaimed wastelands along with the leguminous trees besides salt tolerant which helps in the fixation of nitrogen of the soil. The multi-inter - cropping along with horticultural plantations must be propogated at village level.

Afforestation strategies on the various types of reclaimed wastelands including plantation of *Prosopis Cineraria, Prosopis Juliflora, Azadirachta Indica, Tamrix Indica, Albizia Procera, Pongamia Pinnata, Eucalyptus tereticornis, Shisham, Sagaun, Leucaena Leucacephala* plants should be planted to produce fuelwood, fodder, fibre, to meet the increasing need of the growing cattle and human population.

The waterlogged land should be developed for fisheries cultivation. Pond should be constructed in the waterlogged land in which fisheries culture may be developed and the bunds of the ponds should be utilized for horticultrual and social forestry plantation with the view to restore the ecological imbalances of the area.

Gram Banjar Bhoomi Vikas Yojana, linking with NAREGA (National Rural Employment Gaurantee Act) and allotment of the wastelands on *Patta* and *Tree Patta* basis to the landless agricultural labourers should be promoted and implemented with the involvement of village Panchayat and representatives of the local village Panchayat for successful implementation of the reclamation of wastelands for the Agriculture - Horticulture - Forestry - Fisheries programmes at village level. Greening of Gram Yojana should also be initiated at village level with the involvement of village Panchayat.

Compensatory Fund for Afforestation (COMPA) for diversion of forest land for non-forest use should be developed not only at the state level but at District - Block - Village level to control the deforestation and use of forest land for non-forest purpose and compensate the deforestation through regeneration of the forest cover.

Panchayat Van Yojana should be launched at village level and intensification of agro-afforestation management on wastelands at village level should be propogated and implemented with the involvement of village beneficiaries for ecological restoration and eco-development at village level. Strategies should be formulated to check the indiscriminate deforestation and diversion of forest land for non-forest use and restriction on removal of fuelwood as head loads and availability of the alternate fuels.

Education, training for agro-afforestation management on wastelands for villagers and interested needy beneficiaries should be organised to meet the increasing demand for fuel-wood, fodder, fibre, fruits, fisheries and foodgrains (F^6), growing cattle and human population for restoration of ecological imbalances and regeneration of degraded lands and improving the environmental crisis and improving the socio-economic crisis of the villages for integrated development of the deprived rural multitudes.

9

Conclusions

Introduction

Population growth in India and the growing demand of fuel-wood, fodder, fibre, fruits, fisheries and foodgrains (F^6) has led towards ecological imbalances of the area, over exploitation of natural resources has caused environmental degradation and increase in the wastelands area. Our country has lost 50 per cent of our forest cover which has caused ecological and socio-economic crisis. Out of 75 million hectares which are considered to be forest cover area, about 40 million hectares are considered without sufficient forest/tree cover. We have also lost 26 to 52 per cent of our grazing lands. Therefore, the reclamation of wastelands have alluded and we have to bring our country into an ecological balance and we have to develop 33 per cent of our land resources under forest cover while at the moment we have less than 11 per cent forest cover. The wastelands reclamation agencies could not achieve the earmarked target. The Agri - Horti - Afforestation programmes were not implemented as per the requirement, involvement, peoples participation due to which this programme has very poor impact among the society.

The firewood, requirement of our country is more than 130 million tonnes per year of which only 39 million tonnes are fetched from the forest. We are authorised to utilize the left out natural resources from our ancestors but not snatching the happiness sources of our future generations.

The justified development should be done through maintaining ecological balances of the area to meet the common minimum needs of the people viz. foodgrain, fodder, fuelwood, fibre, fruits and fisheries (f^6). The natural resources are limited and it should be exploited in an appropriate system. The environmental and ecological, socio-economic crisis emerged on account of excessive exploitation of natural land resources leading towards growth of wastelands area.

It is planned to analyse the problems of wastelands at Village level and Block level and the factors responsible for development of wastelands. Analysis of policies/planning for Agro-Afforestation management on wastelands, reclamation of wastelands, agro-afforestation management on wastelands and it cost-benefit analysis and suggesting suitable strategies for the reclamation of wastelands for agro-afforestation management socio-economic crisis of the area. Inter-relationship with different types of wastelands and natural and human factors show a varying trends which is being analysed in this study. The study is based on various sources of data including direct field survey and field work action programmes in five villages viz. Loniapur, Parsanwa, Benipur, Loniapur and Bhaganpur for practical demonstration in the farmers field for reclamation of wastelands for agro-afforestation management to meet the increasing demand of growing cattle and human population.

In ancient times the headquarters town was known as Kasupura or Kushbhawanpur after the name of its founder Kusha, son of Rama. The town was held by Bhars till the end of thirteenth century when two horse dealers Saiyid Muhammad and Saiyid Ala-ud-Din offered some horses for sale to the chief of Bhars, whose seized the horses and killed the both brothers news of which prompted Ala-ud-Din Khilji to punish the Bhars himself. He attacked the Bhars and powered them. After about one year's unsuccessful seize the old town of Kushbhawanpur was reduced to ashes and a new town called Sultanpur came upto existence which was named from the rank of victor or Sultan.

Geologically the District does not reveal anything striking except the ordinary Gangetic alluvium. The Kankar is only the mineral found along the bed of Gomati River. It lies upto a depth of one meter. Reh and Multani Mitti is also found in some parts of the District. Older alluvium and saline and saline alkali soils are found in the area.

Agro-climatic conditions of the District Sultanpur is appropriate for agro-afforestation programmes.

Sitakund on the bank of river Gomati in Sultanpur city is known for religious importance Dhopap situated in Kadipur Tehsil where Ram Chandra obtained absolution for the sin of killing the demon king Ravana and Vijethua Muhaviran temple located in Kadipur etc, are the religiously important places in District Sultanpur.

Thus the District Sultanpur is full of natural and human resources. Appropriate exploitation of these resources will be helpful in restoring the ecological imbalances and socio-economic crisis of the District.

Keeping the above facts into consideration an attempt is being made to analyse the problems of wastelands at village and Block level in District Sultanpur and factors in wastelands development, policies and planning of agro-afforestation, Agro-afforested area and reclamation of wastelands for agro-afforestation management and strategies for the agro-afforestation management on wastelands to restore the environmental and ecological degradation and to improve the socio-economic crisis and to meet the increasing demand of growing cattle and human population for fuelwood, fodder, fibre, fruits, fisheries, and foodgrains (F^6) for the deprived down trodden people of Amethi Block, Sultanpur District.

The symbiotic relationship between man and nature is continued from immemorial time. In the past man and nature relationship has been shattered causing incalculable damage to nature which has caused hardship to man. This trend must be stopped. The remedial measures and effective strategies for restoration of degraded lands must be searched. The problem of wastelands has been appropriately documented. There has been alarming challenge for loss of our agricultural land which is 175 million hectares and 40 million hectares of forest land which is degraded forest land. Thus our country is loosing 1.5 million hectares of forest land and about 12000 million tonnes of top soil is eroded every year. The rural poor depends on the forest resources.

Problems of Wastelands

Thus the problems of wastelands and its reclamation should be taken a challenge to meet the increasing demand of growing cattle and human population in the form of fuel-wood, fodder, fibre, fruits, fisheries, and foodgrains, etc. with the view to restore ecological and environmental degradation and to improve the socio-economic crisis of the area.

The wastelands are those lands which are uncultivable or is presently lying unutilized due to different constraints but it had been used previously, which is giving very low actual return, i.e. it has low economic potential and it is ecologically unstable or whose top soil has completely lost it's fertility status, which has developed toxicity and is therefore unfit for the growth of crops and trees due to environmental or anthropogenic problems, has been advanced and no further use has been found for it.

The classification of wastelands have been derived from land use categories taking culturable waste and fallow land. The culturable wasteland have been sub-divided into — waterlogged, usar, banjar, kankarili, ravine and other types of wastelands while fallow land other than the current fallow has been sub-divided into old fallow land and fallow land excluding current fallow land. These eight categories of wastelands are available in Sultanpur District. While only six categories of wastelands viz. — waterlogged land, usar land, banjar land, old fallow land, fallow land and other types of wastelands are found in Amethi Block of Sultanpur District.

Wastelands are significantly distributed in Sultanpur District. There are 10,3608 hectares of wastelands in Sultanpur District. The fallow lands are found comparatively very high covering 41,044 hectares land followed by old fallow land having 19,089 hectares land and usar land 14,601 hectares land. The waterlogged land is found in 11,291 hectares area and banjar land in 9,594 hectares area. Similarily significant area under ravine land along with the Gomati River is found which spread in 5,310 hectares area and the miscellaneous other types of wastelands are found in 1,925 hectares land while very low area covering 748 hectares Kankarili land is observed in Sultanpur District.

Proportionately the wastelands are very significantly distributed in Amethi Block at village level. There are 11.36 per cent total wastelands found in Amethi Block. Comparatively, fallow land area is very high which is 3.87 per cent to the total area of the block. The old fallow land is found in 2.56 per cent area while usar land is observed in 1.89 per cent area. The other types of wastelands in Amethi Block are recorded 0.35 per cent and waterlogged land covering 0.47 per cent area in Amethi Block of District Sultanpur.

At village level waterlogged land is found very high in Chaturbhujpur, Dehra and Ramdaipur villages while very low waterlogged lands is observed in Kherauna, Parsanwa, Kushi Tali, villages of Amethi Block.

The usar lands are comparatively very high more than 3 per cent in Bhusahari and Umapurganapatti, Trilokpur, and Sarai Khema villages while very low percentage less than 1.0 per cent usar land is observed in Kherauna, Parsanwa,

Hathkila, Loniapur, Katara Maharani, Kushitali, Naraini, Saraiya Duban and Himmatgarh villages of Amethi Block of District Sultanpur.

Banjar lands are significantly distributed in Amethi at village level. Very high percentage of banjar land more than 4 per cent is found in Loniapur, Raipur Fulwari, villages while very low percentage of banjar land less than two per cent is observed in Goderi, Bhusahari, Ramgarh, Himmatgarh, Agahar, Maharajpur, Saraiya Duban, Loharta, Katara Maharani, Sarai Khema and Kherauna villages of Amethi Block.

Proportionately more than 5 per cent old fallow land is seen in Hathkilla village and very low percentage old fallow land less than one per cent is observed in Kherauna, Katarafulkunwar villages of Amethi Block.

Comparatively very high percentage more than 5 per cent of fallow land is seen in Hathkilla Sarai Khema, villagers of Amethi Block while very low percentage less than 5 per cent fallow land is observed in Parsanwa, Benipur, Ramdaipur, Trilokpur, Loharta, Mochwa, Kakwa, Mahmodpur villages of Amethi Block of Sultanpur District.

Other types of wastelands are found very high more than 5 per cent in Kherauna, Parsanwa, Benipur, Katara Fulkunwar, villages while very low less than 2 per cent. Other types of wastelands are seen in Sarai Khema, Trilokpur, Tala, Loharta, Saraiya Duban and Himmatgarh villages of Amethi Block.

The total wastelands are very significantly distributed in Amethi Block. Very high percentage of wastelands more than 15 per cent is seen in Dedhpasar village followed by Hathkilla (14.32 per cent), Loniapur (14.75 per cent) villages while very low percentage of wastelands less than 8 per cent are recorded in Kushi Tali, Loharta, Korarigirdharshah, Nuanwa, Kakwa, Saidpur, Purabgaon, Ramgarh, Himmatgarh, and Goderi villages of Amethi Block of Sultanpur District.

Thus it is observed that the wastelands are significantly distributed at village level not only in Amethi Block but Sultanpur District as whole which has become a challenging problem to the planners and developmental agencies engaged at Sultanpur.

It has been recorded during the field survey and action field work programme that the wastelands of Sultanpur and Amethi Block has been left out of cultivation of very smaller reasons and ignorance of the cultivators. Such wastelands can be easily reclaimed adopting latest scientific and technical methods and applying C-2 scientific technology i.e., the scientific system available within the village or household itself. The adoption of scientific cropping system/pattern, proper ploughing techniques, appropriate doses of organic and inorganic amendments in the form of fertilizer and application of insecticides and pesticides, appropriate high yielding variety of seeds and plants, proper management system including irrigation and post harvest technology will be helpful in bringing out the wastelands under proper use to grow—fuelwood, fodder, fibre, fruits, fisheries, and food grains to meet the increasing demand of growing cattle and-human population on the one hand and restoring the ecological and environmental degradation and imbalances of the area and improving socio-economic crisis of the people's of Amethi in Sultanpur District of Uttar Pradesh.

Factors in Wastelands

The relationship between man and nature is symbiotic. The combination of human and natural factors plays an important role in the spatial distribution of wastelands and its various categories. The correlation matrix and stepwise regression analysis statistically proves that slope and drainage density are the dominant variables in explaining the variations in wastelogged land at village level in Amethi. The main important variables in explaining the proportionate distribution of usar land are the pH value of the soil and scheduled caste population variable in explaining the distribution of banjar land are the pH value of the soil, followed by scheduled caste population. The pH value of the soil, followed by the scheduled caste population and land concentration are the major dominant variables in explaining the variations of old fallow land at village level in Amethi Block. The pH value of the soil and drainage density are the main dominant variables in explaining the proportionate distribution of fallow land at village level in Amethi. The land concentration is one of the main dominant variable followed by the scheduled caste population and pH value of the soil in explaining the distribution of other types of wastelands.

The main dominant variables in explaining the proportionate distribution of wastelands at village level in Amethi Block are the pH value of the soil, land concentration, scheduled caste population and behaviour of water table. Thus the variables which features dominating in explaining the variations in wastelands are the natural factors which are pH value of the soil drainage density, behaviour of the water table and human factors which comprises mainly the land concentration and scheduled caste population. Thus, lastly it can be said that the natural and human factors including some of the other variables directly or indirectly responsible for the proportionate distribution of wastelands at village level in Amethi Block, District Sultanpur.

Agro-Afforestation

The land degradation and deforestation has caused severe ecological, environmental crisis and socio-economic backwardness. The symbiotic relationship between man and nature has been realized because the poor depends on the forest. The scheduled caste communities totally depends on the minor forest produce, to grass and fallen drywood for fuelwood. The relationship between man and nature has been threatened. Agro-afforestation efforts, an endeavour, is rendered is more difficult since the needs of the community are at a variance with each other and it cannot be reclaimed unless poverty amelioration programmes raise the level of living of those who are surviving below poverty line. The agro-afforestation programme must be initiated as a peoples movement.

Agro-afforestation is a system of land use along with the combined growing of agricultural crops with social forestry, horticulture, animal husbandary including vegetables fuel-wood, fodder, fibre, fruits, fisheries, and foodgrains, etc. to fulfil the increasing demand of growing cattle and human population.

There is tremendous pressure of the human population which has led to deforestation and land degradation. The stablization of population and participatory management for the reclamation of wastelands and agro-afforestation management for sustainable development.

The Forest Survey of India, Dehradun indicated in its report that there are 5.86 per cent forest land in Uttar Pradesh. Various programmes has been launched by the government to ensure successful afforestation programmes. There are 1297 sq. km. highly dense forest land out of which 210 sq. km. highly dense forest is found in Shrawasti District followed by 144 sq. km. in Balrampur District. There are 4, 699 sq. km. dense forest in Uttar Pradesh out of which 846 sq. km. dense forest is recorded in Sonbhadra District followed by 502 sq. km. in Kheri, 346 sq. km. in Chitrakoot and 316 sq. km. dense forest is found in Mirzapur District of Uttar Pradesh. There are 8,122 sq. km. open forest in Uttar Pradesh out of which 1,606 sq. km. open forest is found in Sonbhadra District followed by Kheri - 446 sq. km., Shrawasti 347 sq. km., Chandauli 327 sq. km. open forest area. The forest land is found more along with the foodsteps of Himalayas and Vindhayan range and the Chambal and Gomati rivers.

Thus, in Uttar Pradesh, there are 14,118 sq. km. forest area which is 5.86 per cent to the total geographical area of the state which is very insignificant in comparison to the 33 per cent forest land earmarked by the government. Very high afforested area is found in Sonbhadra District 2,469 sq. km. followed by Kheri - 1314 sq. km. forest land and Shrawasti District - 811 sq. km., Mirzapur- 782 sq. km., Pilibhit - 697 sq. km., Balrampur - 532 sq. km., Bijnore - 423 sq. km., Chandauli - 519 sq. km., and Chitrakoot - 554 sq. km., forest area. It has been recorded that during 1977, there was 4.46 per cent forest land and during 2003 there has been 5.86 per cent forest area in Uttar Pradesh having 1.398 per cent growth in the forest land from 1977 to 2003, which is insignificant against 33 per cent forest land earmarked by the National Forest Policy and Uttar Pradesh State Forest Policy. The land degradation and deforestation is a great challenge to the planners and programme implementing institutions.

The agro-afforestation programmes in Sultanpur is not appropriately planned and properly implemented by the implementing agencies, because it requires joint endeavour and efforts of Agriculture - Horticulture - Social - Forestry and Fisheries departments of the District Sultanpur with the involvement of farmers.

The agriculture is the main occupation of the people of Amethi and Sultanpur. The area under cultivation is 73.86 per cent in Sultanpur followed by 0.44 per cent forest area.

The agriculture department has expended Rs. 6.68 lakh for high yielding variety seeds, fertilizer, agricultural implements, irrigation pipes, insecticides and pesticides and field demonstrations. Latest developed agricultural implements, agricultural cropping, etc. are practically demonstrated in the farmers field. Inspite of the above 4619.20 mt. tonnes seed and 5432.25 mt. tonnes fertilizer has been distributed among the farmers and a sum of Rs. 2,873.35 lakhs cropping loan and 59,340 farmers credit cards has been also provided to the farmers. It has been observed that about 25 to 30 per cent loss in the agricultural production is due to the insecticides starting from cultivation–cropping – crop harvesting and storage of the grain. Appropriate application of insecticides and pesticides can reduce the loss in agricultural production.

Sultanpur district has 65.8 per cent net sown area. Proportionately high percentage more than 70 per cent net sown area is found in Baldirai Block and Lambhua Block of the District Sultanpur while very low percentage 55.1 per cent net sown area to the total area is found in Bhadar Block of the District Sultanpur.

Horticultural cropping system has been strengthened in Sultanpur district covering 1000 hectares land under horticultural plantation. Intensive potato cultivation has been ensured in 5,107 hectares land and 305 quintals potato seed has been distributed and hightech potato cultivation has been demonstrated in 520 hectares farmers land. Vegetable development programmes are being launched in 26,500 hectares farmers land providing 52.42 quintals seeds distributed and in the 1800 hectares land horticultural techniques has been demonstrated in the farmers field. Horticultural nurseries has been established through developing 6640 grafted nurseries plants at Kadipur and 34640 grafted plants seedlings and about 10,000 grafted plants and 32000 seedlings nurseries plants has been developed at Bhadar nursery. There are 1.67 per cent horticultural land in Sultanpur District. Very high percentage 6.29 per cent horticultural land is found in Sangrampur Block and 3.41 per cent horticultural area is seen in Amethi Block of the District Sultanpur.

The afforested land in District Sultanpur is 3.97 per cent to the total area. Very high percentage 4.62 per cent forest land is found in Shukul Bazar Block followed by Musafirkhana having 2.43 per cent forest land and Pratappur Kamaicha 1.33 per cent forest land to the total area of the Block. While Amethi Block is having only 0.05 per cent forest area to the total area of the Block which is very insignificant.

Social Forestry Division Sultanpur planted 2.53 lakhs plants covering 118.50 hectares land, and 261.0 hectares land belonging to Gram Panchayat. There are 13 nurseries established in Sultanpur while one nursery at Amethi has also been established. In Amethi Block 8000 plants has been planted covering 5.0 hectares land and 9.03 lakhs plants has been planted covering 593.55 hectares land during 1996-98, in Sultanpur District.

Bhoomi Sanrakshan Adhikari (BSA) planted 70,875 plants covering 1055.50 hectares land.

District Horticulture Officer planted 9115 plants covering 100 hectares land in Sultanpur while 1200 plants has been planted in 12.0 hectares land. Indian Farm and Forestry Development Corporation (IFFDC) planted 19.13 lakh plants covering 1450.03 hectares land in Sultanpur District while Uttar Pradesh Land Development Corporation planted 59509 plants covering 95.22 hectares land. Thus in Sultanpur District 290.56 lakh plants has been planted and 9200 plants has been planted covering 17.0 hectares land in Amethi Block.

The major part of the Sultanpur District was covered with the Dhak, thorny bushes. A large dense forest tract extended in an unbroken strength near Ram Nagar in Tehsil Amethi. The jungles area under Gram Sabha is about 3847 hectares and 1600 hectares forest land is controlled by the Forest Department. While 325 hectares forest land is found in the Tehsil Amethi.

The main species of trees found in the jungles are Dhak, Shisham, Neem, Babool, Bel, Pipal, Bargad, Goolar, Pakar and Mahua. Among the species which has been introduced recently are Mango, Khair, Safed Siris, Kala Siris, Kachnar, Amaltas, Jamun, Sagaun, Semal, Arjun, Bahera, Zezyphus forest departments along the roadsides in the Sultanpur District.

The fish are found in the rivers, lakes, ponds, canals, and artificial reservoirs of the District Sultanpur. The main species of the fish found in the district are bata, rohu, karuanch, singhi, nain, raia, bhakur and belgagra. The fish culture is scientifically and technically promoted and demonstrated in Sultanpur District under various schemes launched by the Fisheries Development Agency, Sultanpur.

The flora and fauna and wildlife in Sultanpur District has greatly decreased in number, which are unimportant in the area.

The ecosystem of the area has been degraded which has led to ecological, environmental crisis and socio-economic backwardness of the area.

Thus, agro-afforestation programmes in Sultanpur District and in Amethi Block has not been properly planned and appropriately implemented because it requires joint venture and efforts of the implementing agencies like — Agriculture - Horticulture - Social - Forestry - and Fisheries and wth the participation, involvement of the local peoples. The agro-afforestation programmes should be implemented for the people, by the people and demonstrated in the farmers field in an integrated manner adopting latest development and innovated scientific techniques.

Policy, Planning for Agro-Afforestation Management on Wastelands

The land degradation and wastelands is caused both by poverty and mismanagement. The degradation cycle of common natural land resources proceeds from hacking, excessive grazing, overcropping, mismanagement, application of high doses of fertilizers, unscientific irrigational practices, cultivation in sub-marginal lands as well as natural calamities all leading to land degradation. The excessive revenue generated through unplanned unscientific cutting of forest, the greater destruction of the forest area, must be stopped. The problem of wastelands is mostly man-made and causes misery to the millions of the deprived rural poor.

The problem of wastelands is not a new one, it has a

long history starting from Apeman to historical invadors, the wastelands has been formed. Emperor Ashoka used the term wastelands as neglected land, while Mughal emperor and Akbar the Great fixed the value of land in *Annas* for revenue collection from Taluqdars. Britishers continued the same practice and no land revenue was charged for the wastelands.

It is observed that wastelands development is the triangular interaction process between man- nature and technology.

After post-independence, Article 48A of the Constitution of India enunciates, "The State shall endeavour to protect and improve the environment to safeguard the forest and wildlife of the country."

National Bureau of Soil Survey and Land Use Planning and All India Soil and Landuse Survey has been engaged in the collection and analysis of the data on wastelands.

National Commission on Agriculture also surveyed the land degradation information. On January 5, 1985 National Wastelands Development Board was established for the reclamation of wastelands. National Level Wastelands Development Mission was launched on 5th October 1989 having 6 Mini Missions, viz. Policy Planning, People's Participation, Technology Extension, Restoration of the Degraded Forests, Greening of the common land and farm forestry. Wasteland development has been also included in the 20-point economic programme. Department of Wastelands Development was established in the Government of India.

In the State of Uttar Pradesh, high level power committee was headed by the Agriculture Production Commissionor of Uttar Pradesh. Later on Department of Wastelands Development was established in the Government of Uttar Pradesh. In the pattern of National Soil Conservation and Landuse Board, Government of India, in the Uttar Pradesh State Landuse Board, is also functional in the Department of Planning, Government of Uttar Pradesh.

The District Land Use Board is also functional at District

level, Bhomi Sanrakshan Adhikari, and Uttar Pradesh Land Development Corporation and Social Forestry Departments are engaged in the restoration of degraded land and reclamation of wastelands.

The Constitution of India lays down provision for environment conservation. The Constitution under article 51 (g) states that "it shall be the duty of every citizen of India to protect and improve the natural environment including forests, lakes, rivers and wildlife to have a compassion for living creatures."

National Forest Policy 1988 and National Conservation Strategy and Policy Statement on Environment 1982 has been formed to protect the environment and conserve the natural resources. National Forest Policy was formed in 1988, while National Environment Protection Act 1986 was also formed, to protect the environment. The National Conservation Strategy and Policy Statement on Environment and Development comprises with strategies for action and policies and systems for conservation and development of environment.

Forest Resource Management and Forestry Development policies includes the main factors for ensuring conservation and sustainable development are use of environment friendly products and processes, low waste generating techniques and proper economic policy and fiscal incentives and disincentives. Raising of the forest cover and conservation of existing forests which are essential life support system and an important source of fuelwood, fodder, fruits, food-grains, fibre, fisheries, etc., a concerted efforts must be initiated.

Compensatory Fund for Afforestation Programme (COMPA) has been developed for deforestation and diversion of forest land for non-forest use.

Integrated Forest Protection Scheme and Intensification of Forest Management has been also launched. National Afforestation and Eco-Development Board has been established in the Ministry of Environment and Forest, Government of India with the objective of National Afforestation Scheme, Greening India and National Action Programme to combat desertification to increase 33 per cent forest cover by 2012, which can be achieved with proper co-ordination and co-operation of the State — District — Tehsil — Block — Village level administrative authorities and sustained involvement of the grassroot level workers, the proposed earmarked target may be achieved and *Panchayat Van Yojana* must be strengthened at grassroot level.

Planning for the reclamation of wastelands is a process of observation, appraisal, analysis with regard to problems, constraints and compatible cause for reclamation of wastelands. The reclamation of wastelands for sustainable development needs a long-term planning for systematic, logical, scientific technological and analytical action plan including identification of wastelands, classification of wastelands and survey and mapping of wastelands, capability classification of wastelands, soil testing, levelling and bunding, cleaning, leaching and flushing, tilling and deep ploughing, drainage system, irrigation system, inorganic amendments, cultivation, greening of wastelands, allotment of wastelands, co-operatives of wasteland developing beneficiaries, peoples movement, extension programmes, policies for reclamation of wastelands and agro-afforestation has been implemented in Parsanwa, Benipur, Loniapur,, Mahmodpur, and Bhaganpur villages for Social Forestry, Forestry-Horti-Agriculture, Agri- Horti-Forestry, Agri- Horticulture and Fisheries-Forestry managements respectively.

Planning for agro-afforestation management has been formulated taking one unit of wastelands in selected five villages of Amethi Block.

Planning of Social Forestry-Horticulture has been formulated and the reclamation of usar land has been implemented in village - *Benipur* of Amethi Block. The reclamation of usar land and land preparation, developing nursery and plantation of suitable social- forestry and horticultural plants has been planted on the reclaimed usar land with the involvement of local village level beneficiaries to meet the increasing demand of growing population for fuelwood, fodder, fruits, etc.

Forestry - Horticulture - Agriculture management planning and reclamation of banjar land has been done in the village Loniapur of Amethi Block of District Sultanpur. The Forestry - Horticulture - Agriculture plantation and cropping has been carried out on the reclaimed banjar land with the involvement of village level beneficiaries to grow fuelwood, fodder, fibre, fruits and foodgrains to meet the increasing demand of growing cattle and human population.

Planning for Horticulture - Agriculture - Forestry management has been implemented in the reclaimed old fallow land in village Mahmodpur of Amethi Block with adequate attention to ecological, and environmental aspects and dynamics of energy flow includes multi-cropping and optimum utilization available natural land resources.

The appropriate planning for Agriculture - Horticulture-Forestry management programme has been implemented on the reclaimed fallow land in village - *Parsanwa* of Amethi Block, for optimum utilization of available natural and human resources, with the view to restore ecological and land degradation and improve socio-economic crisis and to meet the increasing demand of growing cattle and human population.

Planning for the reclamation of waterlogged land has been implemented in village - Bhaganpur of Amethi Block. The waterlogged land has been reclaimed through construction of pond for fisheries cultivation along with horticultural and afforestation programme on the bund and banks of the pond for optimum utilization of waterlogged land to regenerate the bio-mass and improve ecological imbalances of the area.

Thus the planning for reclamation of usar land in Benipur village, Banjar land in Loniapur, old fallow land in Mahmodpur village, fallow land in Parsanwa village and waterlogged land in Bhaganpur villages has been implemented with the involvement of rural poor beneficiaries. The reclamation of various wastelands for Agro-Horti - Forestry - fisheries has been implemented with the view to obtain — fuelwood, fodder, fibre, fruits, foodgrains, fisheries (F^6) to restore the degradation of land and wastelands development to meet the increasing demand of growing cattle and human population to check and control the ecological environmental degradation and improve ecological and socio-economic crisis of the area.

The nation is loosing 1.5 million hectares of forest and 12000 million tonnes of top soil every year due to deforestation and run-off.

The nation's fuelwood requirement is about 130 million tonnes every year of which we are fetching about 50 million tonnes of firewood from the forest. The balance of 80 million tonnes has yet to be generated.

The problem of wastelands is mostly man-made and causes misery to millions of the rural poor. The reclamation of wastelands must be adopted as a strategy for the extension of net sown area according to its suitability to increase the overall agricultural production through agricultural cropping and horticultural and afforestation programmes, predominantly to fetch the fuelwood, fodder, fibre, fruits, fisheries, and foodgrains for the integrated development of the deprived rural poor.

Reclamation of Wastelands

The reclamation capability classification of wastelands has been made, based on the fertility status of the soil, potentialities and limitations, their capability of producing agricultural crops and horticultural and afforestation plantations. It has been observed that the fallow land (1-2 years) are very easily reclaimable for agricultural-horticultural and afforestation programmes. The old fallow land (2-5 years) are easily reclaimable for agricultural-horticultural and forestry plantations. The banjar land which has been left out of cultivation from more than five years are reclaimable with certain difficulty for forestry - horticultural land agricultural cropping system. The usar land is reclaimable with difficulty for forestry and horticultural plantations, while the waterlogged land is reclaimable with moderate difficulty for fisheries, forestry and horticultural plantations.

The eco-sustainability through bio-scientific reclamation of various types of wastelands for Agri-Horti-Afforestation programme for income and employment generation. The Agri-Horti-Afforestation programme is technically and economically viable, scientifically, suitable and socially acceptable, because it will fulfil the increasing demand of the growing cattle and human population.

The reclamation of usar land for social-forestry-horticultural programmes has been demonstrated in the one Bigha of usar land in village Benipur of the Amethi Block. Various reclamation measures such as levelling, bunding, soil testing, application of organic and inorganic, appropriate arrangement of irrigation system leaching and flushing of the top soil and deep ploughing and breaking of the Kankar pan, etc. has been the important task which has been adopted for the reclamation of usar land. Nursery for various social-forestry and horticultural plants and adoption of the tissue culture based techniques has been ensured. Various social forestry plants viz. *Prosopis cineraria, Prosopis Juliflora, Azadirachta Indica, Leucaena Leucocephala* (*Subabool*), *Jetropha, Eucalyptus Tereticornis, Tamrix Indica, Albizia Procera, Pongamia Pinnata* and *Amla, Ber, Karonda, Guvava,* etc. horticultural plants has been planted. Post-harvest technology and follow up action of the reclaimed land has also been practically demonstrated to deprived rural poor beneficiaries.

The reclamation of banjar land has been demonstrated in the village — Loniapur, where 3.27 per cent banjar land has been observed. The reclamation of banjar land in the village Loniapur has been initiated through levelling, bunding, deep ploughing, top dressing of fertilizer, irrigation management, mechanical processing, organic and inorganic amendments and micro-organism based bio-fertilizers and bio-pesticides. Nursery raising various horticultural and social-forestry plants has been implemented. The plantation of various social-forestry and horticultural plants has been planted and agricultural cropping of Sanai/Dhainch for fibre and green mannuring and Barley, urad, mung, etc. has been cropped in the reclaimed banjar land. The bio-scientific management of multi, intercropping on the reclaimed land has also been demonstrated. Proper scientific demonstration of harvesting techniques and recycling of the crop waste for bio-fertilizers has been implemented with the involvement of deprived rural poor beneficiaries. Proper distribution of benefits accrued has been ensured among the involved village beneficiaries. Demonstration of post-harvest technology and proper follow up action has been ensured.

The reclamation of old fallow land which is left out of cultivation from 2–5 years due to some reason or the other has been taken up in the village - Mahmodpur of the Amethi Block. The agricultural cropping quality of the land based on the fertility status of the soil has been analysed.

The land develoment of the old fallow land has been ensured through levelling, bunding, deep ploughing, top dressing of fertilizer, irrigation system, leaching and flushing of the top soil, mechanical processing, green mannuring, organic and inorganic amendments and bio-fertilizer/NPK and micro-organism based bio-fertilizers and bio-pesticides. Land preparation for the nursery raising, irrigation management, mixing of the soil, sand, bio-fertilizers and filling in the polythene bags and seedling of hybrid quality seeds.

Digging of pits, mixing of the soil with organic and

inorganic amendments and filling in the digged pits. Trench making and bio-fencing, hedge plantation on med-bund has been implemented. Various fuelwood, fodder, fibre, fruits plantations has been done and agricultural cropping for paddy, wheat, barley, Mung, Sanai/Dhaincha has been ensured. Inside the land multi-inter-cropping techniques has been adopted. Post-harvest technology and follow up action has been practically demonstrated to its involved beneficiaries.

The reclamation of fallow land, which is left out of cultivation from 1-2 years, for Agri-Horti-Afforestation programmes has been implemented in the village - Parsanwa of the Amethi Block in Sultanpur District. Levelliing, bunding, deep ploughing, irrigation management green mannuring, organic and inorganic amendments, application of micro-organism based on bio-fertilizer and use of insecticides and pesticides has been done for the reclamation of fallow land. Nursery has been developed, irrigation management of nursery plants, mixing of soil, sand, bio-fertilizers and filling in the polythene bags, seedling of the hybrid variety of horticultural and social forestry plants. Arrangements of tissue culture raised horticultural and social-forestry plants and maintenance and management of nursery plants.

The plantation of various horticultural and social forestry plants in the digged pits along with organic and inorganic amendments. Demonstration of agricultural cropping for wheat, paddy, barley, mung, urad and Sanai/Dhaincha, for green mannuring and fibre requirements. Demonstration of bio-scientific plantation techniques on multi-inter-cropping system. Practical demonstration of post-harvest technology and follow up action of the agricultural cropping system and horticultural and social-forestry plantation and distribution of the benefits accrued from it among the involved village beneficiaries.

The reclamation of waterlogged land for fisheries and afforestation has been implemented in village - Bhaganpur of Amethi Block. The land development and construction of pond has been implemented testing of soil and underground water has been done. Nursery raising for horticultural and social forestry plants has been ensured adopting various techniques for nursery raising. The constructed pond has been developed for fisheries and banks of the pond has been utilized for horticultural and social-forestry plantations. Fisheries hatchury has been developed and various types of fish like Rohu, Bhakur, Nain, Karmal Corp, Silver Corp, Grass Corp, etc. has been developed. Requisite scientfic and technological inputs has been applied for the successful development of fisheries programme along with horticultural and afforestation on the banks of the pond. Proper follow up action has also been demonstrated to the involved rural poor village beneficiaries.

Thus the reclamation of various types of wastelands viz. usar land, banjar land, old fallow land, fallow land and waterlogged land has been practically implemented in the Benipur, Loniapur, Mahmodpur, Parsanwa, and Bhaganpur villages of Amethi Block respectively. The Agri-Horti-Afforestation and fisheries cultivation/plantation has been done in the selected villages. It has been observed that the various types of wastelands distributed in the various villages of Amethi Block can be reclaimed with proper scientific and technological inputs. The reclamation of wastelands has been an asset in restoring the degraded land to produce fuelwood, fodder, fibre, wood, fruits, fisheries and foodgrains to meet the increasing demand of growing cattle and human population. The reclamation of wastelands is also an asset in checking and controlling the environmental and ecological crisis and improving the socio-economic crisis of the deprived rural poor villagers of the Amethi.

Economics of Wastelands Reclamation for Agro-Afforestation Management

The restoration of ecological and land degradation is the need of the hour for deprived rural poor because the explosive population growth tremendous deforestation, ecological and environmental degradation has brought us face to face for the scarcity of fuelwood, fodder, fibre, frutis, foodgrains, fisheries, vegetables and wood for the day-to-day requirements of the common people. The over-exploitation and excessive cultivation, high doses of fertilizer, canal irrigation are one of the basic reasons for the growth of wastelands. Such wastelands and degraded cultivated lands has not been within the reach of the common farmers.

The adoption of various reclamation measures for wastelands as accentuate soil erosion is not desirable for the long-term point of view. In view of the above constraints, it is essential that pros and cons of wastelands reclamation are made amply clear to the farmers, so that they can adopt most appropriate remedial measures in the initial stages of reclamation tenure, subsequently, the cultivators will be able to derive considerable benefit from the reclaimed land. The cultivators must be trained, motivated, to adopt various measures for the reclamation of wastelands only by disseminating to them, the information regarding the economic benefits in the form of additional agricultural production, which ultimately paves the way for socio-economic development and restoration of the ecological and environmental crisis of the villagers.

The economics of the reclamation of the different types of wastelands is closely linked to the management aspects. The cost of reclamation of wastelands depends upon the nature and extent of degradation of the wastelands has undergone. The broad criterian has been to reclaim usar land, banjar land, old fallow land, fallow land and the waterlogged land for Agri-Horti-Afforestation-Fisheries cultivation and plantation respectively. The input-output cost analysis for the reclamation of various types of wastelands has been done, after the reclamation of each types of wastelands in the selected villages of Amethi Block. The economics of the reclamation of various types of wastelands has been estimated with the involvement and continued participation of farmers and involved scientific and technical personnel belonging to different implementing agencies engaged in Amethi Block, District Sultanpur.

The most important reclamation measures for the reclamation of usar land with high pH value of the soil has been the land levelling bunding, deep ploughing, appropriate irrigation management, construction of proper drainage, system for inlet and outlet of the water, leaching and flushing of the top sodic soils, breaking of the Kankar pan, and application of organic and inorganic amendments. The quality of the fertilizer, and application of organic and inorganic amendments depends on the requirement of the soil. The cost of the usar land reclamation also varies with the extent of usarization and prevailing cost of commodities and labour.

It has been observed that a sum of Rs. 1,30,300 has been incurred for the usar land reclamation including land preparation, nursery raising, horticultural-afforestation and post-plantation management activities and a sum of Rs. 58,400 has been incurred during the second year of the usar land reclamation process. Thus a total sum of Rs. 18,8,700 has been incurred during the subsequent two years of the usar land reclamation in the one bigha land in village-Benipur of the Amethi Block. It has been noticed that in the initial year of usar land reclamation the input cost was very high which has decreased in the second year but output cost has increased in the next year. It has been recorded that a sum of Rs. 44,500 achieved in the first year while Rs. 61,000 obtain during the second year of plantation while the input cost during the first year was very high but during the second year the input cost has decreased. In the subsequent years also the input cost will decrease and output cost will increase, which indicates that the reclamation of usar land is costly affiar in the initial year but the input cost has decreased and output cost has increased significantly hence it is economically viable and beneficial to reclaim the usar land, to restore the ecological environmental crisis and improving the socio-economic crisis of the villages.

The banjar land reclaimable with certain difficulties has been implemented in the village - Loniapur of the Amethi Block. It has been recorded that a sum of Rs. 92,300 has been incurred for the banjar land development, nursery raising, Afforestation - Horticultural plantation and agricultural cropping and implementation of post harvest techniques during the first year while a sum of Rs. 57,500 has been expended during the first year of the reclamation of banjar land, while Rs. 68,500 has been achieved as output cost from fuelwood, fodder, fibre, and fruits during the first year and Rs. 82,000 has been achieved in the second year of the banjar land reclamation process. It has been noticed that in the first year the benefit was in minus but in the second year it increased and the farmer was benefited with Rs. 24500. Thus during the two subsequent years very nominal benefit has been accrued from the banjar land reclamation.

It has been observed that the reclamation of banjar land for Afforestation-Horticulture- Agricultural cropping was not beneficial during the initial year but in the second year the benefit was increased because in the subsequent year the banjar land reclamation input cost decreases and the output cost has increased simultaneously. Overall the reclamation of banjar land is an economic position because it provides fuelwood, fodder, fibre, fruits and foodgrains to meet the increasing demand of growing cattle and human population and also in improving the ecological and socio-economic crisis of the villages of Amethi.

The old fallow land has been reclaimed in one bigha land of village - Mahmodpur of Amethi Block. The old fallow land has been reclaimed for Agricultural cropping - horticulture and afforestation programmes. It has been recorded that a sum of Rs. 75,600 has been expended for land preparation, nursery raising, Agri-Horti-Afforestation, plantation and agricultural cropping followed by post-harvest technology during the first year of the reclamation of old fallow land and a sum of Rs. 50,000 has been incurred in the second year of the old fallow land reclamation process, while a sum of Rs. 74,000 has been obtained from fuelwood, fodder, fibre, fruits, foodgrains with a negative profit of Rs. 1600 while a sum of Rs. 96,500 achieved as output cost during the second year and there has been net profit of Rs. 46,500 in the second year from the reclaimed old fallow land. It has been recorded that during the subsequent first and second year of old fallow land reclamation a net profit of Rs. 44,900 has been achieved.

The reclamation of old fallow land for Agri-Horti-Afforestation programme in village Mahmodpur of Amethi Block has been economically beneficial to the village beneficiaries and also an asset in improving socio-economic crisis and ecological imbalances of the village.

The reclamation process of fallow land has been implemented in village — Parsanwa of Amethi Block. Agricultural cropping - Horticultural Afforestation activities has been carried out in the reclaimed fallow land. It has been recorded that a sum of Rs. 64,00 has been expended during first year of the reclamation of fallow land reclamation, nursery raising, Agricultural-Horticultural- Afforestation programme and demonstration of post-harvest techniques to the beneficiaries while during the second year a sum of Rs. 42,000 has been incurred out of which a sum of Rs. 69,000 has been achieved as output in the first year and Rs. 88,500 output cost during the second year from the reclaimed fallow land and a total output cost of Rs. 1,57,500 for subsequent two years has been obtained.

It has been observed that a sum of Rs. 4400 has been achieved as net profit during the first year of fallow land reclamation of Rs. 46,500 has been obtained, as a net profit during the second year and a sum of Rs. 50,900 has been achieved as a net profit during the subsequent two years to the reclamation of fallow land in village - Parsanwa of Amethi Block. It has been recorded that the reclamation of fallow land is economically viable in improving the socio-economic crisis of the rural poors and also restoring the ecological crisis of the area.

Reclamation of waterlogged land has been implemented in the village - Bhaganpur of Amethi Block. The waterlogged land reclamation has been initiated mainly through the construction of pond, drainage system, development of the banks of the pond, installation of tubewell and procurement of diesel engine, developing fish hatchury, procurement of fish seeds, arrangement of forestry and horticultural plants and bio-scientific management of fisheries culture and plants etc. for which a sum of Rs. 1,78,000 has been incurred in the first initial year of waterlogged land reclamation, out of which a sum of Rs. 35,000 has been incurred for the construction of pond and installation of tube well and availability of diesel engine Rs. 48,000 has been incurred which are the permanent assets of the beneficiary. Thus a sum of Rs. 83,000 has been incurred as permanent assets expenditure for which no investment is required in the second year and most of the incurred expenses are not required for the subsequent years. It has been observed that a sum of Rs. 63, 500 has been obtained as a output cost from the reclaimed waterlogged land for fisheries and horticultural and social forestry plantation and the output cost will be increased in the subsequent years, the farmers will be able to manage their cost of pond's construction and installed tubewell and diesel engine and the beneficiaries will be able to increase their income from the fisheries cultivation alongwith afforestation and horticultural plantation. It is observed that the waterlogged land reclamation for Fisheries - Horticulture - Afforestation programme is economically viable and beneficial in long-run in improving the ecological crisis and socio-economic crisis of the rural poor beneficiaries.

Thus the reclamation of usar land, banjar land, old fallow

land, fallow land and waterlogged land for Agri- Horti-Afforestation - Fisheries programme has been economically viable and beneficial proposition to village beneficiaries because it has provided fuelwood, fodder, fibre, fruits, food-grains, fish, to the village beneficiaries to meet the increasing demand of growing cattle and human population on the one hand and it has been helpful in restoring the ecological, environmental and land degradation and improving the socio-economic crisis of the deprived rural multitudes of the Amethi, District Sultanpur. The scientific and technical support system and infrastructural availability to the villagers for the reclamation of usar land, banjar land, old fallow land, fallow land, and waterlogged land in the various villages in Amethi Block must be linked with various other programmes being implemented by the line departments will be a milestone in the reclamation of wastelands and restoration of socio-economic and ecological crisis of the villagers of Amethi.

Strategies for Agro-Afforestation Management on Wastelands

The strategies formulation and adoption of various measures for the reclamation of wastelands include the provision of several packages of the most suitable technological and scientific inputs, credit support, building up of a strong social infrastructure and arranging marketing support system. The strategies for the reclamation of wastelands with the involvement of rural poor villagers for agro-afforestation management for appropriate exploitation of natural resources to meet the day-to-day requirements of the common people living in the remote rural villages.

Imaginative strategies for communication with the village beneficiaries should be systematized and extended to grassroot level beneficiaries. Appropriate use of mass media and audio-visual techniques should be made available to motivate the farmers for their enthusiastically in reclamation of wastelands and greening of wastelands. *"Greening of the Wastelands"* with the active involvement of the deprived rural poor people. Peoples participation and involvement is necessary in all operations of the reclamation of wastelands for agro-afforestation management including incentives to the beneficiaries.

Identification of wastelands, classification of wastelands and it's distribution at village level should be analysed i.e., usar land, banjar land, old fallow land, fallow land, waterlogged land and other types of wastelands in the various villages of Amethi has been identified and its distribution has been also analysed.

Various natural and human factors responsible for the growth of wastelands has been explained at village level in Amethi Block of the District Sultanpur.

The genesis of the wastelands and the various determinants responsible for the growth and formation of wastelands has been explained. The genesis of wastelands has been classified into three categories viz., marginally degraded land, partially degraded land and severely degraded lands. The suitable strategies should be worked out for various types of wastelands based on genesis and formation of wastelands.

The capability classification of wastelands as per suitability of the soil to produce the crops has been analysed and strategies must be adopted to be analysed the capability classification of wastelands based on the reclamation capability of the wastelands.

Testing of the soil, land preparation, levelling and bunding, leaching and flushing, green mannuring, organic and inorganic amendments, appropriate irrigation management, bio-scientific management, etc. should be adopted for the reclamation of wastelands.

Action oriented planning within a specification frame should be adopted for reclamation of wastelands. Stepwise proper planning for the reclamation of wastelands starting from land preparation, soil testing, irrigation management, organic and inorganic amendments as per requirement of the soil for agricultural cropping and horticultural - afforestation programmes should be formulated and demonstrated to the needy poor beneficiaries of the villages.

Extension programmes for the reclamation of wastelands for agriculture-horticulture-forestry-fisheries programmes should be practically demonstrated to the deprived resources poor beneficiaries.

Strategies for nursery raising including land preparation, polythene bag filling with mixed sand, soil, fertilizer, and seedlings, and irrigation management and maintenance and management of nursery should be appropriately demonstrated to the village beneficiaries.

Agricultural cropping for the Kharif, Rabi, Jaid cropping seasons especially paddy, wheat, barley, mung and urad and Sanai/Dhainch, etc. should be properly demonstrated on the reclaimed wastelands and agricultural cropping should be planned as capability classification of wastelands and fertility status of the soil.

Strategies for horticultural plantations including — Amla, Papaya, Ber, Mango, Guvava, Karonda, Lemon, Banana, etc., should be demonstrated on the reclaimed wastelands along with the leguminous trees besides being salt tolerant which helps in the fixation of nitrogen of the soil. The multi-inter-cropping along with horticultural plantations must be propogated at village level.

Afforestation strategies on the various types of reclaimed wastelands including plantation of *Prosopis cineraria, Prosopis Juliflora, Azadirachta Indica, Tamrix Indica, Albizia Procera, Pongamia Pinnata, Eucalyptus tereticornis, Shisham, Sagaun, Leucaena Leucacephala* plants should be planted to produce fuelwood, fodder, fibre, to meet the increasing need of the growing cattle and human population.

The waterlogged land should be developed for fisheries

cultivation. Pond should be constructed in the waterlogged land in which fisheries culture may be developed and the bunds of the ponds should be utilized for horticultural and social forestry plantation with the view to restore the ecological imbalances of the area.

Gram Banjar Bhoomi Vikas Yojana, linking with NAREGA (National Rural Employment Gaurantee Act) and allotment of the wastelands on *Patta/Tree Patta* basis to the landless/agricultural labourers should be promoted and implemented with the involvement of village Panchayat and representatives of the local village Panchayat for successful implementation of the reclamation of wastelands for the Agriculture - Horticulture - Forestry - Fisheries programmes at village level. Greening of Gram Yojana should also be initiated at village level with the involvement of village Panchayat.

Compensatory Fund for Afforestation (COMPA) for diversion of forest land for non-forest land use should be developed not only at the state level but also at District - Block - village level to control the deforestation and use of forest land for non-forest purpose and compensate the deforestation through regeneration of the forest cover.

Panchayat Van Yojana should be launched at village level and intensification of agro-afforestation management on wastelands at village level should be propogated and implemented with the involvement of village beneficiaries for ecological restoration and eco-development at village level. Strategies should be formulated to check the indiscriminate deforestation and diversion of forest land for non-forest use and restriction on removal of fuelwood as head loads and availability of the alternate fuels.

Education, training for agro-afforestation management on wastelands for villages and interested needy beneficiaries should be organised to meet the increasing demand, for fuel-wood, fodder, fibre, fruits, fisheries and foodgrains (F^6), growing cattle and human population for restoration of ecological imbalances and regeneration of degraded lands and improving the environmental crisis and improving the socio-economic crisis of the villages for integrated development of the deprived rural multitudes.

Summary of Conclusions

The explosive population growth and over exploitation of natural resources has led to ecological and socio-economic crisis, we have less than 11 per cent forest cover. The fuel-wood requirement of our country is 130 million tonnes per year out of which only 39 million tonnes are fetched from the forest. There has been alarming challenge for loss of our agricultural land which is 175 million hectares and 40 million hectares of forest land. We are loosing 1-5 million hectares of forest land every year.

It has been observed that the wastelands are significantly distributed at village level in Amethi Block and Block level in Sultanpur District which has become a challenging problem to the planners and developmental agencies engaged at Sultanpur. The wastelands in Sultanpur, and Amethi Block has been left out of cultivation for very smaller reasons and ignorance of the farmers, it can be easily reclaimed adopting latest scientific and technical inputs.

The relationship between man and nature is symbolic. The combination of natural and human factors plays an important role in the spatial distribution of wastelands. The pH value of the soil, land concentration, scheduled caste population and behaviour of water table are the dominant variables in explaining the variations in wastelands along with the other natural and human factors. The variables which features dominating in explaining the variations on wastelands are the natural factors viz. pH value of the soil, drainage density, behaviour of water table and human factors which comprises mainly the land concentration and scheduled caste population. There are other natural and human factors responsible for the proportionate distribution of wastelands at village level in Amethi Block, District Sultanpur.

The agro-afforestation in Amethi, Sultanpur has not been properly planned and appropriately implemented because it requires joint venture and efforts of the implementing agencies with the participation of local people. The agro-afforestation programme should be implemented for the people, by the people and demonstration for the people and in the farmers field in an integrated manner adopting latest developed and innovated scientific techniques.

Various policies and planning for agro-afforestation have been formulated and implemented which could not provide significant impact at grassroot level. National Commission on Agriculture, National Wastelands Development Mission, National Forest Policy, Compensatory Fund for Afforestation and Panchayat Van Yojana could not provide significant positive impact among the deprived rural poor who are the common sufferers of the deforestation and land degradation. The agro-afforestation management on wastelands at grassroot level be planned and implemented with the involvement and participation of deprived rural poor beneficiaries.

The reclamation capability classification of wastelands has been analysed as per the fertility status of the soil. The reclamation of usar land in Benipur, banjar land in Loniapur old fallow land in Mahmodpur, fallow land in Parsanwa and waterlogged land in Bhaganpur villages of Amethi Block reclamation has been implemented and practically demonstrated. The Agri-Horti-Forestry- Fisheries cultivation and plantation have been carried out through scientific and technological inputs. The reclamation of wastelands has been an asset in controlling the ecological imbalances and improving the socio-economic crisis of the deprived rural poor villagers of Amethi.

The economics of wastelands reclamation for Agriculture- Horticulture - Forestry - Fisheries has been analysed. It has been observed that in the initial stages of usar land, banjar land and waterlogged land has been comparatively less beneficial because the input cost was high while output cost was low but in the subsequent years of the reclamation process the input cost was lower and output cost was increased and the net profit was increased. The old fallow land and fallow land has been economically beneficial in the initial years and also in the subsequent years of the reclamation of wastelands. It has been observed that the reclamation of wastelands for Agriculture - Horticulture - Forestry - Fisheries cultivation/plantation has been economically beneficial and viable in restoring the ecological crisis and also improving the socio-economic crisis of the villagers of Amethi Block.

The strategies formulation and adoption of various measures for the reclamation of wastelands include the provision of several packages of most suitable technological and scientific inputs, credit support, building up of a strong social infrastructure and arranging marketing system. The strategies for the reclamation of wastelands with the involvement of rural poor villagers for agro-afforestation management for appropriate management for proper exploitation of natural resources to meet the day-to-day requirements of the common people living in the remote rural villages.

Action oriented planning within a specified timeframe should be adopted for reclamation of wastelands for agro-afforestation management. Strategies for land preparation, nursery raising, agricultural cropping, horticultural and forestry plantation and fisheries culture should be properly planned and implemented. Gram Banjar Bhoomi Vikas Yojana, Compensatory Fund for Afforestation for diversion of forest land for Non-forest use, Panchayat Van Yojana and intensification of agro-afforestation management on wastelands at village level should be implemented with the involvement of villagers.

It has been observed that the Amethi Block and District Sultanpur has geographic and historic importance. Various types of wastelands are significantly distributed in Amethi Block and District Sultanpur. Various natural and human factors are responsible for the formation of wastelands. Agricultural cropping, horticultural plantation and afforestation programmes are insignificantly implemented for the needs of the local people. The reclamation of wastelands can be easily implemented through land preparation, appropriate management of irrigation system, propose application of organic and inorganic amendments, and other activities to restore the fertility status of the soil for agricultural cropping, horticultural and forestry plantations and fisheries programmes as per suitability of the land. Several policies and planning has been formulated for the reclamation of wastelands including Wastelands Develop-ment Mission and National Forest Policy, etc. but it has not provided positive impact and message among the common people at village level and it was limited within the official files at National and State level and at maximum extent upto District Level but it could not reach upto the field i.e., grassroot level or at village level for whom the policy and planning for agro-afforestation management has been formulated.

The Hon'ble Supreme Court of India has been also concerned and instructed the Government to develop Compensatory Fund for Afforestation (COMPA) for the diversion of forest land to non-forest use but it is not being implemented at village level successfully.

The *Panchayat Van Yojana, Gram Banjar Bhoomi Vikas Yojana, Greening of Wastelands* programmes must be launched at village level with the sustained involvement of the village Panchayat and interested needy villages. Agri-Horti-Forestry- Fisheries programmes should be implemented as per the requirements of the people, by the people, with the people and for the people. The common land/wastelands must be allotted on *Patta basis* or *Tree Patta* basis to the landless/agricultural labourers and the reclamation of such wastelands should be linked with the 100 days employment scheme of *National Rural Employment Gaurantee Act* (NAREGA) and requisite scientific and technical back up support should be made available not only for the reclamation of wastelands but also Agri-Horti-Forestry-Fisheries cropping and plantation programmes respectively.

It has been observed that the economics of wastelands reclamation is beneficial and viable proposition to the village beneficiaries. Initially the benefit was less because the input cost was very high and output cost was low but from the second and the subsequent years of the wastelands reclamation input cost has been reduced and the output cost was increased, hence, the reclamation of wastelands for Agri- - Horti - Forestry - Fisheries programmes has been beneficial to the villagers. No doubt the reclamation of wastelands, it has been helpful in restoring the ecological, environment crisis and regeneration of the degraded lands and improving the ecological embalances of the area and in improving the socio-economic crisis of the deprived poor villagers on the one hand and it has been a milestone in fulfilling the increasing demand of growing cattle and human population for the fuelwood, fodder, fibre, fruits, foodgrains, fisheries, etc. on the other. Thus the reclamation of wastelands for Agri-Horti - Afforestation and Fisheries programme as per suitability and capability of wastelands is an asset for integrated rural development and eradicating poverty of the resourceless villagers and creating employment generating income among the rural poor masses and also increasing the income of the deprived rural multitudes.

Bibliography

(1) Books

Anderson, J.R., *A Geography of Agriculture* (Durbuque, Iowa), 1971

Bali, J.S., *Ravine reclamation needs for India* (New Delhi), 1972

Bebarat, K.C., *Planning for Forest Resources and Bio-Diversity Management*, published by Concept Pub. Co. Pvt. Ltd., New Delhi, 2002.

Bennett, H.H., *Elements of Soil Conservation*, (McGraw Hill Book Co., New York), 1955

Bhattacharya, J.P., *Study of Soil Conservation for Agricultural Land* (New Delhi), 1964

Blandford, H.F., *The climates and weather of India, Ceylon and Burma* (London), 1889.

Browrigg, F.W., *Settlement report*, District, Sultanpur, 1898.

Chaudhari, P. (Ed.), *Readings in Indian agricultural development* (George Allen and Unwin Ltd., London), 1972.

Chauhan, D.S., *Studies in utilisation of agricultural land* (Aggarwala Publishers, Agra), 1966.

Chislom, M., *Rural settlement and land use* (Hutchinson, Lib.), 1962.

Ganguli, H.N., *Restoration of soil structures with gypsum* (Bikaner Gypsum Ltd., Bikaner), 1954.

Govinda Rajan, S.V. and Gopala Rao, H.G., *Studies on soils of India* (New Delhi), 1978.

Gregor, H.F., *Agricultural geography, themes in research* (Prentice Hall Ltd., London), 1970.

Hadimani, A.S., Studies on the wastelands of Delhi state, M.Sc., Associate, Indian Agricultural Research Institute, New Delhi, 1960.

Hall, A., *The soil*, (London), 1947.

Hartshorne, A., *Perspective on the nature of Geography* (Dutler and Tanner, London), 1959.

Johnston, J., *Economic methods* (McGraw Hill Book Co., New York), 1972.

Kelley, W.P., *The climates of continents* (Oxford University Press, Oxford), 1927.

Kendall, M.G., *A course in multi-variate analysis* (Charles Griffin, London), 1957.

King, Thomson, *Water miracles of nature* (MacMillans and Co., New York), 1953.

Kostrowicki, J., *Hierarchy of world types of agriculture* (Poland), 1979.

Kostrowicki, J., *Land utilisation in East Central Europe Caste Studies* (Geographia Polnica, 5, Warsaw, Poland), 1965.

Krishanan, M.S., *Geology of India and Burma* (Madras), 1960.

Leather, J.W., *Investigation of usar lands in the United Provinces* (Government Press, Allahabad), 1914.

Mahmood, Aslam, *Statistical methods in geographical studies* (Rajesh Publications, New Delhi), 1977.

Medicott, H.B., and Blanford, H.F., *Mannual of geology of India*, 1879.

Mitra, Ashok and Mukherjee, Sheikher, Population, food and land inequality in India, in *A geography of hunger and insecurity, an ICSSAR/JNU/FPF Study*, (Allied Publishers Pvt. Ltd., New Delhi), 1980.

Mohammad, Ali, *Studies in agricultural geography* (Rajesh Publishers, New Delhi), 1978.

Mohammad, Ali, *Dynamics of agricultural development in India*, (Concept Publishing Co. Pvt. Ltd., New Delhi), 1978.

Monk House, F.J., and Wilkinson, H.R., *Maps and diagram*, 2nd edn. (University Paperbacks, Methuen and Co.Ltd., London), 1964.

Mooreland, H.H., *The agriculture of United Provinces* (Allahabad), 1912.

Moore, W.G., *A dictionary of geography* (Penguin Books, London), 1976.

Munshull, R., *Regional Geography* (Hutchinson Lib., London), 1967.

Nevill, H.R., *District Gazetteer of the District Sultanpur* (Allahabad), 1903.

Nigam, N.M., How to reclaim saline and alkali lands in the Delhi state, Thesis Associate, Indian Agricultural Research Institute, New Delhi, 1956.

Pilai, V.R., and Panikar, P.G.K, *Land reclamation in Kerala* (Asia Publishing House, New Delhi), 1965.

Porter, F.W., *Final settlement report of the Sultanpur District,* North Western Provinces and Oudh (Allahabad), 1888.

Raheja, P.C., *Soil productivity and crop growth* (Asia Publishing House, New Delhi), 1966.

Rao, K.L., *India's water wealth : Its assessment, uses and projections* (Orient Longman, New Delhi), 1979.

Raychaudhuri, S.P., *Soils in India* (New Delhi), 1962.

Raychaudhuri, S.P., *Land and soil* (National Book Trust, New Delhi), 1966.

Robinson, G.M., *Mother earth* (London), 1937.

Shafi, M., *Land utilisation in Eastern Uttar Pradesh* (Aligarh Muslim University, Aligarh), 1960.

Sharma, H. S., *Ravine erosion in India* (Concept Publishing Co. Pvt. Ltd., New Delhi), 1980.

Sharma, P. S., *Agricultural regionalisation of India,* (New Heights Publishers and Distributors, Delhi), 1973.

Shome, K.B., and Raychudhury, S.P., *Rating of soils of India* (Indian Agricultural Research Institute, New Delhi), 1960.

Siddiqui, Asiya, *Agrarian change in the Northern Indian State* (U.P. 1819-1933) (Oxford Clarendon Press, New Delhi), 1973.

Singh A.K., *et al; Forest Resource Economy and Environment,* Published by Concept Publishing Co. Pvt. Ltd., New Delhi, 1987.

Singh, Abhalakshmi, *Economics and geography of agricultural land reclamation* (B.R. Publishing Corporation, Vivekanand Nagar, Delhi), 1978.

Singh, Jasbir, *An agricultural atlas of India : A geographical analysis* (Vishal Publications, Kurukshetra, Haryana), 1974.

Singh, Jasbir, *An agricultural geography of Haryana* (Vishal Publications, Kurukshetra, Haryana), 1976.

Singh, M., *Land utilization in Eastern Uttar Pradesh,* Ph.D. thesis.

Singh, N.T., *Reclamation of alkali (kallar) soils* (Punjab Agricultural University, Ludhiana), 1972.

Singh, R.L., *India regional geography* (Varanasi), 1971.

Singh, Shrinath, *Modernization of agriculture : A case study of Eastern Uttar Pradesh* (Heritage Publishers, New Delhi), 1976.

Srivastava, Shyam Sunder, *Agro-Forestry,* Published by Central Book House, Sadar Bazar, Raipur, M.P, 1995.

Spate, O.H.K, and Learmonth, ASJA, *India and Pakistan* (London), 1968.

Stamp, L.D., *Applied geography* (Penguin Books, London), 1960.

Stamp, L.D., *Our developing world* (London), 1960.

Stamp, L.D., *The land of Britain : Its use and misuse* (London), 1962.

Subramanian, C., *The new strategy of Indian agriculture* (Vikas Publishing House, New Delhi), 1979.

Symons, L., *Agricultural Geography* (Bell's London), 1968.

Tejwani, K.G., "*Agro-forestry in India,*" Published by Concept Pub. Co. Pvt. Ltd., New Delhi, 2001.

Wadia, D.N., *Geology of India* (London), 1960.

Yadav, H.R., *Wastelands diagnosis and treatment* (Concept Publishing Co. Pvt. Ltd., New Delhi), 1987.

Yadav, H.R., *Genesis and utilization of wastelands* (Concept Publishing Co. Pvt. Ltd., New Delhi), 1986.

Yadav H.R., *Reclaiming wastelands,* published by Concept Publishing Co. Pvt. Ltd., New Delhi, 1990.

(2) Articles

Abrol, I.P. and Bhumbla, D.R., Paper presented at FAO/ UNDP Seminar of Soil Survey and Soil Fertility Research, 15-20 February 1971, New Delhi, FAO, World Soil Research Rep. No. 46.

Abrol, I.P., Reclamation of wastelands and world food prospects, *Trans. Int. Cong. Soil Sci.*, New Delhi, 1982.

Abrol, I.P. and Joshi, P.K., Economic viability of reclamation of alkali lands with special reference to agriculture and forestry, *Economics of wastelands development* (Society for Promotion of wastelands Development, New Delhi), 1984.

Aggarwal, V.P., *Background note on reclamation of alkali usar area of Uttar Pradesh, in Economics of wasteland development* (Society for Promotion of Wastelands Development, New Delhi), 1984.

Aggarwal, L.T. and Mehrotra, C.L., *Soil Survey and soil work in U.P., Vol. - I* (Allahabad), 1951.

Aggarwal, L.I., *Soil survey and soil work in U.P.*, vol. II (Allahabad), 1952.

Aggarwal, L.I., *Soil survey and soil work in U.P.*, vol. III (Allahabad), 1953.

Aggarwal, L.I., *Soil survey and soil work in U.P.*, vol. IV (Allahabad), 1954.

Aggarwal, R.R., Alkali soils can be reclaimed, *Indian Fmg.* 7(9) (1957).

Aggarwal, R.R., Potential and economic aspects of utilization of saline alkali soils, *Proc. Seminar on Recent Advances in Agronomy and Soil Science*, Simla (Indian Council of Agricultural Research, New Delhi), 1959.

Aggarwal, R.R. and Gupta, C.P., Spread and intensity of soil alkalinity with canal irrigation in Gangetic alluvium of U.P., *Indian J. Agric. Sci.*, 27(1957).

Aggarwal, R.R. and Gupta, R.N., Saline alkali soils in India, *I.C.A.R., Tech Bull (Agricultural Ser.)*, No. 15, 1968.

Aggarwal, R.R. and Mehrotra, C.L., Quality of irrigation waters in U.P., *Indian J. Sci.*, 31 (1966).

Aggarwal, R.R. and Yadav, J.S.P, Saline and alkali soils of the Indian Gangetic alluvium in U.P. J. *Soil Sci.*, 5(2) (1954).

Aggarwal, R.R. and Mehrotra, C.L., *Soil Survey and soil, work in U.P.*, vol. I-IV, (Superintendant, Printing and Stationery, U.P., Allahabad), 1950-58.

Aggarwal, R.R., Singh, M and Pal, C., *Daincha as a green mannure in U.P., Bull Dep. Agri. U.P.*, 1957.

Ahmad, Enayat, Drainage and agriculture, in *Perspective in Agricultural Geography*, vol. II edited by N. Mohammad (New Delhi), 1980.

Akachuku, A.E., *Cost-benefit analysis of wood and food components of agri-siliviculture in Nigerian forest zone, Agroforestry Systems*, 1985.

Anita Kumari and Kohli, R.K. Studies on dormancy and macro-molecular drifts during germination in *Cassia accidentalis*, L. *seeds, J. Tree Sci.* 3(1984); *Reclamation of Kans Land India, Ministry of Agriculture, Series I, Pamph, No. 2,* Delhi, 1949.

Arnold, G.W., *Ethology of Free Ranging Animals*, Division of Land Resource Management (SIRO, Wembley, SA, Australia), 1978.

Auden, J.A. *et al.*, Reports on sodium salts in reh soils in the United Provinces with notes on occurrences in other parts of India, *Rec. geol Surv. India*, 77 (1) (1942).

Blandford, H.F., Hotwinds of Northern India, *Mem. Indian, met Dep.*, vol. 6, 1896.

Blandford, H.F., The rainfall of India, *Mem Indian met Dep.*, vol. 3, 1986-88.

Banerjee, A.K., Reclamation of wastelands in laterite tracts of Eastern India, *Mem. Indian met. Dep.*, 43-122.

Barnes, J.H., and Barkat, Ali, Alkali soils, some biochemical factors in their reclamation, Report on Bihar and Orissa, *Department of Agriculture of Agric. India* (1930-31), 12.

Basu, Subhashrajan, Physical factors affecting agriculture :

A geographical analysis, in *Perspectives in agricultural Geography*, vol. II, Edited by Noor Mohammad (Concept Publishing Co. Pvt. Ltd., New Delhi), 1977.

Bhumbla, D.R., Management of salt affected soils, in *Proc. Indo-Hungrarin Seminar*, CSSRI, Karnal, 1977.

Bhumbla, D.R. and Khare, Arvind, Estimate of wastelands in India, in *Wastelands Diagnosis and Treatment* by H.R. Yadav (Concept Publishing Co. Pvt. Ltd., New Delhi), 1987.

Bhumbla, D.R., Note on reclamation of alkali soils in Uttar Pradesh, *Seminar-cum-workshop on Afforestation of Usar Wastelands* (Society for Promotion of Wasteland Development, New Delhi), 1985.

Bhudhyan, Chattopadhyay and Moonis Raza, Regional Development, *Indian J. Reg. Sci.*, 8 (1) (1975).

Burrard, S.G., *On the origin of Himalayan Mountains, Geological Survey of India, Prof. Paper No.* 12, 1942.

Chinnamani, S., *Forestry, Social Forestry and Agro-forestry in Ravine Reclamation.*

Chopra, D.P., *Promising Horticultural and Plants of Economic Importance for Wastelands.*

Chowdhury, Kamla, Greening of India, *Indian Express*, 21 December, 1982.

Chowdhury, S.G. Alkali soil, I, *Allahabad, Fmg.* (1935), 9.

Chowdhury, S.G., Alkali soil, II, *Allahabad Fmg.* (1935), 9.

Chowdhury, S.G., Alkali soil, III, *Allahabad Fmg.* (1935), 9.

Ciriacy-Wantrup, S.V., Natural Resources in Economic Growth : The Role of Institutions and Policies, in *Perspectives in Agricultural Geography*, edited by N. Mohammad (Concept Publishing Co. Pvt. Ltd., New Delhi), 1980.

Clark, K.G.T, The Vicissitudes of the Summer Rainfall of the Indo-Gangetic Plain and the Valley, *Geography*, 18 (Pt. IV) (1932)

Cowie, N.M., A criticism of Gldham's paper on the structure of Himalayas and of the Gangetic plain as elucidated by geodetic observations in India, *Mem. geol. Surv. India, Professional Paper, No. 18,* Dehradun, 1921.

DacGregor, N.M. and Datta, S.K., The utilization of wastelands, *Indian Tea Ass Tocklai Exp. Sta. Mem. No. 20,* Calcutta, 1947, 19.

Dei, N.K., Fertility and productivity of soil, in *Perspective in Agricultural Geography,* vol. 2, edited by N. Mohammad (Concept Publishing Co. Pvt. Ltd., New Delhi), 1980

Dhir, R.P., Organisations involved or concerned in development of wasteland, in *Perspective in Agricultural Geography,* edited by N. Mohammad (Concept Publishing Co. Pvt. Ltd., New Delhi), 1980

Dhir, R.P., Concept and definition of wasteland, *Proc. ICAR, Sponsored Summer Institute* (Central Arid Zone Research Institute, Jodhpur), 1986.

Dhar, N.R., Mukherjee, S.K. and Biswas, N.N., *Alkali soils and their reclamation, Current Reports* (Academy of Agriculture, New Delhi), 1938, 23

Dhawan, C.L., *Land reclamation,* Central Board of Irrigation *and Power Publication No. 43,* vol. III, 1.

Eliot, J., The hot winds of Northern India, *Indian met. Mem,* 6 (Pt.) (III), (1900)

Gedroiz, K.K., Saline soils and their improvement, *J. exp. Agron,* (in Russian : translated by SA Waksman).

Glennie, E.A., Gravity anomalies in the structure of the earth's crust, *Mem. geol. Surv. India Prof. Paper,* No. 27, Dehradun, 1932.

Grandt, A.F. and Lang A.L., *Reclaiming Illinois stripwal land with legumes and grasses, Agric. Exp. Sta. Illinois Bull,* No. 628, Lerbana, 1958.

Hart, D.R.D and Sands, M.W., "Sustainable Land use system Research and Development" in *International workshop on Sustainable Land use system Research,* Feb. 12-16, p. 13.

Hauser, D.P., Some problems in the use of stepwise regression technique in geographical research, *Can. Geogr.,* 18 (1974), 1.

Hedge, N.G., *Wasteland development : Alternative to Prosopis Juliflora.*

Hill, E.G., The analysis of reh, the alkaline salts in Indian usar land, *Chemical News* (1903), 87.

Hilgard, E.W., *Report of the Reh Committee for Investigating into the causes of the Deterioration of Land by Reh in Aligarh District in Alkali Lands, Irrigation and Drainage,* University of California, Appendix VII to Report for the year 1885: also *Dictionary of Economic Products,* vol. VI, part I, 1886.

Hill, S.A., Variations of rainfall in Northern India, *Indian met. Mem.,* 1 (Pt. III), 1897.

Hoon, R.C., *Land reclamation* (Central Board of Irrigation, India), 2 (43), 1955.

Hyden, H.H., Notes on the relationship of Himalaya to the Indo-Gangetic plain and the Indian Peninsula, *Mem. geol. Surv. India, Prof. Paper No. 27,* Dehradun, 1932.

Jana, M.M., Physical factors affecting agriculture in a backward region, in *Perspective in Agricultural Geography,* vol. 2, edited by Noor Mohammad (Concept Publishing Co. Pvt. Ltd., New Delhi), 1980.

Khanduri, H.C., Reclamation of usar land for agriculture by afforestation, in *Perspectives in Agricultural Geography,* (Concept Publishing Co. Pvt. Ltd., New Delhi), 1980.

Kamps, L.F., Mud distribution and land reclamation in Eastern Wadden Shallows, *Netherlands International Institute for Land Reclamation and Improvement Publication,* No. 9, Wageningen, 1963.

Kanwar, J.S., Reclaiming deteriorated soils, *Fertil News,* 6, (21) (1961).

Kanwar, J.S., *Reclamation of saline alkali soils : Quality of water required for leaching,* Paper presented at Symposium on Alkalinity and Salinity (Indian Agricultural Research Institute, New Delhi), 1962.

Kanwar, J.S., *Reclamation of saline, alkali soils, amendments, kinds amounts and costs,* Paper presented at Symposium on Salinity and Alkanity (Indian Agricultural Research Institute, New Delhi), 1959.

Kar, Amal, Land man and desert degradation : Geomorphic problems of agriculture in western Rajasthan, in *Perspectives in Agricultural Geography*, vol. 2, edited by N. Mohammad (Concept Publishing Co. Pvt. Ltd., New Delhi), 1980.

Kar, Anita & Kar, Amal, Relevance of geomorphology in agricultural planning. Some global examples, in *Perspectives in Agricultural Geography*, Vol II, edited by N Mohammad (Concept Publishing Co. Pvt. Ltd., New Delhi) 1980.

Kaul, K.N., *Scheme for reclamation and development of usar lands, Report, Indian Council of Agricultural Research Scheme, Delhi,* 1961.

Kennedy, K., Australia's wasteland is now bountiful, *Indian Fmg.*, 11(10) (1962), 29.

Khan, A.D., *Usar soils, their indentification and reclamation,* Agriculture, Animal Husbundry, U.P., 1950, 5.

Khan, A.D., It can certainly be done, *J. Soil Wat Conserv. in India,* 8 (1960).

Khan, A.D., Diagnosis and reclamation of usar soils, Bureau of Agricultural Information, *Tech. Bull No.* 4, Lucknow, 1951.

Leather, J.W., Reclamation of usar resource. Land, Bureau of Agricultural Information, *Tech. Ball, No.* 4, 1951, 7, 9, 13, 37.

Leather, J.W., Agricultural Soils, in *Agrl. Ledger,* 3(1898).

Leather, J.W., Reclamation of reh or usar soils, *Agrl. Ledger,* (1893), 12, 13.

Mathur, R.K., Economics of agroforestry for wasteland reclamation, *Agrl. Ledger,* (1983), 175-87.

Milne, R.A. and Rapp, E., Salinity and drainage problems, causes, effects, managements, *United States Department of Agriculture Farmers Bull, No.* 1314, Washington, 1968.

Mishra, Rajbans, Dayan, S.N., and Bhola, *Economics of ravine afforestation with special reference to Chambal ravines,* Soil Conservation Research, Demonstration and Training Centre, Kota, 1967.

...k farming in wasteland development ...esearch Demonstration, Training

...g Back the Wasteland, Lecture ... a meet organized by the Society for ...otion of Wastelands Development, India International Centre, New Delhi, 27, December, 1982.

Oldham, R.D., The structure of Himalayas and Gangetic plain, *Mem. geol. Surv. India and Burma*, 3rd Edn., Vol. I, Delhi, 1917.

Oldham, R.D., The deep boring at Lucknow, *Rec. geol. Surv. India*, vol. 23.

Pant, S.C., Role of NABARD in reclamation of wasteland, *Rec. geol. Surv. India*, vol. 23.

Parshad, R. and Yadav, J.S.P, *Alkali soil reclamation questions and answers* (Central Soil Research Institute, Karnal).

Poscoe, E.H., *A mannual of geology of India and Burma*, 3rd Edn. vol. I, (Delhi), 1950.

Raheja, R.C., *et al*, *Study of suitable trees, grasses and crops for saline and alkali land*, Working Group on Waste Land including Saline, Alkali and Waterlogged Lands, Government of India, 1962.

Raj, S.K.T, *Ganga Khadir, A study on land reclamation in India, Ministry of Information and Broadcasting Pamph*, No. 4, New Delhi, 1951, 44.

Raychaudhuri, S.P., Extensions of cultivated area for increased agricultural production, *Proc. Symposium on Science and India's Food Problem*, (ICAR, New Delhi), 1971.

Raychaudhury, S.P., and Biswas, N.R.D., Saline alkali soils of Asia with particular reference to India, *Trans. 5th International Congress*, 1954.

Raychaudhuri, S.P., Final report of the All India Soil Survey Scheme, *Bull Indian Council agric. Res.*, 1952, 13.

Sarkar, Vinod, Vegetation of semi-arid wastelands and indicators of degradation.

Sen, A.K., Land utilization mapping to estimate the

wasteland of arid zone by photo interpr technique, 49-53.

Sen, A.K., Typology of wastelands and mapping procedu in Rajasthan.

Saxena, S.K., Economic attributes of some multipurpose plants needed for wasteland Development.

Shah, Parmesh, Economics of wasteland development projects undertaken by Gujarat State Rural Development Corporation, 189-213.

Shafi, M., The problem of wastelands in India, in *The Geographer,* (Sp. No.) 21 (1968), International Geographical Congress India, 15 (November 1968). Aligarh Muslim University Geographical Society, Aligarh (India).

Shankarnarayan, K.A., *Agroforestry, the key to rehabilitation of wasteland.*

Shankarnarayan, K.A., Sen, A.K., and Balakram, *Analysis of wastelands in arid zone by remote sensing techniques*, 55-64.

Sharma, H.S., Genesis of ravines of the Lower Chambal Valley, India, Selected papers, *Proc. 21st International Geographical Union Congress,* 1 (1968), 114-18.

Sharma, K., Prospects of integrating agroforestry with goal husbandry for economic upliftment or rural poor in wasteland of India.

Shrivastava, K.B., *Role of Prosopis in Wastelands development.*

Signond, A.A., Joe, The alkali soils in Hungary and their reclamation measures, *Soil Sci.* 18(1924), 379-81.

Srivastava, P.B.L, Mehrotra, C.L., and Agarwal, R.R., The effect of leaching saline, alkali soil with irrigation waters of different kinds on the premeability and composition of the soils and the composition of leachets, *Jl India Sec. Soil Sci.,* (1962), 10.

Singh, R.P., *Dryland agriculture and wasteland development.*

Stamp, L.D., The land utilization survey of Britain, *Geograph, J., Land,* 78 (1931)

Subhashranjan, Basu, Physical factors affecting agriculture :

A geographical analysis in, *Perspectives in Agricultural Geography,* edited by Noor Mohammad (Concept Publishing Co. Pvt. Ltd., New Delhi), 1980.

Swaminathan, M.S., 1990, "Opening Remarks," International workshop on Sustainable Land use System Research, New Delhi, Feb. 12-16.

Venkataraman, K.G., Designing, planning and financing of tree plantation over state lands, in *Perspectives in Agricultural Geography,* edited by Noor Mohammad (Concept Publishing Co. Pvt. Ltd., New Delhi), 1980, 221-25.

Verma, Balvir, *Principles and practices in gully relcamation.*

Thomas, K.M., and Srinivasan, A.S., Weed Killers, *Indian Fmg.,* 10(2) (1949)

Taylor, C.C., Weed control, *Indian Fmg.,* 9(4) (1948)

Taylor, C.S., Effects of salt on soils, *Q J Dep. Agric., Bengal* (1919)

Taylor, E.M., Making land reclamation profitable, *Ind. tan. Fmg.,* 1(9) (1940)

Tewari, D.N., "Technology for Sustainable Development", National Seminar on Technology for sustainable Development, March, 12-18, Guru Ghasi Das University, 1980, p. 17.

Uppal, H.L., Reclaiming alkali wastelands, *ICAR Bull* No. 85, New Delhi, 1961.

Uppal, H.L., *Reclamation of saline and alkali soils* (Land Reclamation, Irrigation and Power Research Institute, Punjab), 1962.

Uppal, H.L., *et al. Reclamation of saline and alkaline lands, India,* (Directorate of Extension Farm, No. 66, New Delhi), 1961.

Uppal, H.L., Agarwal, R.R. and Kibe, M., *Alkaline Lands Farm Bull* No. 66, Farming Information Unit Directorate of Extension, Ministry of Food and Agriculture, New Delhi, 1961.

Wadia, D.N., and Auden, J.B., Geology structure of Northern India, *Mem. geol. Surv. India,* 78 (1939)

Whyte, R.D., and Sisam, J.W.C, The establishment of vegetation on industrial wasteland, *Common Agr. Bur. Joint* Pub. No. 14, 1949.

Yadav, J.S.P, Usar soils their characteristics and exploitation in forestry, *Proc. 9th Science Congress,* Part I, 1956.

Yadav, J.S.P and Aggarwal, R.R., Dynamics of soil changes in the reclamation of saline alkali soils of the Indo-Gangetic alluvium, *Indian Sc. Soil Sci.* (1979) 7.

Yadav, J.S.P and Agarwal, R.R., A comparative study of effectivness of gypsum and dhaincha in the reclamation of saline-alkali soils, *J Indian Soc. Soil Sci.,* (1961), 9.

(3) Government and U.N., Publication

Academy of Sciences of the USSR, *The application of drainage in the reclamation of salinized soils,* translated from Russian, Moscow, 1958.

Agricultural Census of Uttar Pradesh, 1970-71 *Agricultural Statistics of Uttar Pradesh,* 1971.

Bulletin of Agricultural Statistics for Uttar Pradesh (1970-71) Joint Director for Statistics, Directorate of Agriculture, U.P., (India), 1972, 16.

Census of India, 1981, *Series I-India,* Part IIB(t)., *Primary Census Abstract.* General Population Table, 1981.

District Census Handbook, Sultanpur District, 1971, Series 21 U.P., Part X-B, *Primary Census Abstract,* 1971.

F.A.O., A Framework for land evaluation, *Soil Bull* No. 1, 1976.

Government of India, *Indian Agriculture in Brief,* Eighth Edition.

I.C.A.R., *Final Report of All India Soil Survey Scheme,* 1958.

I.C.A.R., *Handbook of Agriculture,* 1969

Indian National Science Academy, *Proc. Symposium on Reclamation and Use of Wastelands in India,* Bulletin No. 44, INSA, New Delhi, 1968.

Ministry of Food and Agriculture, Government of India, Waste-land Survey and Reclamation Committee, *Report on the location and utilization of wastelands in the* Part X. U.P., New Delhi, 1961.

National Botanic Gardens Lucknow, *Conquest of Usar (An experiment in reclamation of alkali land at Benthara, Lucknow District by biological and agronomic methods)*, 1961, 24.

National Thematic and Maps Grganisation, Govt. of India.

Planning Commission, Programme Evaluation Organization, *Study of soil conservation programme for agricultural land,* New Delhi, 1964.

Planning Commission, Committee on Natural Resources, *Study of survey and reclamation of ravines in India,* 1965.

Planning Commission, Committee on Natural Resources, *Study of wastelands, including saline, alkali and waterlogged lands and their reclamation measures,* New Delhi, 1963.

Proc. natn Inst. Sci. India, 26 (*Suppl.*) (Pt. A) : *Physical Sciences,* National Institute of Sciences of India, New Delhi, 1960.

Recommendations Regarding the Revision of the National Forest Policy, Department of Environment, Govt. of India, New Delhi.

Research and Reference Division, Ministry of Information and Broadcasting, Government of India, *India,* 1972: *A Reference Mannual,* 1972, 250.

State Soil Conservation Research, *Annual Report, State Soil Conservation Research,* U.P., 1961.

Statistical Book, District Sultanpur, Sultanpur, 1981-82.

Survey of India : *Topographical Sheets,* No. 63F/11, 63 F/10, 63F/12, 63 F/14, 63F/15, 63F/16, 63J/3, 63J/4, 63J/8, 63J/11, 63/12, 63K/5, 63K/9.

The Times of India, Directory and Year Book including who's who, 1972, 192.

United Provinces of Agra and Oudh, Department of Agriculture, 1909, *Reclamation of usar land, Report of Agra and Oudh,* Department of Agriculture, U.P., 1908-09.

Usar Land Reclamation Committee, U.P., *Report of Usar Land*

and Reclamation Committee, (Superintendent, Printing and Stationary, Allahabad), 1938.

U.S.A., Salinity Lab, *Diagnosis and improvement of saline and alkali soils Handbook,* U.S. Department of Agriculture No. 60, 1954.

U.S.D.A., *A Mannual on conservation of soil and water, Handbook of Professional Agricultural Workers,* (Oxford Publishing Co.) 1984.

The Imperial Gazetteer of India, vol. XXIII, *Singhbhumi to Trashi-Chod-Zong,* Reprint Edition (Today and Tomorrow Printers and Publishers, New Delhi), 1974, 130-37.

Village Khasara Map of Amethi Tehsil, District Sultanpur.

Wasteland Survey and Reclamation Committee, Ministry of Food and Agriculture, *Report on location and utilisation of wasteland in India,* Part X, Uttar Pradesh, 1961.

Index